Women, Beauty and Power in Early Modern England

Also by Edith Snook

WOMEN, READING AND THE CULTURAL POLITICS OF EARLY MODERN
ENGLAND

Women, Beauty and Power in Early Modern England

A Feminist Literary History

Edith Snook

palgrave
macmillan

Softcover reprint of the hardcover 1st edition 2011 978-0-230-28285-8

First published 2011 by
PALGRAVE MACMILLAN

Palgrave Macmillan in the UK is an imprint of Macmillan Publishers Limited, registered in England, company number 785998, of Houndmills, Basingstoke, Hampshire RG21 6XS.

Palgrave Macmillan in the US is a division of St Martin's Press LLC, 175 Fifth Avenue, New York, NY 10010.

Palgrave Macmillan is the global academic imprint of the above companies and has companies and representatives throughout the world.

Palgrave® and Macmillan® are registered trademarks in the United States, the United Kingdom, Europe and other countries.

ISBN 978-1-349-32866-6   ISBN 978-0-230-30223-5 (eBook)
DOI 10.1057/9780230302235

This book is printed on paper suitable for recycling and made from fully managed and sustained forest sources. Logging, pulping and manufacturing processes are expected to conform to the environmental regulations of the country of origin.

A catalogue record for this book is available from the British Library.

Library of Congress Cataloging-in-Publication Data
Snook, Edith.
  Women, beauty and power in early modern England : a feminist
  literary history / Edith Snook.
      p. cm.
  Includes index.

  1. English literature—Early modern, 1500–1700—History and criticism.
  2. English literature—Women authors—History and criticism.
  3. Beauty, Personal, in literature.   4. Women in literature.
  5. Women—England—Intellectual life.   I. Title.
PR113.S567 2011
  820.9'928709031—dc22   2011002012

10   9   8   7   6   5   4   3   2   1
20   19   18   17   16   15   14   13   12   11
Transferred to Digital Printing in 2011

For Jeff

List of Contents

List of Illustrations

Acknowledgements

Research for this book was materially aided by a Standard Research Grant from the Social Sciences and Humanities Research Council of Canada, the University of New Brunswick University Research Fund and the UNB Faculty of Arts Busteed Publication Fund. This essential funding enabled me to travel to archives in the UK and the US and to afford the very able assistance of Vicky Simpson and Madeline Bassnett, for which I am very grateful. Jason Simmonds, Lisa Jodoin and Javad Ghatta also provided valuable research assistance through the UNB Department of English. I am indebted to the students of English 6246 at the University of New Brunswick for thinking about early modern beauty with me, and to Karen Bamford for inviting me to talk to her students about Anne Clifford. Thank you to Madeline Bassnett, Natasha Hurley, Christine Horne and Goran Stanivukovic for reading various parts of this book in its different incarnations. I am especially indebted to Karen Robertson and Susan Frye, who invited me to participate in their session at the Still Kissing the Rod Conference at St. Hilda's College, Oxford in 2005, to Caroline Bowden who invited me to the Health and Medicine in Early Modern England Conference she organized at All Soul's College, Oxford in 2005, and to the participants in my workshop session at the Shakespeare Association of America Conference in New Orleans in 2004. The discussions at these conferences occurred at an early stage in the research and writing of this book and were formative to my thinking. So, too, were the helpful criticisms of the anonymous readers at *Seventeenth Century* and *The Journal of Women's History*. I am beholden as always to Theresa Keenan and Janet Noiles for their good-humoured assistance with organizing our department and graduate programme. Most of all I am indebted to Jeff Lilburn for taking on far more than his share of the cooking most of the time and for seeing to the moving of our household in the final week that I had with this book. Touched by your fair tendance I gladlier grew.

Introduction

Female beauty occupies a central place in the literary culture of early modern England. Inspired by the gold hair, rosy cheeks and fair eyes of Petrarch's Laura, English poets praised beautiful women in feats of poetic virtuosity.[1] In *Astrophil and Stella,* Sidney gave Stella an architectural face, comparing her skin to a front of alabaster, her hair to a gold roof, her lips to a door of red porphir, her cheeks to porches of red and white marble and her eyes to touch, which ignites fires in the poet made of straw.[2] A sonnet in Edmund Spenser's *Amoretti* made Elizabeth a treasure: she contains in her eyes, lips, teeth, forehead, hair and hands the sapphires, rubies, pearls, ivory, gold and silver which merchants vainly seek from afar.[3] John Donne's Elegy 14 describes a woman of dazzlingly global proportions with hair like a forest, a nose like a 'meridian' running between the hemispheres of her cheeks, lips like islands to anchor on and breasts that are the Sestos and Abydos one meets on the way to the Atlantic of her navel and the India below.[4] Milton made Eve 'for sweet attractive grace'.[5] If less frequently, poets do trace the outlines of male beauty. Shakespeare's sonnets address the fair young man whose eyes are 'more bright' than those of women, who is 'A man in hue, all hues in his controlling',[6] and his Adonis is 'more white and red than doves or roses are'.[7] Marlowe's 'amorous' Leander is 'beautiful and young' and has 'dangling tresses', while the 'fair large front and eye sublime' of Milton's Adam 'declared/Absolute rule'.[8] Frequently anthologized and taught in courses on Renaissance literature, these writers are pivotal figures within the traditional canon of English literature, and their poetry has received scholarly attention for many years. Still, Nancy Vickers's assessment seems undeniable: '[t]he canonical legacy of description in praise of beauty is [...] a legacy shaped predominantly by the male imagination for the male imagination; it is,

1

in large part, the product of men talking to men about women' – and about other men.[9]

This book turns to an archive produced by women. Women in early modern England created texts about beauty that survive in print and manuscript form – works of fiction, drama and verse, the formal prose of maternal advice, historical chronicles and letters, and domestic writing, such as recipes and accounts. Scholars of early modern women's writing have observed that in poetry early modern women did not devise an alternative canon of male beauties to stand as objects of female desire. Lady Mary Wroth's sonnet sequence *Pamphilia to Amphilanthus* draws on Petrarch's techniques of poetic self-construction, but she does not put Amphilanthus's appearance on display.[10] When Elizabeth (Carey) Berkeley translated two of Petrarch's sonnets, she redefined Laura as an icon of Protestant virtue and an aristocratic bride.[11] Aemelia Lanyer's *Salve Deus Rex Judaeorum*, exceptionally, represents male beauty, evoking Petrarch and the Canticles in her meditation on the body of Christ. Women wrote about female beauty more often, frequently with reference to race. Through this lens, scholars have studied Elizabeth Cary's *The Tragedy of Mariam*, Mary Wroth's prose romance, as well as her sonnets, and Aphra Behn's prose fiction, *Oroonoko*.[12] Continuing this discussion, this book shifts the focus somewhat from beauty's literary traditions to its practices with three sections on cosmetics, clothing and hair.

'Nature's Coin': The Traditions of Early Modern Beauty

Early modern beauty is a theoretical, conservative construct. In praising beauty, male writers often looked to tradition, to the poets, princes, painters and philosophers who pondered its signs in England and Europe, particularly in Italy.[13] Although fiction and drama also represented beautiful people, poetry was beauty's most powerful advocate, with the blazon serving as beauty's principle form. In anatomizing the female body, the blazon constructed beauty according to a rigid formula; whatever the rhetorical figures, Petrarch's Laura, Sidney's Stella, Spenser's Elizabeth and the rest, seemed to possess the same colours and proportions. Sara F. Matthews Grieco outlines the code: 'In Italy, France, Spain, Germany, and England the basic aesthetic was the same: white skin, blond hair, red lips and cheeks, black eyebrows.'[14] Chapter 5 will suggest that curled hair is as important as blonde, but Grieco is basically correct. Writing in 1541, Agnolo Firenzuola's *On the Beauty of Women* attempts to explain the rationale of these qualities. Working in the

Neoplatonic tradition, and alongside Petrarch, Boccaccio, Ficino and Castiglione, Firenzuola establishes that beauty is harmony and that the most 'pleasing unity, that propriety, that moderation we call beauty. I say this is mysterious because we cannot explain why that white chin, those red lips, those black eyes, that wide hip, that little foot should produce or arouse, or result in beauty. And yet, we see it is like this.'[15] Although Petrarch's influence on English verse fades, and fashions in hair and clothing change, the codified physical attributes of female beauty remain entrenched in early modern England.

Poets do employ the paradoxical encomium to praise women with non-normative looks, in poems that range from the vulgar to the satiric to the serious, but they rely very much on the same narrow definition.[16] Poets such as John Collop, Edward Herbert, Baron of Cherbury and John Carew wrote in praise of ladies who were 'Thick and Short', yellow-skinned, black, or suffering from green sickness. John Donne's anagram on 'Flavia' disorganizes beauty's parts: small eyes, a large mouth, black teeth, yellow skin and red hair.[17] Most famously, Shakespeare's Dark Lady is a mistress whose eyes are 'nothing like the sun', her hair is 'wires' and her cheeks, not red and white.[18] Blackness represented the most significant challenge to beauty's circumscribed terms. Thomas Buoni's *Problemes of Beautie* (1606) asked whether the beauty of women could consist in different colours, and he concluded that 'to the eye of the Moore, the blacke, or tawny countenance of his Moorish damosell pleaseth best, to the eye of another, a colour as white as the Lilly, or the driven snowe'.[19] He introduces relativism into beauty's definition on the assumption of segregation. Margreta de Grazia posits that Shakespeare's longings for a black mistress, who may be African, are more transgressive, for they 'threaten to raze the very distinctions his poems to the fair boy strain to preserve'.[20] Yet Kim F. Hall argues that the placement of black beauty at the centre of verse is 'concomitant with the increasing appropriation of black bodies in Atlantic trade',[21] and most non-normative beauties merely provide a ready opportunity for the poet to assert his dominance. Shakespeare concludes Sonnet 130 by insisting his love is 'as rare/As any she belied with false compare', making the poem less some early modern version of a 'campaign for real beauty' than advocacy for a literary aesthetic that eschews extravagant, falsifying metaphors.[22] Neither are Flavia's looks praiseworthy for their own sake. They certify the poet's poetic and social originality: in choosing to praise an ugly wife, he can retire from competition with other men, assured of her chastity. 'Things in fashion', he concludes, 'every man will wear'.[23] The paradoxical encomium establishes the poet's control over women most baldly when John Collop tells the yellow-skinned lady, who is 'with Childes cack [...] yellow'd o're', 'I made thee gold, 'tis I can make thee brasse.'[24] Heather Dubrow argues that the paradoxical encomium attempted to reincorporate the other into a cultural norm by the denial of difference, to dominate and exert textual control over non-normative women and to deflect anxieties about normative beauty onto other bodies.[25] Poems addressed to non-normative beauties do little radically to challenge beauty's catalogue of parts, but they do expose just how firmly beauty's language depends on hierarchies of class and race and on cultural preferences and how beauty's definition articulates power, to the degree that appearance was used by European colonizers to justify violent subjection.[26]

So delimited, normative beauty was, on the one hand, idealized as the physical sign of truth and virtue. On the other, it inspired a myriad of anxieties, even vitriol in announcements of women's failures to accommodate the ideal. Physical beauty could be the outward manifestation of a soul beautiful in its virtue. Baldesar Castiglione's *Book of the Courtier*, translated into English by Thomas Hoby and published in 1561, is perhaps the most influential articulation of this theory. Castiglione's Pietro Bembo translates Diotima's speech in Plato's *Symposium* to a heterosexual, Christian context when he urges the courtier to develop from looking at beautiful women an understanding of universal beauty and divine truth. The question of whether or not women might understand truth through gazing at beauty is left unanswered; Gaspare proposes women are too full of passions, but Giuliano reminds them of the example of Diotima, and the meeting concludes, the conflict unresolved.[27] In verse, just as Petrarch indicated that Laura led him to the highest good, Astrophil recommended that men who look in the book of nature to see how beauty could be lodged with virtue should look to Stella, who possesses 'fair lines which true goodness show'; her beauty wins men to reason and makes them love the good.[28] Within this framework, looks are an outward manifestation of a spiritual state.

Yet this philosophical idealization of female beauty frequently finds women themselves wanting. If beauty's virtuous ideal includes chastity, a beautiful woman will inevitably frustrate the desire of the man who praises her. Consequently, the beautiful woman is often cruel. Each quatrain of Spenser's Sonnet 56 begins on the refrain 'fayre ye be sure', to which he adds a 'but': she is also 'cruel and unkind', 'proud and pittilesse', and 'hard and obstinate' because she is, like Laura, chaste, and he, like Petrarch, is shipwrecked – a model Spenser will ultimately reject to become a married Protestant lover.[29] Neither can idealized beauty

cope with female agency in what Ovid calls women's 'self-cultivation' –
their use of cosmetics, fashions and hairstyling.[30] Although Ovid's *Ars
Amatoria* (The Art of Love) might have provided literary authority for
beauty practices, and there were sixteenth-century Italian paintings
that used the theme of the lady at her toilette to praise women, early
modern English dramatists, poets, ministers and polemicists tended
instead to denounce painting, ornament and fine clothes as deceptive,
vain and proud because they were not natural.[31] Frances Dolan argues
that '[d]efenses of poetry associate the feminine with nature' which
masculine poets can respond to with their art; women who are 'authors
of themselves' are attacked as presumptuous. Art belongs to the male
poet, not to the beautiful woman who paints her face.[32]

In addition to stripping women of agency as ethical thinkers and artists, idealized beauty commodifies women with figurative language that
translates body parts into things, into precious metals and stones, flowers and colonized countries. Patricia Parker has written about how the
blazon uses the economic rhetoric of the commodity to put women on
display and to claim 'economic, sexual, and epistemological possession,
a gendering which goes beyond a simple matter of language minimized
as such into the actual relations of power in a culture which displays
and controls women and other strange things'.[33] As a commodity,
female beauty can be exchanged by men, but female chastity not yet
controlled by a husband is a waste. Like Shakespeare's sonnets to the
fair young man, Milton's *A Masque Presented at Ludlow Castle* debates
beauty's proper use. The Second Brother asserts that his sister's beauty
is 'like the fair Hesperian tree/Laden with blooming gold' and must be
protected, but for Comus, the Lady's beauty must be shared: 'Beauty is
Nature's coin, must not be hoarded,/But must be current, and the good
thereof/Consists in mutual and partaken bliss.'[34] When Shakespeare's
Collatine blazons 'the clear unmatched red and white' of Lucrece, he
'[u]nlocked the treasure of his happy state' and exposed her to Tarquin's
lust; beauty and honour 'in the owner's arms/ are weakly fortressed
from a world of harms'.[35] The fragile treasure of female beauty exists
under threat of destruction, by assault and by time because women
are weak, men not always able to protect and time inexorable. The
ephemerality of youthful, reproductive beauty threatens its economic
value. When Samuel Daniel compares Della's beauty to a half-blown
rose, most beautiful the moment before it is destroyed, he ends with a
plea: 'O let not then such riches waste in vaine;/But love whilst thou
maist be lov'd againe.'[36] Robert Herrick's 'To the Virgins, to Make Much
of Time' instructs virgins to '[g]ather ye Rose-buds while ye may' and

marry while they are young, while in Andrew Marvell's 'To His Coy Mistress', the poet, after abandoning his extravagant promise to spend centuries on blazoning her beauty, insists 'Thy Beauty shall no more be found;/Nor, in thy marble vault, shall sound/My echoing song: then worms shall try/That long-preserved virginity.'[37] The beautiful and chaste are menaced with the end of their exchange value, the end of the poet's song and, in Marvell's case, a grotesque rape by necrophilic worms. Placed firmly within the heterosexual economy of desire, literary renditions of female beauty presume that female beauty always faces towards men, and, as much as male poets praise female beauty, they also define male authority to control, to use and to exchange women's bodies. Obviously, the poetry of female beauty by men says more about the male writers than it does about women. Nancy Vickers argues that 'bodies fetishized by a poetic voice logically do not have a voice of their own; the world of making words, of making texts is not theirs'.[38] Making texts about beauty we know displays the poet's mastery of literary tradition, channels the poet's anxieties about his artistic and social ambitions and explores inwardness and male poetic subjectivity.[39] Yet literature in praise of beauty is also something of an echo chamber, where beauty is codified and aestheticized in ways that connect poets more to other men than to women's literary or social history.

Beauty's Practices: A Feminist Literary History

Women's writing engages the Neoplatonic, Petrarchan, theological and political ideas of beauty that subtend the dominant literary culture. But women also reflect on the manufacture of beauty and produce writing from their beauty practices, recording their creation and purchase of skin products, their acquisition of clothing and their manipulation of their hair. For women, beauty was – as for men, who also attended to their appearance – not only a matter of conforming to an aesthetic theory, but also a practice of everyday life. Practices could both engage beauty's ideals and question its problems – commodification, sexual violence, ageing and the denial of agency and voice among them. Michel de Certeau says that many of the practices of everyday life are 'tactics'. A tactic, he says, 'is an art of the weak': 'A tactic insinuates itself into the other's place, fragmentarily, without taking it over in its entirety, without being able to keep it at a distance [...] because it does not have a place, a tactic depends on time – it is always on the watch for opportunities that can be seized "on the wing".'[40] Not existing in a separate cultural space from beauty's dominant literary and philosophical forms, women's beauty practices are tactics informed by patriarchal aesthetic theory, but they are also an opportunity because they can require knowledge and actions of various kinds, including writing.

For men and women in early modern England, getting dressed – putting on clothes and making the skin and hair appropriate – was far from trivial. It required one to understand one's place within the social order and, on occasion, allowed one to demonstrate one's understanding of the body, its physiology and its cultural meanings; to evaluate the ideal relationship between art and nature and between inward identity and outward appearance, two of the period's fundamental philosophical questions; and to articulate an inevitably political point of view on structures of power. Attention to appearance could provide a means to express female subjectivity and self-governance. It could provide the means to contest the trivialization of women's work, the disenfranchisement of the older woman and the violence directed at the beautiful woman. Beauty practices were a form of knowledge that allowed women to participate in scholarly culture, to raise politically knowing sons, to exert control within a household and community, to be creative and ethical with their own appearance and to encourage the same in others. With their beauty practices, early modern women fracture the perspective that female beauty functioned only within the patriarchal economy of desire. Hilda Smith asked in 2007 how 'women's historians create interest in women's intellectual life, while still representing their daily lives within the family and at work?'[41] I want to answer her question by making women's intellectual life visible within their beauty practices, activities often decried as merely foolish.

Women in early modern England do not engage in an overt assault on beauty's dominant definition, unlike, for instance, the second-wave feminist demonstration against the 1968 Miss America pageant, in which a 'freedom trash can' became the receptacle for copies of *Cosmopolitan*, hair curlers and restrictive undergarments. To have engaged in such a critique in early modern England would have required an absolutely radical rejection of literary history, of an intellectual and religious culture that linked beauty and goodness, and of a society ordered along hierarchies of class, gender and race. The women in this book are not especially subversive on that front. Indeed, their construction of beauty is most often deeply invested in distinctions based in class and race, and consequently beauty relies for its authority on invidious distinctions between men and women of different cultures, religions and class positions, with English women often preferring much the same beauty ideal as male writers. The focus in this book is on middle- and upper-class women, for they had the economic means both to participate in beauty culture and to gain access to the literacy that allowed them to use its literary forms and to record their ideas. This book, I think, cannot be the final word on early modern women's thinking about beauty, but it does show just how thoroughly the ideals and practices of English beauty depend on class privilege.

The historical scope of women's preoccupation with beauty practices is thinly understood within the analysis of beauty that has emerged with second- and third-wave feminism. Early modern women provide precedents for the deep positional rifts in the analysis of beauty and its practices, sharing with contemporary feminists both a critique and a sense of beauty's possibilities. Many modern-day feminists – Germaine Greer, Andrea Dworkin, Robin Lakoff and Raquel Scherr, Wendy Chapkis, Susan Brownmiller, Naomi Wolf, and Patricia Hill Collins – have detailed and contested the dilemmas adhering to beauty, including standards informed by racist, classist and sexist ideals, the veneration of thinness and youth, the violence adhering to its production, including cosmetic surgery, and its economic consequences, including the trivialization of women's work, the drain on female resources and the commodification of the beautiful woman in media culture.[42] At its most acute, the critique of beauty has rejected virtually all beauty practices, as in the work of Andrea Dworkin and, more recently, Sheila Jeffreys, who proposes that wearing lipstick is akin to foot binding and female genital mutilation.[43]

Other contemporary feminists have found some redeeming value in the attention that women give to their looks and argued that beauty practices can be a means of economic advancement for women, the occasion for fashioning female rituals and a source of pleasure, power and play. One critique of absolute repudiations of beauty practices attends the way that women interested in their appearance emerge from such complete denunciations as the dupes of patriarchal culture and the beauty industry. Linda M. Scott confronts this view with the examples of Florence Graham (the daughter of a Welsh immigrant to Canada), who created the Elizabeth Arden brand, and Sarah Breedlove (the daughter of slaves, later known as Madame C. J. Walker) who became the first African American female millionaire through selling hair products. For each of them the cosmetics industry was a means not only for social advancement and wealth, but facilitated, in the first instance, a woman-centred social life and, in the second, the development of the African American community and support for the anti-lynching movement.[44] Complicating the unqualified rejection of beauty pageants that was the hallmark of Anglo-American second-wave feminism, Valerie

Felita Kinloch argues that the involvement of Black women in beauty pageants – not least in the Miss Black America pageant held on the very same day as the 1968 Miss America pageant famous for its freedom trash can – made the pageant into a site of contestation in a way that it was not for white women.[45] Drawing into question the view that women beautify only for men, *Lesbians, Levis, and Lipstick* looks at some of the ways that lesbians redefine and are made anxious by dominant ideals of beauty – but also do not live outside a context concerned with appearance.[46] Liz Frost focuses on the pleasure of 'doing looks' and, while agreeing with some elements of the critique of beauty, still questions another assumption inherent in the most categorical rejections of beauty practices: that 'appearance is detachable, something women can simply not have anything to do with if they choose to'; for her, this smacks of a reinstatement of the mind/body dualism, in which the self is located elsewhere than the body, a position that feminism claims to critique.[47] For Pamela Church Gibson, the more polemical rejections of beauty are paradoxically reminiscent of both misogyny and Puritanism.[48] People in early modern England took as given that appearance could not be disentangled from identity. Both men and women thought a great deal about how the self was represented on the body's surfaces, in the skin, the clothes and the hair. This book investigates this component of intellectual history through women's writing, their account books, recipes, life-writings, letters, advice and fiction.

The book is divided into three sections, each consisting of two chapters. The chapters in Part One on cosmetics rethink the common characterization of cosmetic practices in sixteenth- and seventeenth-century England as dangerously unhealthy and women themselves as dupes destroying their health to decorate their faces with cosmetic products containing mercury and lead. Annette Drew-Bear's *Painted Faces on the Renaissance Stage* (1994), Farah Karim-Cooper's *Cosmetics in Shakespearean and Renaissance Drama* (2006) and Patricia Phillippy's *Painting Women: Cosmetics, Canvases, and Early Modern Culture* (2006) – and others writing in essay form – have effectively detailed patriarchal anxieties about female sexual power, ruptures in patriarchal control, the transformation of women into commodities and the delimiting of all forms of female art. Using recipes, the first section demonstrates that the anti-cosmetic polemics and sallies typically used as evidence of beauty practices have distorted our understanding of the historical relationship between health and beauty. Recipes, for their part, were a form in which women and men authoritatively constructed knowledge about beauty and about health, race and class.

Chapter 1 focuses on recipes for products which make the face fair by removing freckles, pimples, redness and other blemishes. Found in both women's domestic collections and in printed volumes of cures by male physicians, these recipes need to be understood not as directions for paint but as beautifying physic and, as such, a recognized component of early modern medical practice. Even the beautifying recipes involving mercury were not, as scholars have assumed, merely a sign of women's wilful destruction of their health. Mercury, if controversial, was also a prestigious and useful treatment employed by physicians and surgeons, and the abuse women incurred for its use was, at least in part, informed by their intrusion into an esoteric domain of medical practice deemed the preserve of the male scholar. When read within the conflicts over professionalizing in early modern medical culture, women's recipes for beauty products emerge as logical investments in the health of the whole body and women's writing as an experimental art intended to improve nature.

Chapter 2 draws attention to the political structures undergirding the cultural evaluation of fair (that is, white and unblemished) skin. Race in early modern England is, as Ania Loomba defines it, a category of origins of blood and of distinctions of religion, nation, class and gender, as well as ethnicity. The chapter looks at how fair skin is politically constructed as whiteness, where fair beauty is a privilege of class – of an aristocratic race. The beautifying recipes in *The Queens Closet Opened* (1655), printed as the recipe collection of Queen Henrietta Maria, her last masque, *Salmacida Spolia* (1639/40) by William Davenant, and Aphra Behn's posthumously published prose narrative *The Wandring Beauty* (1698) polemically align the Stuart monarchy and its loyalists with fantasies of fair skin to advocate a harmonious social order based on absolute, natural and indestructible class privilege. This vision of class-based whiteness provides authority to racial difference.

If beautifying physic could become a means for some women to contest their intellectual authority and their place within early modern culture, so, too, could their clothes. Costume historians have taught us about the clothes men and women wore, while scholars of early modern drama have explored the multiple meanings of cross-dressing on the stage. But we know much less of how women inhabited female dress. To be sure, recent publications, such as those by Amanda Bailey and Sue Vincent, have been attentive to issues of gender in the history of fashion.[49] Ann Rosalind Jones and Peter Stallybrass's *Renaissance Clothing and the Materials of Memory* was a landmark book in drawing out the cultural significance of clothing. Still, these works attend to only limited evidence produced by early modern women themselves. Part Two uses the resources of women's fiction, advice and account books to further the discussion of women's approach to dress.

Chapter 3 delves into relationships between clothing and subjectivity in Lady Mary Wroth's prose romance, *The Countess of Montgomery's Urania* (1621), and a manuscript account book by a young woman, Margaret Spencer (British Library, Additional MS 62092, c.1610–1613). With the story of Nereana, Wroth explores how donning aristocratic clothing confers a powerful social identity, as well as the need for a version of female subjectivity forged independent of clothes. The entries recording the procurement of clothes in Margaret Spencer's account book confirm Wroth's model of power dressing to show practically how clothes, and the means by which they were acquired, allowed elite, beautiful women to become dominant, as well as subordinate, subjects within a social fabric structured by class, as well as gender.

Chapter 4 turns from women's writing about the subjective functions of women's clothes to their theorizing in works of maternal advice the public role of children's dress. The chapter looks at the printed advice book of Elizabeth Jocelin, *The Mother's Legacie, to her Unborn Child* (1624), and unpublished epistolary advice to her son Edward by Brilliana Harley, Lady Harley, who also composed in manuscript a short advice book (British Library, Additional MS 70118). Their maternal advice invests in clothing the capacity to manifest parental ideals of education, faith and order. The chapter assesses maternal advice about clothes, not as the expression of a peculiarly feminine concern, but as a form of governance functioning in concord with other social institutions, such as the church, the law and the university, which likewise sought to establish how the young should dress. For both mothers, advice to children about how to dress is informed by how they think about education. For Elizabeth Jocelin, clothes should not undermine the education of a daughter, whereas for Lady Harley they provide an entrance into masculine scholarly and political cultures. Lady Harley's advice to her son, moreover, allowed her legitimately to contemplate, and even control, how a young man should look, in a world where women very rarely wrote extensively about male appearance.

Part Three examines literary representations of the hair on the head, maintaining the book's attention to the social functions of beauty by exploring how hair marked and produced political and social power, first as a racial signifier and then as an economic one. Very little work has been done on the meanings of women's hair in the early modern period, with most historical research on hair taking the form of catalogues and sweeping surveys, such as Richard Corson's *Fashions in Hair: The First Five Thousand Years* (1965, 2001), although research on later periods sees hair as a cultural artefact. Hair has not been a component in scholarship of either the analysis of early modern race, despite the importance that contemporary feminists give hair as a racial marker, or of cross-dressing, although the man who dons female clothes and the woman who wears breeches must both change their hair to perform new gender roles convincingly.

Chapter 5 examines the function of hair in cross-dressing stories by Lady Mary Wroth and Margaret Cavendish, Duchess of Newcastle upon Tyne. The *Urania* and 'Assaulted and Pursued Chastity' treat soft, thick and slightly curled natural hair as a physiological sign of an elite European identity central to the cross-dresser's success in manipulating his or her gender identity and to the author's reconsideration of female subordination. When Leonius in Mary Wroth's *Urania* dons female clothes and convincingly styles his long, naturally thick and wavy hair in a feminine style, Wroth posits that hair has an absolute power to signify his class but does not allow it to define sexual difference or female subordination as it most often did. Drawing on contemporary travel narratives that constituted knowledge about the hair of inhabitants of the New World and Africa, Margaret Cavendish employs the natural hair of the cross-dressed aristocratic, European woman in her escape from sexual exploitation as an instrument of imperial power and cultural sway over people who have markedly different hair than her own.

Chapter 6 looks at the different approaches that Anne Clifford, Countess of Pembroke, Dorset and Montgomery took to hairstyling when she was a maid and a widow and argues that Clifford understood her hair as a component of her changing relationship to her inheritance and to luxury. The chapter compares the records of hair-related purchases in an account book from her youth (Beinecke Library, Osborn MS B27, 1600–1602) with a second account book's records from when she was older (Cumbria Record Office WD/Hoth/A988/17, 1665, 1667–1668) and reads these account book entries through the lens of portraits and life-writing, particularly her three volume manuscript family chronicle, *The Great Books of Record* (Cumbria Record Office WD/Hoth/A988/10). In her youth, her naturally luxurious hair embodies for her the legitimate possession of luxury goods and property, but when she was older, Anne Clifford covers and eventually shaves off her hair. This more ascetic approach is not a wholesale rejection of luxury, but a demonstration of her control of goods and herself, her autonomy and her place outside of the patriarchal economy of commodification and desire.

'The Poetry of Women'

A seventeenth-century needlework picture of Susanna and the Elders adorns the cover of this book because it exemplifies beauty's problems, because for early modern women, Susanna's story legitimized female speech against the false accusations of men, and because, for us, its material suggests an approach to women's literary history. Susanna's story, from the apocryphal thirteenth book of Daniel, is an iconic tale of how men approach female beauty. '[E]xceeding fayre' and well instructed by her parents in the law of Moses, Susanna was the wife of an honourable man whose home was a meeting place for all the men of judgement.[50] His fine house appears in the background of the needlework image behind two judges, their positions marked by their substantial robes, hats and beards. Inflamed with lust, the two old men spy on her daily in her husband's orchard. The image captures a time before the calamitous moment when Susanna sent out her maids to fetch the 'oile, and washing bals' she needed to bathe and was left alone with the lechers, who had hidden themselves in the garden.[51] The judges use Susanna's isolation as an opportunity to threaten her, as Collatine does Shakespeare's Lucrece: she must lie with them or they will accuse her of adultery. When she refuses and cries out, she is denounced by the judges and condemned to death for her purported adultery until, in response to her prayer, God sends a young Daniel first to name the foolishness of the people of Israel for 'not judging, not discerning that which is the truth' and then to expose the truth of Susanna's claims of innocence by revealing the inconsistencies in the judges' lies.[52] Ending with the execution of the corrupt judges, the reformation of the people and the restoration of Susanna to her family, the story precisely recounts some of beauty's more common early modern dilemmas – how the beautiful woman attracts unwanted and dangerous male attention, how it is difficult for the chaste woman within a patriarchal society to defend her honour, how men speak with more authority than women and how transgressive male desire for beauty can undermine the social order, disrupting families, making a travesty of justice and corroding the nation's faith. In her speech and chastity, as well as the divine favour with which her prayers are rewarded, Susanna possesses a remedy, however contingent, to her disenfranchisement.

This particular picture of Susanna and the elders, created around 1660, was embroidered on satin, with coloured silk, metal purl, couched work and watercolour details, probably by a professional embroiderer.[53] It records Susanna's beauty, that she is 'exceeding delicate, and beautiful of face', in the carefully wrought curls in her hair, the pearl necklace, the large falling collar, long sleeves and delicate blue apron over a voluminous skirt.[54] But the embroidered image also, more surely than many seventeenth-century paintings on the theme, asserts Susanna's chastity and virtue. Unlike the compliant, vain, curious, impassive, coy or weak Susannas depicted in the nude by Jacopo Tintoretto (1555–1556), Paolo Veronese (1580), Henrick Goltzius (1615), Lodovico Carracci (1616) or Geurcino (1617), or even the terrified, exposed Susannas painted by Peter Paul Rubens (1607) and Anthony Van Dyck (1620–1621), the proper clothes of this Susanna establish her virtue and preclude the paintings' suggestions of culpability, as do the maids who seem to tend her hair.[55] Neither does the image provide the opportunity for viewers to gaze on Susanna as the old men did.

Needlework was the quintessentially feminine activity, signifying industrious silence, but it could also provide the occasion for something more. Heroic women, such as Judith, Esther, Jael, Ruth or Susanna, were among the most popular Old Testament subjects for seventeenth-century needlework – more popular than stories of perfidious women, such as Delilah, or of men, such as Moses.[56] Embroidering such biblical exemplars, says Susan Frye, 'formed visual expressions of narratives offering alternatives to the passivity, privacy, and silence that needlework was supposed to enforce'.[57] As Lisa Klein contends, through making and exchanging needlework, women 'fashioned themselves as subjects, promoted their interests, and fostered social relationships [...]'.[58] For these critics, as well as for Elizabeth Mazzola and Jennifer Munroe, needlework is one of the practices that underpin women's literary history; it informs how women imagined themselves as writers, how they wrote and how their texts circulated.[59] Beauty practices are not entirely unlike needlework, if they were not so readily deemed moral and proper. Both afford tactical opportunities for intellectual and spiritual engagement, for artistic creativity and for enhancing social relationships. Beauty practices are part of the history of women's literary production, not as the opposite of literature but as activities, like writing, through which women could understand themselves as creative, skilful and authoritative. In this sense, women's material culture can be productive, at once imaginative and imagined in women's writing.

Margaret Cavendish, Duchess of Newcastle perhaps can best explain the connections between beauty practices and literature for early modern women. She thought a great deal about beauty. She wrote about it, too, much more than I have been able to consider in this book. She also put her theories into practice with her own appearance. With 'Of Painting', an essay in *The Worlds Olio* (1655), Cavendish confronts with wit and irony the dominant critique of cosmetic use, that painting is artificial, dissembling and an enticement to evil desires. She highlights the political, anti-feminist illogic of the polemic. Masculine arts are esteemed, she insists, even when the result is not advantageous. Those who created the 'Art of Gunpowder, Guns, Swords, and all Engins of War for Mischief' are esteemed as 'Petty Gods', while the creators of adornments and dressings are derided, even though the art of war 'destroyes Mankind' and the arts of beauty 'increaseth it; the one brings Love, the other begets Hate'. Gender politics, she insinuates, police the otherwise arbitrary boundaries of what counts as natural and moral. She concludes, 'I believe all Adornments of Beauty are lawfull for Women, if the Intention be good.' Adornments can even be commended as art, as 'the Poetry of Women, in shewing the Fancyes' and as directed towards the public good. They are 'the cause of imploying the greater part of a Commonwealth, for in four parts, three of them are in the Arts of Adornments'.[60] Cavendish defends beautifying by insisting on women's moral agency, allowing for their creativity and highlighting their consumption as a force for social order. Her argument is not that beautifying should be the most important thing in a woman's life – she contests that point in other essays – but she resists the sexualizing of women's appearance and the moralizing of women's attention to clothes, hair and cosmetics as inevitably vain, corrupt and sinful.

If Margaret Cavendish thought that beautifying was the poetry of women, her originality with the form garnered her little respect. The Duchess of Newcastle was better known for centuries for her appearance than for her writing because Samuel Pepys recorded in his famous diary what he thought of how she looked. He pursued a glimpse of the Duchess for almost two months. His quest began on 11 April 1667, when he went to Whitehall hoping to see her; on 26 April, 1 May and 10 May 1667 he tried again to see her, but he was inhibited first because she was in her coach and then because she was surrounded by others; on 10 May 1667, he 'drove hard' towards Clerkenwell upon seeing her coach, but only saw the '100 boys and girls running looking upon her'.[61] Pepys wanted to confirm what he had heard of her 'antique dress' and 'extravagancies': 'her velvet-cap, her hair about her ears; many black patches because of pimples about her mouth; naked necked, without anything about it, and a black juste-au-corps'.[62] Although he concluded that '[s]he seemed to me a very comely woman', his attraction evaporated when he achieved his goal on 30 May 1667. This was the occasion of the historic meeting of the Royal Society at Arundel House which Cavendish attended. Pepys seems disappointed: 'She is indeed black and hath good black little eyes, but otherwise but a very ordinary woman I do think; but they say sings well. The Duchesse hath been a good, comely woman; but her dress so antic, and her deportment so unordinary, that I do not like her at all.' She is pretty enough but strange – a woman interested in science – and consequently suspect. His assessment of her appearance frames his understanding of her speech, for Pepys adds, 'nor did I hear her say any thing that was worth hearing, but that she was full of admiration, all admiration'.[63] Later Pepys also denounces her biography of her husband as 'ridiculous'. It 'shows her', he says, 'to be a mad, conceited, ridiculous woman'.[64] Thus Pepys came to define the Duchess of Newcastle for centuries as 'Mad Madge', while Cavendish's own intellectual history, her thoughts on her cultivated look went unexamined.

Beautifying was for Margaret Cavendish a form of intellectual labour and creativity. In her autobiography, 'A True Relation of My Birth, Breeding, and Life', printed with *Nature's Picture Drawn By Fancies Pencil* (1655), she explains that she likes to dress. As she says:

> [M]y serious study could not be much, by reason I took great delight in attiring, fine dressing and fashions, especially such fashions as I did invent myself, not taking that pleasure in such fashions as were invented by others: also I did dislike that any should follow my Fashions, for I always took delight in a singularity, even in accoutrements of habits [...].[65]

Unremorseful about her enthusiasm for fine dressing, she sees her keen interest in appearance not only as lawful, honest, honourable and modest, but also as a study requiring imagination and invention.[66] Provided that the expense is within the bounds of what her estate can afford, dressing is profitable because she lives in a world that tends to look more to the outside than the inside – as Pepys's account of her palpably demonstrates.[67]

Appearance is also a means to identify one's power. Margaret Cavendish linked fair skin to Royalist politics, much like the women discussed in Chapter 2, when she represents her mother as a woman with perfect skin and politics. For her, Lady Elizabeth Lucas was a martyred Royalist, a widow deprived of all her goods for her loyalty to Charles I. She possessed, nevertheless, a 'Magestick Grandeur'. Her beauty, evidence of her social status, will strike awe in beholders

> and command respect from the rudest, I mean the rudest of civiliz'd people, I mean not such Barbarous people, as plundered her, and

used her cruelly, for they would have pulled God out of Heaven, had they had power, as they did Royaltie out of his Throne: also her beauty was beyond the ruin of time, for she had a well favoured loveliness in her face, a pleasing sweetness in her countenance, and a well temper'd complexion, as neither too red, nor too pale, even to her dying hour.[68]

Here Cavendish construes beauty as a physical feature, linked to moderation and divine favour, as a political value, connected to physiological and social temperance and respect for a timeless hierarchy with God and king at its apex. She would have her mother remembered as beautiful not to affirm that she was desirable to men, but to insist historically on her legitimacy as a political subject. While Pepys's diary demonstrates that he was himself deeply interested in fashion, he simply cannot read the Duchess's appearance. This book asks questions about women's thinking that Pepys will not. The Duchess is quite right to note that early modern England was deeply invested in appearances. How one dressed, the fairness of one's skin and the shape and texture of one's hair could signal differences of gender, class, race, and political, religious and moral identity. The women I discuss in this book recognize this and, working within a patriarchal culture and literary tradition, use beautifying creatively to forge a place for their own art – for their own social place and identity and for their writing practices. They do so in reference to literary history and to the beauty culture of everyday life. A feminist literary history might account for both.

Part One: Cosmetics

1
'The Beautifying Part of Physic': Women's Cosmetic Practices in Early Modern England

Investigations into female cosmetic practices in sixteenth- and seventeenth-century England have used their critics for evidence: satirical treatments of face painting in plays by Shakespeare, Jonson and Webster; Thomas Tuke's rancorous *A Discourse Against Painting*, printed in 1616; Richard Haydocke's 'Discourse of the Artificiall Beauty of Women' (his addition to his translation of *A Tracte Containing the Artes of Curious Painting*, again printed only once, in 1598); John Bulwer's ethnographic *Anthropometamorphosis* (1650, 1653), and Phillip Stubbes's somewhat more often reprinted *The Anatomie of Abuses* (1583, 1584, 1585, 1595). With these resources at hand, scholars have detailed how women who painted were derided for being vain, deceptive, seductive and akin to prostitutes, and how anxieties about paint were aligned with more general apprehensions about female power.[1] Scholars have also shown how these debates affected women. Kim F. Hall argues that the language of whiteness in the discourse of face painting commodifies women and signifies racial and cultural difference between them.[2] Frances Dolan contends that anti-cosmetic satire contrives to delimit all female art, while Patricia Phillippy illustrates how female writers and painters had to challenge this anti-painting tradition with their entry into print and visual art.[3]

What has not been sufficiently explored is how early modern women themselves approached beauty practices. By relying on the evidence provided by male critics of painting, rather than beauty's female practitioners, we have better detailed patriarchal anxieties than women's theories or their material praxis. Besides occluding women's agency in the production of beauty, relying on critical polemics has had a particularly distorting effect on our understanding of the relationship between health and beauty. Women appeared, even to sympathetic investigators, to be victims of their own needs or desires, as they destroyed their health by decorating their faces with cosmetics containing lead and mercury.[4] Carroll Camden contends, for instance, that if more women had heeded the advice of their critics, they would have used fewer cosmetics, 'with the resulting improvement in the general health of ladies'.[5] Sujata Iyengar convincingly offers one possible explanation for this seemingly self-damaging behaviour: women painted because it allowed them 'to rewrite the texts that men attempt to read on their faces'.[6] Yet she too relies on anti-cosmetic tracts and evidence from the early modern stage and does not question the assumption that women were acting against medical advice. Domestic recipe collections compiled by or belonging to women suggest an alternative point of view. Montserrat Cabré has argued that a fourteenth-century Catalan manuscript addressed to women construed recipes treating the body's surfaces as a means to preserve health.[7] Early modern manuscript recipe books in which were recorded cookery, medical and beautifying receipts, amongst other things, similarly attest to the role of beautifying physic in health care. Face painting scarcely appears in these documents. Indeed, I have found only one recipe that identifies itself as being for paint and that in a collection of alchemical recipes. More prominent are recipes for face washes and ointments, beautifying concoctions that transform the skin rather than cover it, and these are manifestly a component of medical practice. Extending the discussion beyond face painting, this chapter will argue that women's recipes demonstrate that beautifying, including work with mercurial cures, was a forum for the exercise of female authority in domestic medicine and for experiments in natural philosophy. As contemporary feminists have taught us, cosmetics are inflected by structures of power. In early modern England, even as beautifying physic encoded conformity it could also become an expression of female expertise in areas demarcated and claimed by professionalizing male physicians, surgeons and scientists.

The 'Choicest and Select'd Receps' of Women

Both female practitioners and cosmetic recipes have a place within seventeenth-century medical culture, and this fact must be used to reconfigure our unexamined assumption that women who used cosmetics were acting against the advice of medical practitioners. George Hartman's *Family Physitian* (1696) includes an entire section on the 'choicest and select'd Receps for making the rarest and safest Cosmeticks, to beautify, smoothen, soften, and whiten the Face and Skin'.[8] The subtitle of

Johann Wecker's 1660 collections of cosmetic receipts, variously entitled *Arts Master-piece: Or the Beautifying Part of Physick* and *Cosmeticks, or, The Beautifying Part of Physick,* gives the name to the concept discussed here: what I will call beautifying physic.[9] John Bulwer (1653) defines a similar idea, 'Cosmeticall Physic', as 'the exornatorie part of Physick, whose Office is, that whatsoever is according to Nature, that it is to preserve in the Body, and so consequently to cherish and maintaine the native Beautie thereof'.[10] Far from forging a unique connection between medical and beauty practices, these collections are extracting and highlighting a long-standing strand of medieval and early modern medical publication and practice. Beautifying physic encompasses the writing and work of physicians, surgeons (who administered topical medicines for the body's 'outer covering' and were, unlike physicians, legally limited to the use of external medicines) and apothecaries (whose function was, officially, to dispense medicine, but often included issuing medical advice).[11] Significantly, women practised these occupations or had the skills associated with them, although they were not typically licensed.[12] There was, as the work of Doreen Evenden Nagy, Lucinda McCray Beier and Andrew Wear proves, little difference between women's receipts and those used by men, whether they were professional or lay practitioners; moreover, lay treatment by family members, neighbours and women was widespread.[13]

Beautifying physic is part of this medical culture of diagnosis and treatment shared by lay and licensed practitioners, who employed products, like pomatum and face washes, which did not inspire the vitriolic anti-feminist attack that paint did. Moreover, practical distinctions between paint and medical treatments are surprisingly enigmatic, for paint can be a medicine and washes and pomatums, paints. For example, face washes are uncontroversial in one of the prefaces to Tuke's *A Discourse Against Painting,* Elizabeth Arnold's translation of an invective against painting by a Spanish physician, Andreas de Laguna. While Laguna announces that '[t]he Ceruse or white Lead, wherewith women use to paint themselves was, without doubt, brought in use by the divell' and that the use of mercury sublimate is 'like to originall sinne', he recommends washing the face and allows that 'honest women should wash themselves, and seeke to make their faces smooth'.[14] Yet the recipes for face washes catalogued here indicate that face washes, like paint, could include mercury, and that, although the aim was to alter rather than cover the skin, the end was still a fair face, as much as a clean one. Pomatums, too, are used in beautifying physic, but they are sometimes derided in the same terms as face paint and even identified as paints themselves. Mary Evelyn and Margaret Cavendish both mock pomatum as expensive and deceptive, as if it were paint, while Hugh Plat's *Delightes for Ladies* uses the words 'pomatum' and 'fucus' inter-changeably.[15] A recipe for 'An excellent Pomatum to clear the skinne', made of barrow's grease washed in May dew and marshmallow roots, is 'of a great professour of Arte ... as the best fucus this day in use'.[16] While 'fucus' denotes paint, the phrase 'clear the skinne' suggests a trans-formative function more aligned with medicine. Plat's identification of his source, the professor of art, also connects the product to science or medicine. Indeed, when this same recipe appears in Hannah Wolley's *The Accomplish'd Lady's Delight,* which reprints many of Plat's recipes, it appears in the section entitled 'The Phisical Cabinet: Containing Excellent Receipts in Physick and Chyrurgery'.[17] In recipe books the difference between concoctions that cover the skin and those that pre-serve and cure it – and thus mobilize the moralized distinction between nature and artifice – are constantly rendered imprecise; pomatums, for instance, both cover and transform. More important than the material difference between artificial and natural beauty, or between noxious paints and salutary medicines, is how those with power attempt to police the boundaries of the natural. Margaret Cavendish observed this in the seventeenth century, when she questioned why it was considered more artificial to beautify than to cut one's hair, pare one's nails, shave one's beard, or wash one's face – all activities allowed to men.[18]

Neither do there appear to be substantive differences between the female and male practice of beautifying physic. Recipes for pomatums and washes are not exclusive to a feminized medical practice or to books for women. Printed medical treatises by male practitioners include them and then often without an explicitly gendered audience. Some recipes in Hugh Plat's *Delightes for Ladies* come from male sources: M. Foster, the Essex man who cured his high and fiery colour with a liter; Master Rich who 'helped himselfe and a gallant Ladie' to remedy the mor-phew; and the traveller who rid himself of freckles.[19] Likewise the ointment to 'make a man's visage white' in *Natura Exenterata* implies masculine concern with fairness.[20] The integration of male and female practices that scholars have observed of medical practices generally holds true in the more specific area of cosmetic receipts, which are found in collections made by surgeons, physicians and apothecaries, and produced for male, as well as female, audiences. *The English Man's Treasure,* addressed to surgeons by Thomas Vicary, Sergeant Surgeon to Henry VIII, was published first in 1586. It has a water that will 'make the face faire and the breath sweete', a 'remedie for a red face or red nose', another for 'chappes', a rosemary water that will make a clean face and cures for 'coppered' and swollen faces.[21] Addressed to female readers and dedicated to Richard Wistow, 'one of the assistants of the Companie of the Barbers and Surgions', John Partridge's *The Treasurie of Commodious Conceits,* has the same recipe 'to make the face faire and the breath sweete';[22] his *Treasurie of Hidden Secrets* reprints the recipe, along with still more waters to make the face fair, to remove high colour, heat or pimples, and to make the hands white and fair.[23] Nicholas Culpeper's enormously popular *The English Physician* provides 22 different concoctions said to remedy such dermatological issues as freckles, deformity, discolouring, morphew, spots, scurf (characterized by scales), pimples, wrinkles and sunburn.[24] Culpeper consistently employs words like 'heal' and 'cure'. A distilled water of kidneywort 'healeth Pimples, Redness, S. Anthonies fire, and other outward heats and Inflammations' and the juice of fumitory 'cureth' pimples, itches or wheals that appear on the face.[25] *Pharmacopoeia Londinensis* (1618), translated by Culpeper in 1649, lists the preparations sanctioned by the College of Physicians in London and includes cures for pimples, freckles, morphew and sunburn. 'Oyl of Tartar' (a potassium carbonate solution made from the deposits in wine barrels), the pharmacopoeia recommends in its English translation, is 'common to be had at every Apothecaries, and Virgins buy it to take away the sunburn and freckles from their faces'.[26] Although the oil is identified as a product uniquely for female use, it remains an institutionally sanctioned pharmaceutical. The face-water recipes have a diverse array of ingredients but the same aim: to make the face fair – white, smooth and without marks. This fairness signals health, as well as beauty.

Recipes for pomatums, as for face waters, are printed in medical treatises by professional practitioners. The 'safe cosmetick remedies' recommended in George Hartman's *Family Physitian* include a pomatum consisting of the marrow of six dozen sheep's feet, cold-seeds, lemon rind, borax (a mineral), lily root and rose water, which 'nourishes, smoothens, softens and whitens the Skin'.[27] *The Physicall Directory* lists a pomatum amongst the ointments approved by the College of Physicians. Made of suet, the fat of a sow, apples, rose water, almond oil and wax – although Culpeper adds that there are many better than this – this pomatum is used to 'soften and supple the roughness of the skin, and take away the chops of the lips, hands, face or other parts'; Culpeper's difficulty with the recipe, it should be noted, is with its effectiveness and not with the morality of treating the skin.[28] Culpeper's *The English Physician* similarly notes in its entry on apples that 'The oyntment called Pomatum, if sweet and well made, helpeth the chops in the lips or hands, and maketh smooth and supple the rough skin of the hands or face parched with winde or other accidents.'[29] John Tanner's *The Hidden Treasures of the Art of Physick* indicates that 'Unguentum Pomorum, commonly called Pomatum' is 'good to anoint the Nose and Lips, being chopped by the Wind'.[30] While fair skin is an aesthetic end, it is also a medicalized state, for chapped or dry skin requires a cure.

Both face waters and pomatums are evident in popular herbals, as well. The tables at the end of *The Greate Herball* and of the herbals compiled by Rembert Dodoens, John Gerard (a prominent member of the company of Barber-Surgeons) and John Parkinson (a member of the Society of Apothecaries) all index the face and direct the reader to many herbs that can be used in waters, as well as in ointments, to cleanse the face of freckles, redness, morphew, pimples, deformities and the like.[31] The contexts in which the recipes appear, as well as the language that they employ, configure face waters and pomatums as components in the production of health, most without mentioning a specifically gendered audience. These medical recipe collections and herbals, moreover, are considerably more numerous and exponentially more popular than the few polemical anti-painting treatises.

When women's manuscript recipe collections include recipes for pomatums and washes, they document not just women's knowledge of beautifying physic but their active participation in medical culture, as dispensers of cures and experimenters in pharmacology. Recipe collections, including those that record recipes for beautifying products, are presented by their owners as valued medical knowledge, not as a form of 'desperate madnesse' or as contempt for nature, as Laguna insists cosmetics are.[32] In several different hands, Lady Frances Catchmay's manuscript, entitled *Booke of Medicens,* includes 23 products for the face. The recipe collection was a bequest to her children, to be delivered to her son Sir William Catchmay, who was charged to allow all of his brothers and sisters to copy it.[33] The language of these receipts is also consistently therapeutic: 'A soveraigne medicen for the heate in the face proved by many & often tymes', 'A very good water for the heate in the face, or for the morphew', several 'medicen[s] to coole & repell the reddnes of the face that proceedethe of heate in the liver', 'Another medicen to destroy a heate in the face' and 'other good medicens to make the face fayer & to take away heate'.[34] Wellcome MS 373, into which the inscription 'Jane Jackson: her Booke: written in the yeer 1642' has been pasted, is entitled *A very shorte and compendious Method of Phisicke and Chirurgery.*[35] The manuscript provides notes on weights and measures, explains humoural physiology and offers several diagnostic tests.[36] Measurements are needed, the text explains, because errors 'in the true quantitie ... doth much hurte to the body and many times putteth the life in ieopardy'.[37] Thus approaching the practice of medicine systematically, this receipt book includes several face washes to remove freckles, others for redness and to 'abate blood in the face' and one for 'red blemes [blemishes] in a man's face'.[38] *Elizabeth Digby's Housebook*, c.1650, contains a plaster 'For any swelling, or breaking forth on the face, blasting, or other corrupted meanes', while Margaret Baker's medical and culinary recipes, c.1672 – a receipt book that preserves a wide array of medical receipts from diverse sources – includes a snail water for the face, two face washes for morphew, sunburn and freckles, others for freckles, and face washes based on borax and pippins.[39] *Cookery Receipts of Lady Ranelagh* includes quite a number of medical receipts, for scurvy, rhume, deafness, consumption, cough and gout, for instance. It also has 'A water for heat in the faces + breaking out with pimpills' and waters for a red face, for heat in the face, for a 'red pimpled face' and 'Red face, by a hot (lever)'.[40] Mary Doggett's *Book of Receipts*, c.1682, includes, in its section on medical receipts, 'A water to take Sunburne off ye Face & hands', 'A Mercury Water good for ye killing of any Itch or Ringworm Redness or salt Flamed Face', a puppy water used as a face wash, a drink 'For cooleing ye Liver & Flushing in ye Face' and a wash 'For an inflama[ti]on or Breaking out in ye Face'.[41] Mary Glover's book of recipes, autographed as 'Mary Glover, her Booke of Receipts: Anno Domini 1688', but in various hands, has two recipes to take away freckles.[42] In short, there are numerous recipes for face washes in women's domestic receipt books, and their language, like those of recipes in collections by licensed practitioners, is that of medicine.

For both unlicensed female medical practitioners and their professional male contemporaries, the absence of fairness in the skin can be attributed to humoural imbalance of one kind or another, usually an excess of heat or dryness. Within the Galenic model of physical health, the skin is the signifier of the complexion, upon which depends good overall health.[43] As *The Touchstone of Complexions* puts it, 'There is no surer way (sayth Galene) certainly to knowe the humours and juyce in a Creature, then by the colour and outward complexion.' Accordingly, a very white complexion betokens a phlegmatic humour, paleness or yellowness, melancholic and choleric humours, and blackness, a choleric humour.[44] The colour shifts with the ruling humour, which also inflects personality and gender identity, and is itself influenced by food, activity and the environment. *Artificiall Embellishments,* a text devoted to beauty practices, begins by recommending 'those things which Physitians usually terme *res non naturales*' – air, watching and sleep, exercise or repose, evacuation or retention of excrements, passions, meat and drink.[45] Beyond thus invoking Galen's 'non-naturals', the text explains how beautifying functions within a humoural medical context: 'Such colours when they annoy the complexion principally proceed from ill humours, which abound in the body & are expelled forth to the external supersicies of the skin; wherefore those that desire to correct any vitious colour that offends their bodies, must in the first place by some purgation evacuate that humour, whereto their distemper ows its original.'[46] A woman's concern for the appearance of her face, therefore, can be a way of caring for the health of her body as a whole and constituting identity, not just performatively or theatrically – as facilitated by paint – but inwardly and physiologically. 'A Beauty Water for the Face, by Madam G.' in Hannah Wolley's *The Accomplished Ladys Delight* says that '[i]t is good to wash the Head, and to comfort the Brain and Memory.'[47] Both the ideal of beauty and its attainment have a physical and emotional logic.

Mercury's Artists

Even when women employ mercury in beautifying physic, they are working within a rational model of appropriate early modern medical practice. The rejection of beautifying physic on the basis of mercury's harm strains to delimit women's medical and scientific knowledge more than it strives accurately to reflect the prevailing early modern views of mercury. It is true that mercury was acknowledged to be dangerous, even by those not against female power or feminine artifice. Margaret Cavendish's 'Of Painting' from *The World's Olio* (1655) debunks most of the arguments against cosmetic use, but the duchess still speaks out against paints that employ mercury because they cause consumption, swelling and rotten teeth.[48] Yet mercury was not regarded only with suspicion. Mary Trye's *Medicatrix or the Woman Physician* (1675) is a defence of the chemical medicine practiced by Paracelsus, Van Helmont and her father, who taught his cures to her.[49] Indeed, mercury was a common medicinal ingredient. As Andrew Wear observes, 'Whilst [physicians] accepted that [mercury] produced dangerous side-effects for the patient, they swore by it.'[50]

   When employed in the chemical therapies of Paracelsian medicine, mercury – along with sulphur and salt – was one of the three principles of which bodies were thought to consist. Mercury constituted bodies as fluid and vaporous; its rule produced paralysis, tumours, stupefaction and corrosion and thus functioned as their cure, for according to Walter Pagel, in Paracelsian medicine, 'in the source of the disease lies its remedy'.[51] An English translation of one of Paracelsus's works contends that mercury, linked to fire and to purity, preserves the body from corruption, 'defendeth wounds and ulcers from accidents, and expelleth such diseases as are under its degree and power, and disperseth the root thereof'.[52] Within the dominant Galenic paradigm, mercury and lead were a remedy for the heat caused by an imbalance in the humours. Mercury, particularly, is an evacuative medicine.[53] Two works appended to *A Briefe and Necessarie Treatise, Touching the Cure of the Disease called Morbus Gallicus* (1585), by William Clowes, defend the use of mercury beyond the treatment of syphilis. John Banester, a master in surgery, writes one of these epilogues. Mercury, he says, can dissolve and expel humours, especially those next to the skin; it is 'not onely not to be discommended, but also with admiration to be entertained of all those which faithfully studie and earnestly enjoyne themselves to the reliefe & comfort of afflicted persons'.[54] John Woodall's *The Surgions Mate* includes a poem, 'In Laudem Mercurii: Or in Praise of Quicksilver or Mercurie', which suggests that although mercury makes a patient 'seeme like death,/with ugly face, with stinking breath' it soon restores him to health, curing him of pox, gout, leprosy, scabs, itch, wounds and ulcers. Mercury dries moist humours and purges them down because it is both moist and dry, hot and cold.[55] The damaging effects of mercury censured in anti-cosmetic discourse are, in these medical treatises, but short-term consequences to a long-term cure for ailments that require a purge.

Like mercury, lead is an ingredient in beautifying physic that is dangerous from a contemporary perspective but commonly utilised in early modern medicine. Lead – ceruse, white lead, red lead and litharge of lead – is an ingredient in plasters for drying and for cold, for pain, old sores, morphew, ulcers in the arms and children's faces, and the serpigo. Vicary prescribes it as an ingredient in a green water, in a concoction to 'take away heate and inflamation of a member', 'Vergent milke' (used to take away pimples and redness), a 'searccloth [*sic*] for aches' and a cold ointment.[56] While in translating *The Physicall Directory* Culpeper adds sceptical metacommentary about the use of mercury, the many recipes for chemical preparations, ointments and plasters based on lead approved by the College of Physicians receive a different assessment; lead, Culpeper asserts is 'of an healing nature, applied to the place it helps any inflamation, and dries up humors'.[57] When *The Greate Herball* proposes 'to take awaye overmuche readnesse' with lily root, 'scomme of golde', 'camfre in oyl' and 'quenched quickesilver', the recipe is not resorting to some particularly desperate remedy to feed the voracious vanity of women but, in the use of quicksilver at least, recommending a fairly standard medical practice.[58]

The use of mercury and lead in recipes belonging to women functions according to the same physiological presuppositions. One of the recipes in Lady Ranelagh's collection of recipes addresses heat in the face and explicitly relates the red face to a hot liver, a recommendation seemingly based on the idea that fairness will result from cooling the humours.[59] Lady Frances Catchmay has a recipe for mercury water, which will 'kill all heat' and 'make yor face much fayrer and smoother then the other sorte'; a 'Spetiall medicine for the rednes of the Face or nose' employs mercury, too.[60] Margaret Baker's recipes posit that freckles can be 'dr[ied] away' and employ mercury in a cure for morphew, sunburn, freckles and worms in the face, as well as in a recipe that will 'destroy' freckles.[61] A drink in Mary Doggett's recipes proposes to cool the liver and so flush the face and the same collection includes 'A Mercury Water good for ye killing of any Itch or Ringworm Redness or salt Flamed Face'.[62]

Beyond demonstrating women's knowledge about the medical uses of mercury and lead, recipes for beautifying physic exhibit women's engagement with scientific experiment. Lady Frances Catchmay's recipes report of 'a ge[n]tle wooman of my acquaintance' as a researcher who tried an 'experiment' to create an ointment to make the skin even more fair, clear, white and smooth than the original version, which 'they saie is used by my Lady: p: Riche'.[63] This experimental approach is also suggested by the repeated use of the Latin tag, *probatum*, for 'having been approved' – used in many manuscript recipe collections – in reference to a salve for sore lips and a cure for spots on the face.[64] This tag appears, too, in Lady Ranelagh's recipes: 'Red face. Prob.'[65] Physic recipes, because they are exchanged, are also traces of knowledge networks that link manuscript and print culture and male and female medical practitioners. Montserrat Cabré shows how women's medical recipes in Iberia between 1350 and 1650, exchanged in letters and through 'open' collections of recipes (compiled by different women over long periods of time), could provide empowering knowledge; recipes could be exchanged as gifts and when the recipe was a secret, used for self-promotion. They are evidence, too, of 'women's learning communities'.[66] They are, as Sara Pennell says of cookery recipes, a form tested and validated by women who used the receipt and 'as important to understand in the history of early modern cultures of knowledge as

the ways in which their natural philosophical contemporaries deployed
such texts at the heart of their experimental revisionism'.[67] A particular
part of this culture, beautifying physic is an accessible mode for the
development and expression of women's knowledge in medicine and
natural philosophy.

Outside the domestic context, beautifying physic could provide a
means for gaining an economic livelihood as one element of women's
medical practices. According to Margaret Pelling, there may have been
about 300 women practising medicine in London between 1550 and
1640.[68] Helping women to make a living as healers by advertising their
services, handbills from the later decades of the seventeenth century
intimate that beautifying physic comprised a notable component of
the medical practices of women.[69] The language of the bills draws no
distinction between expertise in medicine and in beautifying physic.
One handbill advertises the service of a 'Gentlewoman' in 'Surry-street,
in the Strand' who '[h]ath a most excellent Wash to beautifie the face,
which cures all Redness, Flushings, or Pimples. Takes off any Yellowness,
Morphew, Sun-burn, or spots on the Skin, and takes away the Wrinkles
and Driness, caused too often by Mercurial Poysonous Washes.' As it
continues, the advertisement enumerates more of the 'gentlewoman's'
wares: masks and forehead pieces, red pomatum for the lips, paste to
whiten the hands, cosmetics to anoint the face after smallpox, pre-
ventatives for baldness, tooth powder, hair remover and colouring, and
the ability to pluck eyebrows perfectly. The bill concludes by advertising cures for sore eyes, consumption, scurvy and barrenness, and
her knowledge of 'many other secrets in Physick'.[70] Another bill, by a
gentlewoman in 'great Suffolk Street' advertises her years of experience
and study, her cures for the ague, stone and ulceration of the kidney,
amongst other indispositions, and her 'most rare Secrets in the World
for beautifying the Face'. She cures teeth and faces ruined by poisonous
washes and red faces, and she has pomatums, lip pomatum and face
waters (for half-a-crown to £5 per bottle).[71] Still another woman, identifying herself as 'Agnodice' – a female gynaecologist who inhabited classical Athens – and a physician, insists that she can cure scotch disease,
itch, surfeit, leprosy and either venereal disease or pregnancy, while
also offering an 'Italian wash' '[w]hich takes away all Cutaneous Effects,
or Blemishes in the Skin, as Freckles, Scorbutick Spots, Morphew, and
all other spots; also Dark and Swarthiness of the Skin, making the Face
most Fair and Clear'.[72] For these women, and others, beautifying physic
is plainly part of the medical marketplace and the unlicensed practice
of early modern healing.

We need to reconfigure our understanding of early modern beauty practices within larger cultural conflicts surrounding the recondite and secret nature of knowledge of mercury, institutional postures towards legitimate uses and users and gendered struggles for medical authority. From this angle, the critique of women who make and use cosmetics which employ mercury seems contingent on their transgression into a realm of knowledge reserved for educated men, as much as on anxiety about mercury itself. Mercury is construed as a special ingredient that should be only in the hands of authoritative users, whose possession signals their intellectual prestige. After all, Robert Boyle, living at his sister, Lady Ranelagh's house, conducted experiments with mercury, as did Sir Isaac Newton and King Charles II, although both suffered detrimental effects on their health as a result.[73] Sometimes the art of mercury is accessible for a popular audience, as in the herbal's call for 'quenched' quicksilver and Thomas Vicary's recommendation of 'quicksilver killed with fasting spettle' as part of a cure for the 'coppered face' and in other recipes; Mrs Carlyon's recipe to 'cure a face that is redd, and full of Pimples' similarly explains how to kill quicksilver with fasting spittle, presumably all attempts to mitigate the damaging effects of mercury to what is actually efficacious.[74] More often, however, mercury is represented as an arcane substance, simply dangerous to those who use it without learning. G. Baker, a 'Maister in Chirurgerie' who contributed another epilogue to Clowes's work, allows that 'through the undiscrete handling of it, manie evills may happen, the which is not to be attributed to the thing, but to the worker'.[75] For Woodall, it is a 'secret rare' discovered by the 'Artist wise'.[76] And while for Banester 'women, ignorant people, & runners about' might succeed with it only because of fortune, for those who 'faithfully studie', it yields 'health to the bodie after a mervailous maner … if it be ministred according to arte'.[77] As Andrew Wear puts it, when it came to mercury, 'learning, as in other areas of medical practice, provided safety'.[78] Female practitioners, by virtue of their exclusion from institutional education, could never be qualified to use mercury, and consequently, their creation and use of beautifying physic based on mercury will always be suspect.

The aura of mystery and esoteric power attached to mercury may also derive from its use in chemistry and alchemy – another gendered category of knowledge. John Webster's *Metallographia,* an English translation of a Latin collection of writing about chemistry dedicated to Prince Rupert (the son of Elizabeth, Queen of Bohemia), begins with the assertion that metals are 'the most abstruse and most excellent part of all Naturall Philosophy'.[79] Paracelsus describes the one who works with mercury and other chemical medicines as 'an Artist in this Profession' who can 'imitate Nature in all her Operations', for one who 'searcheth a thing so secret and difficult' must 'be a Scholar not only of Art, but of Nature'.[80] This scholar has power over feminine nature, at its most illustrious in mercury. For William Fulke, too, quicksilver is feminine, the 'mother of all metals', and for Joseph De Chesne, sulphur is to quicksilver as 'the man to the woman, and as the proper agent to the proper matter'.[81] If for Paracelsus, mercury is the 'sperm' in chemical transmutation – a differently gendered scientific metaphor – mercury continues to have a generative power.[82] Either way, women's use of mercury is transgressive. The scholars controlling feminine nature are implicitly masculine, while mercury forges a form of reproduction known exclusively by men as a masculine secret.

As medical and alchemical secrets, cosmetic recipes are knowledge inappropriate for women. *Naturall Magick: Where are set forth all the Riches and Delights of the Natural Sciences* (1658) prints a chapter on female beautifying alongside explorations of the generation of animals and plants, the changing of minerals and counterfeiting of gold, amongst other topics. *Eighteen Books of the Secrets of Art & Nature: being the Summe and Substance of Naturall Philosophy* (1660), 'first designed by John Wecker Dr in Physick, and now much Augmented and Inlarged by Dr. R. Reid', has a frontispiece picturing on either side of its title, William Harvey and Francis Bacon, presumably to convey the gravity and scientific authority of its contents. Along with chapters on astronomy, anatomy, animals, fish, birds, metals and other topics, is a chapter on the secrets of life and death, which includes recipes for beautifying the body.[83] *A Choice Collection of Rare Chymical Secrets and Experiments in Philosophy* (1682), 'Collected and Experimented' by Sir Kenelm Digby and published posthumously by George Hartman, also includes cosmetic recipes. The volume presents an array of highly complex alchemical processes, printed with the use of alchemical symbols and figures illustrating the required tools. This is a work, says the address to the reader, of 'rare and profitable Secrets in Philosophy and Chymistry', to be praised for its clarity, for the secrets can lead the understanding reader to 'be conducted as with an Ariadnean Line into the most intricate and hitherto fatigating Arcana of Chymistry'.[84] These chemical secrets include, along with innumerable experiments with mercury, three oils of talc 'Excellent for the Face and Skin', a 'Cosmetick prepared out of [silver]' that is 'Excellent to whiten the Face', and one of Sir Kenelm Digby's own remedies, which includes in its merits curing inflamed red faces.[85] While Hartman warns in *Family Physician* against the use of mercury in beautifying physic, his qualms do not extend beyond domestic medicine to include products catalogued as the arcana of chemistry.

The exclusion of women from the use of mercurial remedies which might be employed by learned men is a component of cosmetic discourse directed to a female audience, as well. When *Artificiall Embellishments* remarks that 'experienced Physitians' commend mercurial ointments, it is invoking mercury's medical and scientific posture. The writer lists two ointments which contain quicksilver, but if the writer finds them 'much extol'd', he warns women to try other things first 'because of the quicksilver'; experienced physicians might be the skilful artists – straining mercury through a sheepskin, boiling it with vinegar and various herbs, again straining it, and finally mortifying the concoction with lemon juice or fasting spittle – but women cannot be, since they are warned from the use of what physicians recommend.[86] 'Simple women', Richard Haydocke similarly implies, employ mercury sublimate and lead unwitting of their harm, although, he acknowledges, surgeons use the former as a corrosive and the latter to dry up moist sores.[87] It is not that mercury is dangerous and should not be used – as we might think – but that surgeons and physicians may use mercury in their practice while women cannot. The purgative effect of mercury in beautifying physic is the same as in other cures, but women are presumed to be ever unwitting users. Women cannot be practising physic when they use mercury because women are not capable of the category of knowledge to which it belongs. This is certainly how George Hartman sees things: 'the more curious Women and pretenders to the most exquisite knowledge in the Cosmetick Art, are scarce satisfied with any Remedies for the Skin but Mercurial'.[88] Hartman's comment is derogatory – again, women can only be pretenders to knowledge – but it does seem to imply that women may have found a certain pleasure specifically in mercurial products because their use demonstrated authority in a realm of sophisticated, scientific knowledge that was made accessible to them through beautifying physic. That it is Lady Ranelagh's alchemical recipe collection that contains the only recipe which I have found for paint certainly highlights this special alignment between beautifying and science. Lynette Hunter describes Lady Ranelagh as a practitioner of experimental chemistry, and the recipes in Ranelagh's collection employ alchemical symbols, as well as other abbreviations.[89] For other women, too, mercurial remedies are not just topical applications but esoteric forms of knowledge.

In short, cultural anxieties about female beauty practices overlap at several points with gendered attempts to undermine and delimit the knowledge and intellectual authority of women in the fields of medicine and natural philosophy. Beautifying physic is often the knowledge of secrets. As Allison Kavey has shown, women participate in secrets, a common trope in scientific discourse, on different terms than men – as gossips and the holders of domestic knowledge, rather than as gentlemen scholars who have intellectual authority in natural philosophy because of their social and economic independence.[90] When they rely on mercury, beautifying recipes become masculine knowledge. Margaret Pelling describes as 'hybrid or cross-gendered instances of practice' those medical practices that cross stereotypes of simple feminized medicine based on experience and difficult masculine, authoritative remedies; her example is women's use of powerful remedies, including mercury.[91] This is the very ingredient at the heart of attacks on painting. Although we might assume that cosmetics were female knowledge, they are often more of a hybrid form and, as such, sure to incite anxiety. Physicians themselves, according to Pelling, were concerned that their activities were deemed too feminine and responded accordingly to constitute their profession in masculine terms to exclude women; male physicians, surgeons and apothecaries were 'compromised by gender', by the association of physic with women's work – the nurturing and care of the body, servitude and gossip within the household.[92] There is a similar taint of effeminization surrounding experimental natural philosophy. As Deborah Harkness writes of the sixteenth and seventeenth centuries, 'the household bridged the gap between monastery and laboratory as a site for the practice of natural philosophy'.[93] Far from signalling women's ignorance, the use of chemical ingredients alongside herbal ones in the practice of beautifying physic illustrates a form of experimental and intellectual authority and a challenge to attempts by scientists and physicians to delineate exclusionary, gendered categories of knowledge. Mercury is a hazardous ingredient. But to say, as early modern commentators did, that its use in beautifying is straightforward evidence of women's moral corruption, ignorance or desperation is to ignore the range of its uses in early modern medical practice, debates over that use and struggles around women's participation in creating and conveying medical knowledge.

Conclusion

Beautifying physic is without a doubt a deeply ambivalent practice. Some of these conflicts will be discussed further in the next chapter. The creation and use of beautifying physic must inculcate a class identity. Not only can the female producer afford to purchase the ingredients, she can enhance and highlight her class position by transforming her body in culturally signifying ways. The author of *Artificiall Embellishments* expresses concern that even in addressing the question of '[h]ow to repair the beauty of an itchy or scabby skin', his lady readers will think he is addressing himself to their 'kitchin maids' because such 'exulcerations are more frequently incident' to them.[94] For this author and, he assumes, his readers, to have scabby skin is to risk being identified as lower class. To have fair skin is to avoid such ready designation, and so cosmetics potentially enable the transgression of class distinctions marked in appearance. But if the woman of Surry-Street's face water costs 'half a Crown, to five Pound a Bottle', beautifying products are materially the preserve of those with the money to buy them or the ingredients with which they are made. The face water also creates a racialized identity. When Agnodice promises a medicine to remove the 'Dark and Swarthiness of the Skin', she uses beautifying physic to materialize racial difference, just as Kim F. Hall suggests is the purpose of paint. Because the healthy body is signified by fairness, the appropriate shade of white, health itself is fundamentally a racialized construct. In addition to standing in opposition to blackness, early modern fairness gathers meaning against alternatives of whiteness, redness, marks and colours that signal an unhealthy complexion or overall ill health. Red skin is attached to yet another configuration of cultural power, for when blemishes are seen to be products of blood, the production of the fair face is linked to anxieties about female chastity in a world where lust is connected to an excess of blood. The 'clean, straight, unmarked body', as Margaret Pelling observes, ideally signified both health and beauty and was that 'which the searchers were seemingly to have in mind during witchcraft trials' – with fairness portending in this context that one was not a witch.[95] The production of fairness might be an attempt to make one's goodness visible. And finally, the production of beauty, even when it requires knowledge of esoteric subjects usually reserved for men, can still aim at allowing women to function within a normative, patriarchal social order. Indeed, one handbill by a woman selling her medical skills explicitly defends the distribution and use of face waters by suggesting that women's beauty can stabilize the patriarchal family:

> God the Author of all things, to make Man in love with his Wife, in her state of Innocency, he made her smooth, soft, delicate and fair, to intice him to imbrace her; I therefore, that Women might be pleasing to their Husbands, and that they might not be offended at their Deformities, and turn into other Womens Chambers, do commend

unto you the Virtue of an eminent and highly approved Balsamick Essence, with several other incomparable Cosmeticks, faithfully prepared without Mercury.[96]

In all of these ways, the creation of fairness is a means by which women position themselves within a hierarchical social order by inscribing the markers of class, race and appropriate femininity in their flesh.

Nevertheless, if all this aligns with Susan Brownmiller's observation that fair skin, 'of the sort poets have praised', has long signified a healthy absence of deadly contagion, and is but 'a sentimental attribute of virginal innocence and aristocratic fragility', we should not let this be the whole story.[97] While plainly not a practice without politics, which will be developed in Chapter 2, beautifying physic could be contrived within the discourse of health. There it tactically occupies a cultural space, available to literate women of some economic means, where attempts to attain fair skin are not only endeavours to match the arbitrary whims of painters and writers who celebrated the fair-skinned Petrarchan lady. In beautifying physic, women access a holistic logic of good health and, by attending to their skin, care for their whole body. Beautifying physic is itself an art, requiring specialized skill and physiological, chemical and herbal knowledge, which, in practice, provides evidence of women's minds and their ability to function creatively and knowingly, whether in the household or in the marketplace, in a medical field competitively claimed by men. Recipe sharing could be the basis of intellectual relationships between women, and so in many ways, beautifying physic disrupts the dichotomy that Sara Halprin sees as having prevailed for many centuries, that in which women have to be 'naturally beautiful', while men make art out of beautiful women.[98] As physicians, early modern women are the artists ensuring that purportedly natural beauty, in themselves and others. Rather than regarding cosmetics as a component of the monolithic, oppressive structures of patriarchal power, we might see beautifying physic in early modern England as a site of contest for women living in a patriarchal society which sought strictly to limit their knowledge. We might well be sceptical, as Mary Wollstonecraft is, about the history of beauty practices, but it is worth recognizing that in the seventeenth century, at least, they are not only about shaping the mind to a body that is a gilt cage. The body could produce practices which enabled women to be literate, rational, intelligent and creative.

2
'Soveraigne Receipts', Fair Beauty and Race in Stuart England

I turn now to three texts that confer authority on the definition of beauty as fair and healthy to examine the strategies by which fair beauty becomes powerful and normative. Queen Henrietta Maria's last masque, *Salmacida Spolia* (1639/40) by William Davenant, has the Queen embodying Amazonian fair, healthy beauty against an anti-masque of recipes. *The Queens Closet Opened* (1655), printed as the recipe collection of Queen Henrietta Maria, includes recipes for beautifying physic and fashions the Queen as a medical authority. Reflecting on the political conflicts of the Civil War and Interregnum, Aphra Behn's posthumously published prose narrative, *The Wandring Beauty* (1698), rewrites heroic tales of Charles II's 1651 escape from Worcester through a well-born Royalist maid whose fair skin and medical expertise allow her, while disguised as the daughter of a yeoman, to escape a forced marriage and find her own more suitable match. It may seem curious to include *Salmacida Spolia* and *The Queens Closet Opened* in a book about women's writing. But if Queen Henrietta Maria did not write the masque, critics have positioned her as a producer of masques and through her performances the aesthetics of the Stuart court.[1] Likewise, if the Queen did not write the recipes in *The Queens Closet Opened,* she was their collector, and she provided them with authority. To be a collector of recipes is also to engage in an act of cultural production. For Susan Pearce, early modern collectors used objects 'as material witnesses to the truth of historical narrative, concrete assertions of the morals which can be drawn from the stories themselves'.[2] For W. M., who published the recipes, the collection recalls during the Interregnum the historical truth of the English monarchy; he puts the volume into print 'as it might continue my Sovereign Ladies remembrance in the brests and loves of those persons of honour and quality, that presented most of these rare receipts to her'.[3] The strategies by which *Salmacida Spolia* and *The Queens Closet Opened* construct the authority of the beautiful woman underpin the representation of health, beauty and politics in *The Wandring Beauty*. The texts together present fairness as an attribute of a powerful, authoritative elite who will maintain a social order structured by class and hereditary monarchy. Margreta de Grazia wrote of Shakespeare's sonnets that '[f]air is the distinguishing attribute of the dominant class', an attribute that 'serves both to distinguish the dominant class and, by distinguishing it, to keep it dominant'.[4] In Stuart England, these texts construct fair beauty as a physical norm consequent on humoural physiology and a political one: whiteness.

I use the word 'whiteness' to explore how the fair beauty so admired in early modern England is part of the historical constitution of white as a racial term. Valerie Babb defines whiteness as 'more than appearance; it is a system of privileges accorded to those with white skin' and as 'an invented construct blending history, culture, assumptions, and attitudes'.[5] With respect to early modern England, scholars such as Kim F. Hall and Joyce Green MacDonald have argued that discussions of race in early modern England should include the analysis of fair-skinned people as well as dark, 'not only', MacDonald says, 'because this concentration of color as the chief determinant of race is a modern rather than a Renaissance phenomenon, but because assuming that race is only about skin color leaves whiteness – the physically unmarked category, the engine which drives and dictates racial definition and stratification – immune from examination'.[6] As an engine of stratification, white skin would come to be associated in racist ideology with rationality, order, freedom and power, but it did not always have these meanings.[7] It was in the seventeenth century, with the advent of colonial trade, that white came to refer to Europeans exclusively and to function as a generic, collective, racialized adjective (as in 'white people').[8]

Race and class were mutually constituting structures in early modern England, implied even in the definition of the word 'race', which encompassed a somewhat broad array of categories of origin and of distinction based on the blood, such as lineage, religion, nation, gender and class, as well as colour.[9] Sujata Iyengar argues that 'the alignment of various nonsystematic xenophobias – mythologies of color, nationality, religion, class, and gender – into a coherent mythology of race is an emergent structure' in the early modern period.[10] Thus, skin colour could function in identifying racial difference in the modern sense but race could also define other forms of difference: groups differentiated from the English by nation or religion, such as the Irish or Jews, might be identified as black, while African women in the Renaissance could be given the white skin of the Petrarchan beauty because sexual, political and behavioural features were identified as racial markers, too.[11] The most common meaning of the word 'race' was as a synonym for class.[12] Because neither class nor whiteness have received as much attention as racial identities as have the African, Moor, Amazon, Native American or the Jew, part of my purpose here is to mark whiteness as a racial category deployed strategically in beauty practices and women's writing.[13] Another is to suggest that opposition with blackness was not the only means by which early modern writers constructed the privilege of white skin. Richard Dyer argues that opposition is 'characteristic of white culture, but it is not the whole story and may reinforce the notion that whiteness is only racial when it is "marked" by the presence of the truly raced, that is, the non-white subject'.[14] The texts discussed in this chapter establish fair beauty ideologically as a privileged form of whiteness because skin colour is made to signify class as well as ethnic difference and because fairness defines the normative, healthy state. Moreover, within the particular historical context of Stuart politics, *Salmacida Spolia, The Queens Closet Opened* and *The Wandring Beauty* elevate fair skin as a form of natural social power linked to class hierarchy and authorize it as the privilege of those loyal to Stuart monarchs.

Physic and the Queen's Amazonian Beauty in *Salmacida Spolia*

Fair beauty triumphs in *Salmacida Spolia* as a political and epistemological structure. Skin colour was not a new concern for the masque form. Jesse Swan contends that 'a poetics of color underwrote the "wit" and sensation of masques', that there was a 'royalist color complex'.[15] *The Masque of Blackness,* devised by Ben Jonson and Inigo Jones, in which Queen Anne performed with her ladies in blackface, and *The Masque of Beauty,* the sequel in which the Queen and ladies are made white, are central to the study of both beauty and blackness in the Stuart period. Before James took the throne, Queen Elizabeth represented herself as beautiful, ageless and fair to evoke ideas of virginity and goodness. As Peter Erickson comments, '[t]he cult of Elizabeth is a cult of whiteness', for her 'emblematic facial whiteness' was refracted through her portraits and her public appearances.[16] Put on display in the Ditchley portrait, Kim F. Hall adds, Elizabeth's whiteness is shared by England.[17] Fair beauty was a persistent component of Queen Henrietta Maria's political identity, too. Erica Veevers has shown that Henrietta Maria's performances in the masques embodied the spiritual qualities of Beauty and Light, correlatives of Neoplatonic and Counter-Reformation Catholic ideals, which also encompassed the Laudian preference for beauty in holiness: 'Charles was, in fact, restoring the arts to the English Church as well as to the country, and his deepest wish was that Anglicanism should be a religion in which Truth and Beauty were one. The action and images of these masques seem to reflect such an ideal, uniting English moral reform with "divine" beauty, and creating an image, in the union of the King and Queen, of a new and resplendent "British" heaven.'[18] With the exception of Ben Jonson's *Chloridia* (the Queen's Shrovetide masque of 1631), in which Henrietta Maria took the role of Chloris, goddess of the flowers, all of the masques in which she performed and for which we have surviving records saw her play a character identified as beautiful. When the Queen played Divine Beauty in *Tempe Restored* (Aurelian Townsend's Shrovetide masque of 1632), she was accompanied by her ladies, 14 stars of a happy constellation, and she dissolved Circe's sensual enchantments to demonstrate the superiority of the rational to the concupiscent. 'Corporal beauty', Townsend concludes, 'consisting in symmetry, colour, and certain expressable graces, shining in the Queen's majesty, may draw us to the contemplation of the beauty of the soul, unto which it hath analogy'.[19] *The Temple of Love* (the Queen's Shrovetide masque of 1635 prepared by Inigo Jones and William Davenant) had the Queen playing Indamora, Queen of Narsinga, and her ladies, the lesser lights. Their beauty will re-establish the Temple of Chaste Love, which has been controlled by magicians who used it to intemperate ends; her arrival, prefaced by the advent of Orpheus, impresses poets: 'each princess in her train hath all/That wise enamoured poets beauty call!'[20] The Queen played the role of beauty and light in Davenant's *Luminalia,* performed first on Shrove Tuesday in 1638, dispelling sleep and night and, with the King, 'making this happy island a pattern to all nations'.[21] Dedicated to the ladies of *Luminalia,* Francis Lenton's *Great Britaines Beauties, or The Female Glory Epitomized* (1638) collects encomiastic, anagrammatical and acrostic poems praising the Queen and the masquers with the language of fair beauty; their beauty is praised as timeless, noble, virtuous, true, blessed and as a chaste but erotic power that brings them influence over husbands, poets and the observers of the masque.[22]

In *Salmacida Spolia* – the last of the Stuart court masques, the King and Queen's Twelfth Night Masque of 1639/40 – the Queen plays herself, dressed in Amazonian habits. A tale of the triumph of civility over barbarism, the moral is that 'his majesty, out of his mercy and clemency approving the first proverb, seeks by all means to reduce tempestuous and turbulent natures into a sweet calm of civil concord'. Salmacis is a stream on Halicarnassus, in Asia, taken by the Greeks but perpetually attacked by 'barbarians [...] of fierce and cruel natures'. By drinking the sweet stream, the barbarians 'were reduced of their own accord to the sweetness of the Grecian customs'.[23] Discord and Queen Henrietta Maria embody the difference between chaotic incivility and calm civility. When Discord, a Fury, appears on stage in the first scene, there is no sun, 'as if darkness, confusion, and deformity, had possessed the world and driven light to heaven'. Discord's appearance represents chaos and the absence of light: 'her hair upright, mixed with snakes, her body lean, wrinkled and of a swarthy colour. Her breasts hung bagging down to her waist, to which with a knot of serpents was girt red bases' (lines 118–21). Chaos has swarthy, dark skin and unruly hair; she is unclothed, and she is animal. The Queen, on the other hand, is the 'fair partner of our monarch's throne'. Instead of snakey, standing hair, rays of light shine from her head. The Queen, luminous, light and beautiful, is dressed in 'Amazonian habits of carnation' embroidered with silver (line 393), and, as she descends, the song asks: 'All those who can her virtue doubt,/Her mind will in her face advise' (lines 416–17); her face is evidence of her virtue and the source of her power: 'Why stand you still, and at these beauties gaze,/As if you were afraid,/Or they were made/Much more for wonder than delight?' (lines 433–6).[24] The carnation colour of the Queen's gown amplifies the distance of the Queen's own skin colour from swarthy Discord. The proper colour of English skin, carnation is, according to Nicholas Hilliard, 'the flesh couller': 'very littel Red lead only added maketh the fairest carnations'. In his instructions on painting, Henry Peacham recommends painting fair faces first in 'Carnation or Flesh colour'; the colour of swarthy flesh requires an altogether different combination of paints.[25] The Queen's fair beauty – her face, her skin, her carnation dress and the lights that draw attention to it all – symbolize the order, reason, truth and virtue that triumph over swarthy, disorderly, unclothed and barbaric Discord.

Salmacida Spolia is engaged with dominant modes of beauty – racial, Neoplatonic, Marian and political – as the other masques are, but it also constructs the power of fairness through recipes and medicine. The premise of William Davenant's plot is that the world is disordered by envy of the blessings and the tranquillity that England has long enjoyed and that the King's governance will restore order. Central to the conflict and its resolution, physic functions first at the level of metaphor: the nation is a body. Fury 'stir[s] the humours' in the nation 'overgrown with peace', and makes the great suspicious, the rich avaricious, the poor ambitious and religion vice (lines 138–53). After Concord and the 'Good Genius of Great Britain' arrive and go off to incite the beloved people to a cure, an anti-masque arrives, which places recipes on the stage. In this anti-masque – with an ancient Irishman, Scotsman and Englishman, a nurse and children, a country gentleman and others – Wolfgangus Vandergoose uses his medical receipts to attempt to cure the defects of nature. This is not a wholly new dramatic deployment of physic, for the anti-masque of *The Temple of Love* also includes 'amorous men and women in ridiculous habits, and alchemists', whose place outside the Temple of Chaste Love is determined by the excess of their approach to dress and nature.[26] Vandergoose's confections are not so obviously misplaced as the alchemist's, for his essences, julips, waters, electuaries and powders seem to have some good effects, entertaining lovers and making eunuchs engender. His 'Pomado of the bark of comeliness, the sweetness of wormwood, with the fat of gravity, to anoint those that have an ill mind' uses the pomatum figuratively (lines 212–13). Made of beauty rather than producing it, the pomatum improves the mind, with the result that Vandergoose's recipe accords beauty a curative power. Still, Vandergoose's medical knowledge is surpassed by the physiological wisdom of the King and Queen. Just as in *Tempe Restored* Circe's disorderliness was articulated in her call for medicine – 'Bring me some physic! though that bring no health' – Vandergoose's physic can only be ineffectual because it is limited by his social position; far from august, Vandergoose is costumed like a dwarf anti-masquer in *Chloridia*.[27] The effective remedy begins instead with the beloved people, who turn to their rulers. Led by Concord and the Good Genius of Great Britain, the people address themselves first to Marie de Médicis and then to the King, who can calm the people's 'giddy fury' and the murmuring that is a 'sickness epidemical' (lines 361, 364). The King is the authoritative physician, a source of true knowledge of nature: 'He's fit to govern there and rule alone/Whom inward helps, not outward force, doth raise' (lines 378–9). Finally, the Queen and her ladies arrive and the beloved people praise her wise studiousness, her virtue and her power to inspire good in the people, chastity in lovers and sight in men. The Queen's fair beauty, as much as her husband's political power, is a cure for the nation's sickness. She does not instigate fear, but as King and Queen join together in a heaven of deities, she subdues all that is harsh and rude, teaches obedience and is loved 'even by those who should your justice fear' (line 482). Her beauty is the perfection of Vandergoose's pomatum. She brings true beautifying physic to a country most healthy when its subjects choose civility, obedience and love of the royal couple – civic virtues she inspires with her appearance.

Both beauty and physic are key components of this drama, although critics have tended to treat them as unrelated elements. Martin Butler contends that the anti-masque represents the problems of England, not as a real threat, but as grotesques and follies; the masque itself is an inadequate attempt to ease the strains of the Stuart court, with its ambiguously passive King.[28] For Graham Parry, the anti-masque is 'of a harmless, sportive nature, suggestive perhaps of the simple recreations that Charles recommended to his subjects'; Parry, however, sees little ambiguity in the end, for it shows Charles relying on 'magic: the divine right of kings that James had inculcated in him so thoroughly, the special providence of God that favoured the Stuarts [...] The King's touch would heal the country'.[29] These critics read the masque exclusively in terms of its representation of the King, minimizing the feminine and Neoplatonic elements. Butler, for instance, neglects entirely all of the female masquers and does not discuss the arrival of the Queen and her ladies as the penultimate movement of the masque, although it is this, as much as the arrival of the King, which leads to the resolution of the conflict. Karen Britland and Erica Veevers are more attentive to the role of the Queen and her ladies. Veevers concentrates on the depiction of beauty, although the recipes do not figure in her reading. She argues that in *Salmacida Spolia* Inigo Jones 'demonstrat[es] the power of Beauty to appeal through the eye to the soul, and creat[es] for the Queen a Platonic image of great visual force'.[30] Recipes, but not beauty, feature in Britland's approach. Picking up on Enid Welsford's observation that the recipes that appear in the anti-masque of *Salmacida Spolia* are translations of French recipes that were part of the *Ballet de la Foire Saint Germain*, performed about 1606, Britland argues that the masque is 'in dialogue with continental forms of monarchical representation, recirculating iconological images in a manner which connected the English court to Bourbon spectacle in France, and to the grand Florentine productions of the Médicis'.[31] Engaging Parry's interest in the masque's concern with national health, Veevers' in the Neoplatonic beauty, and Britland's in the recipes, I see the Queen's fair beauty as the perfected cure that counters the limitations of the recipes of the anti-masque. Queen Henrietta Maria possesses the social authority the physician lacks, and consequently her knowledge of England's cure surpasses his. Her physical beauty is the Neoplatonic embodiment of abstract truth and a visual performance of a medical culture in which what can count as medical knowledge hangs on social power as much as the efficaciousness of the cure.

The Queen's Neoplatonic beauty has a specific shape, as well as a carnation colouring: she is the Amazon queen, a warrior in pink. Besides her carnation gown, she and her ladies don 'plumed helms, baldrics with antique swords hanging by their sides, all as rich as might be', a 'strangeness [...] most admired' (lines 393–6). Their gowns are not so strange, their skirts merely suggesting armour rather than being fully masculine garb.[32] But the Amazonian dress does invoke its cognate, the Amazon River, for the Queen is a river, too. The beloved people in the masque told the Queen Mother the Queen is '[t]he stream from whence your blessings flow' (line 318). Kathryn Schwarz argues that such semantic slippage between river and woman is common to the word 'Amazon', which can 'refer to history or myth or the new world or your queen or your wife'; even in a single text Amazon can be both river and population so that the word cannot signify in a straightforward way.[33] So in *Salmacida Spolia,* Queen Henrietta Maria is at once Amazon queen and river, a construction of her identity that brings together the ideas of beauty, power and health the masque explores. The Amazon river is the sometime geographic home of the elusive race of female warriors. Sir Walter Raleigh's *Discoverie of the Large, Rich, and Bewtiful Empire of Guiana* recounts his search for 'those warlike women' and locates them on the south side of the Amazon River. In addition to being the home of Amazon women, the Amazon River is – like Salmacis, 'famous fountain of most clear water and exquisite taste' – a famous fountain of fresh water.[34] Robert Harcourt, whose 1613 account of Guyana is dedicated to Charles I, then Prince Charles, represents the Amazon as 'the great and famous river' and a 'mighty streame of fresh water' that can change the salty sea to water 'as fresh and good as in a spring or poole' – a claim that John Smith repeats in his *True Travels*.[35] Like the regenerative stream, Salmacis, which turns barbarians towards sweet customs, the Amazon transforms. And like Henrietta Maria, the Amazon River is a queen, an imperial and feminine locale. *A Publication of Guiana's Plantation*, which reworks Harcourt's material, calls the Amazon, not just 'that great and famous River' but 'the Empresse and Queene of all Flouds' and 'the greatest River [...] of the whole world'.[36] As the queen of rivers, the Amazon is English. Harcourt had gained a patent from Prince Henry for the coast of Guyana and 'the famous River of Amazones, to him and his heires'.[37] The Queen is a river, the river is a queen, and both are powerful, sweet, regenerative and made English.

The propitious powers of the Amazon extend beyond its freshness to encompass physic. Raleigh's *Discoverie of the Large, Rich, and Bewtiful Empire of Guiana* catalogues amongst that nation's treasures, the fruits, flowers and trees that line the Amazon river, 'sufficient to make ten volumes of herbals', medicines that counteract poison, quench fevers and heal internal wounds, and even cosmetics: it has 'great quantities of Brasilwood, and divers berries, that die a most perfect crimson and Carnation: And for painting, all France, Italy, or the east Indies yeeld none such: For the more the skin is washed, the fairer the cullour appeareth, and with which, even those browne & tawnie women spot themselves, and cullour their cheeks.'[38] That is to say, the Amazon is the source of health and of fair beauty. Speaking generally of the area, Raleigh asserts, 'both for health, good ayre, pleasure, and riches, I am resolved it cannot bee equalled by any region eyther in the east or west.'[39] *A Publication of Guiana's Plantation* reiterates this point, characterizing Guyana as 'both healthfull and pleasant; for God in wisdome hath so ordered the heavens in their horizon, as that by meanes of a brieze (or fresh gale of winde) blowing in the day time, it quallifieth the heate, and maketh the climate much more temperate, as with us is often felt the like in heate of summer.'[40] Robert Harcourt adopts a similar stance, including medicine in his list of Guyana's commodities: '[f]or phisick there be also many excellent Druggs, [...] Druggs and simples also of strange and rare vertue, in these parts unknowen'.[41] The Amazon then is not only powerful, feminine and English, it is also a temperate source of health. As such, the Amazon is a compelling analogy for the Queen in a play about a stream and the country's ills. Curing the nation's 'sickness epidemical', the Amazon queen ultimately becomes a bridge over a river, a link between divine and human, which the people can pass over. Not foreign but fair and powerful, the Amazon represents true knowledge, efficacious cures and imperial control – but not autonomy, for as the Amazon and the Queen, Henrietta Maria is powerful because she has been made English.

The narrative and dramaturgy of the Stuart Court masque typically established royal authority. In *Salmacida Spolia* this ideological direction enhances the social authority of fair beauty as a form of health. Queen Henrietta Maria's carnation gown and her Amazonian identity construct her beauty as politically effective, for she makes visible the legitimacy of hereditary monarchy and the epistemological authority of the crown in medical questions. The Queen's fair beauty is supposed to be politically persuasive, not just because the play purports that beauty inspires admiration, but also because the drama links skin colour to the civility and health of the English social order. Discord is swarthy, the Queen is not. She is of a pink flesh colour, a colour highlighted by her gown. If not technically white, the masque confers meaning on carnation, so that it represents what is elite, orderly, truthful, healthy and powerful; in this, the masque creates a text about whiteness, in Babb's sense of the term. The play establishes the Queen's fair beauty within a system of privileges.

The Politics of Beauty in *The Queens Closet Opened*

The Queens Closet Opened was printed first in 1655 as 'Incomparable Secrets [...] as they were presented to the Queen By the most Experienced Persons of our Times' (A2). This collection of cosmetic, medical and food recipes is published with reference to a court at which material culture was political. R. Malcolm Smuts argues that while the reign of Charles I saw the development of a culture of art collecting and patronage, this innovation coexisted with an older court culture in which the display of power was effected through public ceremonies. 'On the eve of the Civil War', he writes, 'splendour at court continued to mean much the same thing that it had in the reign of Henry VIII. It meant gilt barges, embroidered cloths of state, yeomen of the guard in resplendent liveries, tables piled high with food, and rooms crowded with people in opulent clothes and jewels.'[42] A recipe collection, such as *The Queen's Closet Opened*, is uniquely able to bring together the forms of culture Smuts identifies – collecting, patronage and ceremonial display – and to configure the Queen's closet as the central repository of knowledge of material culture at court. Recalling the Queen's role as patron and collector of recipes, *The Queens Closet Opened* remembers the Queen's authority in matters of health.

During the 1650s, a number of recipe books were published to political ends. Madeline Bassnett has argued that in the period 'recipe books were well-suited to demonstrate the integral relationship between royalty and good household management to a broad audience and thereby to participate in what Elizabeth Sauer has called the "war of words" that extended into the 1650s'.[43] *The Queens Closet Opened* does not begin in an argumentative tone, however. W. M., the volume's editor, explains that the recipes were 'transcribed into her book by my self, the Original papers being most of them preserved in my own hands, which I kept as so many Reliques' (A3*v*). Along with a pro forma apology for publishing his mistress's secrets because of the putative circulation of two unauthorized versions (A4–A4*v*), W. M.'s emphasis on 'true copies', '[o]riginal papers' and the unauthorized version eulogizes the Queen's closet as a place of origin and intellectual authority, while the act of remembering includes both the Queen and her court, those of 'Honour and Quality' who gave her the recipes (A3). Jayne Archer has argued that W. M. is Walter Montague, sometime secretary to the Queen, the author of *Shepherd's Paradise*, a pastoral play performed by the Queen and her ladies in 1633, and the translator of Jacques DuBosq's *The Accomplished Woman* (1655).[44] Archer's attribution is certainly plausible, and Montague's involvement fits nicely with my overall contention that *The Queens Closet Opened* can, in part, be understood through the ideology of court drama. Leah Marcus contends that Interregnum Royalists had a habit of looking back to Stuart rule: 'royalists and royalist sympathizers coped with the loss of public ritual and festivity by recasting old ceremonies in more private forms and surrounding them with cryptic language and hermetic symbolism – barriers against the intrusion of hostile outsiders'.[45] The collection is a recollection of what has been lost.

The recipes for beautifying physic remedies found in *The Queens Closet Opened* are actually unexceptional, in that they are of the kind commonly found in medical treatises of the day, and they are little different to the recipes discussed in the previous chapter. Richard Dyer provides a way into thinking about how to situate what seems merely normal within the history of race. Whiteness, he contends, has been treated as a 'natural, inevitable, ordinary way of being human': 'Power in contemporary society habitually passes itself off as embodied in the normal as opposed to the superior. This is common to all forms of power, but it works in a peculiarly seductive way with whiteness, because of the way it seems rooted, in common-sense thought, in things other than ethnic difference.' '[T]he invisibility of whiteness', he adds, 'colonises the definition of other norms – class, gender, heterosexuality, nationality and so on – it also masks whiteness as itself a category.'[46] Sara Ahmed adds another perspective to Dyer's claim that whiteness is invisible: 'whiteness is only invisible for those who inhabit it. For those who don't, it is hard not to see whiteness; it even seems everywhere.' Yet the colonizing effects she points to are like those which Dyer acknowledges. Ahmed adds: 'Seeing whiteness is about living its effects, as effects that allow white bodies to extend into spaces that have already taken their shape, spaces in which black bodies stand out, stand apart, unless they pass, which means passing through space by passing as white.'[47] Recipes for beautifying physic function in this way, shaping the space of health to fit people with white skin. In *The Queens Closet Opened* they do so under the Queen's authority and the authority of the physicians who serve her. Theodore Turquet de Mayerne, the contributor of a purge to *The Queens Closet Opened*, created cosmetic receipts for Queen Anne and Queen

Henrietta Maria, which are preserved in *An original record book of cases and consultations of Sir Theodore Mayerne* (Royal College of Physicians MS 444, c.1607–1651), in 15 pages entitled, 'Cosmetica à me proescripta Regin: Magnaoe Britann: Anna & Henriettae Mariae ab anno 1612 ad 1643'. A French Huguenot physician, Mayerne became chief physician to James I, was knighted by him in 1624 and then was appointed physician to Queen Henrietta Maria.[48] The beautifying physic of queens is the concern of their chief physician, amongst others.

In *The Queens Closet Opened*, as in the recipe collections I discussed in Chapter 1, cosmetic recipes are better defined as beautifying physic for they appear without distinction in the section 'Physical, & Chirurgical Receipts'. Primarily herbal cures for heat, the recipes address redness or dryness in the face: 'To make the face fair, and for a stinking breath' – a mixture of white wine and rosemary that can be drunk or used to wash the face (53); 'For heat in the Face, and redness, and shining of the Nose' – a cloth wet with morning dew to wash the face (53–4); 'An excellent Oyl to take away the heat and shining of the Nose' – an oil of almonds and gourd seed (54); two recipes 'For heat or pimples in the Face' – one a face wash made of liverwort and the other a distilled face wash of several herbs, strawberry leaves and milk (54, 173); 'For Sweating in the Face' – a herbal steam bath (55); 'To make the Face fair' – a distilled face wash from bean blossoms (115); and 'For heat or scurfe in the Face' – an ointment made of cream and camomile (173–4). Beautifying here involves remedying excess heat. Within the humoural system of Galenic physiology, heat is a problem that must be addressed to restore balance to the body, and thus a concern for the appearance of the face and skin is not simply aesthetic.[49] The recipe in *The Queens Closet Opened* to make the face fair and the breath sweet is in Thomas Vicary's *The English Man's Treasure* and Peter Levens' *Right Profitable Booke for all Diseases, called, The Path-way to Health*. John Partridge's *Treasurie of Hidden Secrets* reprints the recipe (it is also in his *The Treasurie of Commodious Conceits*), along with other waters to make the face white or fair, to remove high colour, heat or pimples and to make the hands white and fair.[50]

Neither are marks, like freckles, merely aesthetic affairs. They are constructed as medical problems. *The Queens Closet Opened* contains a recipe 'To take away Freckles or Morphew' (146) – a face wash based on May dew and oil of tartar – as well as two medicines to prevent the scars from 'small pocks' (137, 138), based on spermaceti and bacon, respectively. A recipe 'For a knock or bruise in the Face' (144) involves brown paper and beer.[51] All of these marks seem to belong to the same category of problem, as things 'foul' – marks of corruption or putrefaction in the body that can be remedied by 'cleansing'. The 1618 *Pharmacopoeia Londinensis,* which listed the preparations sanctioned by the College of Physicians in London, provides many similar cures for pimples, freckles, morphew and sunburn, as does Nicholas Culpeper's contemporaneous and extremely popular *The English Physician.* Culpeper refers often to foulness in *The English Physician;* the root of briony, for instance, 'cleanseth the skin wonderfully from all black and blue spots, freckles, morphew, Leprosie, foul scars, or other deformity'.[52] Cleansing is not just a simple question of the removal of dirt but a more substantial, necessary medical operation. The fairness intended to result from these concoctions is not aligned with artifice, sexuality or luxury, but with health and nature. Fairness is a consequence of the restoration of a bodily order disrupted by imbalance, such as excess heat. *Artificiall Embellishments* writes of the beautifying recipes the volume provides that '[i]f ever then your ill disposed humors grow so strong, to break their way through the inclosing skin, it will do you no harm to have something in readiness that may check their presumption'.[53] Imbalance is a type of social rebellion within the body. Recipes work towards the restoration of order. The fair beauty that results is, as a consequence, orderly and healthy; skin not deemed fair is, by this logic, disorderly, unbalanced and unhealthy (like that of swarthy-skinned Discord in *Salmacida Spolia*).

   The Queens Closet Opened uses recipes to recall not just the material practices of the Queen's household but also her place of authority in intellectual and social relationships. As I showed in the previous chapter, recipes generally are evidence of knowledge networks that link manuscript and print culture and male and female medical practitioners of medicine and cookery. What is interesting then about the physic recipes in *The Queens Closet Opened* is how knowledge is produced through social processes, how state, class and patronage underpin what Ludmilla Jordanova calls the 'social construction of medical knowledge'.[54] These recipes are knowledge because they are treasured Royalist relics. Fair beauty is healthy, at least in part, because it is the knowledge of the Queen and her court, as well as of physicians. Margaret Pelling argues that powerful patrons influenced the careers of physicians by advancing irregular practitioners or those whose activities were questioned by the College and by facilitating the promotion of physicians as candidates or fellows of the College; the College itself sought to thwart these outside influences, while also maintaining such patronage relationships to buttress their own authority.[55] Recipes are proof of the medical knowledge of the practitioner, an authority based on experience, but in *The Queens Closet Opened* they are also revealed to be bids for royal and aristocratic favour. Looking at the identities of some of the contributors, Laura Lunger Knoppers sees the volume as a kind of bridge, 'assimilating the Queen into a multigenerational social network, distinguished above all, by its Englishness'.[56] The volume does function in this way, as does the Queen in the final image of the bridge in *Salmacida Spolia*. Because the contributions to *The Queens Closet Opened* come from medical practitioners who served English monarchs, as well as those who received aristocratic patronage, as presidents and members of the College of Physicians and as irregular practitioners, the volume demonstrates royal authority over medical knowledge.[57] The recipes, including those for beautifying physic, become authoritative through the social contexts that *The Queens Closet Opened* encodes. She is connected to English and Scottish society and served by physicians, whose concern for the Queen's health is legitimate and historically rooted. Medical interest in royal beauty persists across reigns and requires the attention, not just of her ladies but prominent men and institutions, such as the College of Physicians. These recipes are indeed, 'sovereign receipts'. They are the accumulated knowledge authorized by a queen.

In these ways, *The Queens Closet Opened* strategically enhances the Queen's authority in questions of medicine. The Queen provides authority to the medicalized construction of beauty as fair. Famous as a beauty, Queen Henrietta Maria's image appears with the volume. In the image, she wears widow's garb but she is also, according to Knoppers, wearing a costume similar to the one she wore in *Tempe Restored,* where she played Divine Beauty herself.[58] If the recipes convey how she preserves and maintains her health, the picture is a reminder of more abstract parts of her identity, that she is a queen whose beauty was the embodiment of divinity and power. Diane Purkiss contends that publication of the recipes is 'not an apolitical move' precisely because of its beauty treatments, which, she says, 'signify the kind of "colouring" stigmatised in pre-Civil War criticisms of the Queen and the King she ruled: dissembling or artifice'.[59] But if such recipes are not paint but beautifying physic authorized by monarchs and medical culture, the collection assumes a rather different political posture. The Queen's beauty is a legitimate medical matter, and the collection uses the strategies of authority pertinent to medical culture to authorize her knowledge of beautifying as healthy and legitimate. Kevin Sharpe has warned against equating royal absolutism with decadence, immorality and the court, and puritanism with sobriety, asceticism, godliness and the country, and *The Queen's Closet*

Opened certainly disrupts this dichotomy.[60] Eschewing overt, artificial and gaudy display in the name of true, natural and healthy nobility, the recipes, like the masque, situate beauty and fairness as components of the Queen's knowledge of the restoration of a vital constitution, in physic and, obliquely, in the nation. Although *The Queens Closet Opened* does not overtly draw attention to itself as part of the archive of the history of race, it belongs there. The social processes of recipe collecting and the strategies for authorizing knowledge employed in medical culture ensure that the aesthetic ideal of fair beauty is underpinned by the structures of royal and aristocratic, as well as medical, authority. In *The Queens Closet Opened* fair beauty becomes whiteness because the strategies of authority unique to medical culture construct knowledge of fair beauty as the privileged form of health and order and as knowledge possessed by a queen.

Whiteness in Aphra Behn's *The Wandring Beauty*

Aphra Behn's *The Wandring Beauty* is a little studied, short work of prose fiction first printed posthumously in 1698, as one of several of Behn's stories printed by Samuel Briscoe after 1696.[61] When it was reprinted in *Histories, Novels and Translations* in 1700, it had the subtitle 'The Lucky Fair One'. Behn has been central to studies of race in early modern England. Several critics have observed how the political conflicts over royal authority and Stuart succession, particularly in *Oroonoko* (1688) and *The Widow Ranter* (1689), are refracted through her representations of Africans and the indigenous people of the Americas.[62] *The Wandring Beauty* does not overtly reflect on England's colonial endeavours in the way that these other works do. Nor does it include any racial Others. Still, like *Oroonoko* and *The Widow Ranter, The Wandring Beauty* relies on class and political ideology to develop an idea of race. The narrative recounts the adventures of the aptly named Arabella Fairname, a pretty, well-born young woman who runs away from home when her parents are persuaded by the lure of future wealth to arrange a marriage with an elderly neighbour, Sir Robert Richland. Arabella Fairname sets out walking. At the end of the first day, a husbandman offers her food and shelter, while his daughter exchanges her best clothes with the more aristocratic Arabella. She also darkens her skin with walnut juice before continuing her perambulation, walking from the West Country of her home to Lancashire. There she is welcomed into the household of Sir Christian Kindly as Peregrina Goodhouse. With her knowledge of physic, she cures their 4-year-old daughter of an eye infection and consequently becomes a companion for the older daughter, Eleanora. Arabella soon receives an offer of marriage from Mr. Prayfast, a clergyman. He changes his mind, however, when he hears from Sir Christian Arabella's story of her humble parentage. Soon after, Arabella accepts a better offer of marriage from Sir Lucius Lovewell, a man as eminently suitable as his name suggests: a young gentleman with wit, learning and £3,000 a year. The marriage is quickly effected, and soon after Arabella is reunited with her parents, her disobedience forgiven and old Sir Robert conveniently dead.

The plot is simple and details few – it is a story without the narrative complexity of *Oroonoko* – but Behn gives Arabella's beauty a political valence that engages race as a matter of origins and birth. Behn develops explicit connections between beauty and power in *The Lady's Looking-Glass, to Dress Herself by: Or, the Whole Art of Charming,* printed first in 1697 and in 1700 with *The Wandring Beauty* in *Histories, Novels, and Translations. The Lady's Looking-Glass* is Behn's genre-bending contribution to the conduct book form. Its title recalls looking glasses for women, but instead of obedience it explores, like *Salmacida Spolia,* the relationship of female beauty and power within a Neoplatonic framework.[63] Behn's *The Lady's Looking-Glass* is a series of apostrophes to Iris in prose and verse which praise her beauty and her virtues, by turn her shape, complexion, hair, eyes, mouth, neck, arms and hands, grace, discretion, goodness, wit and modesty. Iris is both English, residing on the Thames, and powerful, the goddess of the rainbow.[64] Her complexion is 'infinitely fine, [...] Skin soft and smooth, as polisht Wax, or Ivory, extreamly white and clear', and her 'Quantity of lovely fair brown hair' reveals she is 'born to Rule; and to repair the Faults of Fortune, that has not given you a Diadem'; Iris's complexion is 'neither so cold, to be insensible; nor so hot, to have too much Fire; that is, neither too white, nor too black', and her eyes 'strike an unresistable Awe upon the Soul'. Her smiles make 'conquests'.[65] In Behn's version of a conduct book, beauty provides women with absolute romantic power: 'Heav'n for Sovereignty, has made your form:/And you were more than for dull Empire born./O'er Hearts your Kingdom shall extend,/Your vast Dominion know no end.' Eschewing hours of dressing, Iris also knows 'how to gain a Conquest with your Pen, more absolutely, than all the industrious Fair, who trust to Dress and Equipage'.[66] Iris is an absolute Stuart monarch of marriage, ruling hearts, not England, with her physiological balance, fairness and writing.

In *The Wandring Beauty,* Behn translates this construction of whiteness to a fictional context. Arabella Fairname's fair skin is both a sign of her gentle birth and a political force. Just as the Queen's beauty is efficacious in *Salmacida Spolia*, curing the nation, in *The Wandring Beauty* fair beauty works to return Arabella to the class position of her birth and to cure her father's overweening authority in the question of her marriage. While Behn's vision of fair beauty affirms class and king as components of order, it also inserts into that order the agency of upper-class women. *The Wandring Beauty* marks these simultaneous commitments to female agency and to class hierarchy in its various utopian impulses, not least in raising the possibility of class-based conflict only to erase it. Behn's story repeatedly creates moments that initiate competition between beautiful women of ostensibly different classes but, like *Salmacida Spolia,* calms the discord. She draws Peregrina and her mistress directly into conflict when Sir Lucius Lovewell arrives at Sir Christian's with the intention of making his addresses to Eleanora Kindly but instead prefers Peregrina. Not at all displeased, Eleanora is delighted because it provides her with the occasion to make her own marriage for love: 'her Heart was already pre-engag'd elsewhere; and [...] she did equally desire the good Fortune of her Beautiful Attendant with her own'.[67] Like her father, Eleanora displays a generosity that seems utterly indifferent to the traditions of rank; she does not begrudge her maid a suitor suitable for herself. Yet even as her liberality inserts charity into social hierarchy, her ostensible indifference to rank functions in the narrative less to undermine the difference between mistress and maid than to allow Peregrina to return to the social position of her birth.

The relationship between Arabella, newly a servant, and her mistress in *Wandring Beauty* reflects on and idealizes class relations. Certainly early modern single people did migrate long distances in search of work, particularly towards London, and Arabella is able to elude her parents because that is where they expect her to go. But going into service was not the assuredly happy solution to an unwanted marriage that it is for Arabella.[68] Rather the opposite. For many young people, distances from family connections meant reduced nuptial opportunities, not a better marriage of one's choice.[69] Employers could also insist on the unmarried status of their servants, and female servants, in particular, faced sexual advances from masters, sons and fellow servants; such possibilities also helped to make mistresses suspicious of beautiful female servants and placed women in positions of competition, rather than cooperation.[70] Arabella confronts none of this and, even more, accrues all the security and status of belonging to the Kindly family. Even though she joins the Kindly household as a servant, Sir Christian provides her with a dowry of £300 when she marries Lovewell and keeps the wedding for a week at his house, before it moves for another week to Lovewell's own estate (403–4). Naomi Tadmor argues that in eighteenth-century England, family was understood to encompass not just relationships of blood and marriage, but also attachments that were contractual, instrumental and occupational.[71] So servants were part of the family unit, but Behn's representation of Peregrina's relationship to the Kindly household demonstrates this model at its most remarkably inclusive – and unlikely – form. The Kindlys are exemplary in their charity, and the Fairnames, eventually no longer insisting on Arabella's unwanted union, become more kindly. Despite her disobedience, Arabella is immediately reconciled to them when her husband reintroduces her, and Arabella's father, learning charity at last, promises her husband £10,000 of ready money because of the worthiness of the match. In easing the conflict between women over men and labour, Behn aligns the two gentlewomen as advocates for choice in marriage for elite women and facilitates an easy readjustment of a natural order for Arabella.

The father's usurpation of her choice is a kind of malignant sore introducing disorder, but the social cure is effected through fair beauty that protects Arabella, provides her with a new family, initiates a better marriage and ameliorates the consequences of her rebellion. In creating the possibility of these idealized, harmonious social relations, Arabella's beauty has two essential attributes: cleanliness and white skin. The story constructs cleanliness as the visual outcome of virtue and as a quality shared with the charitable husbandman and his daughter, who dwell in a 'poor, but cleanly Habitation'. With the 'very cleanly, though not very fine' daughter, Arabella exchanges two of her own shifts, 'new and clean', hoods, a headdress and shoes for the hardy maid's Sunday clothes, holiday shoes, shifts, two pinners and her best straw hat (393). For both the husbandman's daughter and Arabella, cleanliness is the sign of inward virtue. This is certainly how Sir Christian Kindly reads Arabella's hygiene. She arrives at his house in a 'very mean, though cleanly habit', which allows him to conclude that she is 'of very humble, yet honest, Parentage' (400). Cleanliness is the outward evidence of virtue that can be shared by people across the social spectrum.

Yet Arabella's cleanliness has a further dimension not shared with the husbandman's tidy daughter. She can walk several hundred miles – in England – in a single outfit and pair of 'holiday' shoes, without gathering even a layer of dust. Behn tabulates the number of miles that her heroine must walk: first ten miles, then nine the next morning and ten more before that evening. She walks 12 miles more the next day, and then the narrator stops counting; '[t]hus she continued her Errantry for above a Fortnight' (397). Needless to say, this wandering beauty accomplishes a journey of some physical difficulty. If she grows weary – after the first ten miles, her 'Soft and Beautiful Limb[s], began now to be tired, and her Tender Feet to be galled' (393) – she does not get dirty. The incredible resilience of her cleanliness facilitates the restoration of her status. Clean, she does not need 'Ornaments of Cloaths to set her Beauty off', and once she arrives in the Kindly household she is welcomed by them because she is still clean, so they recognize her virtue. Even more, Peregrina is soon able to abandon the clothes of the husbandman's daughter to be dressed 'altogether as Costly, though not so Richly (perhaps) as Eleanora' (399). When she gets married, she gets still better clothes, for Lovewell sets the wedding date two months hence so that he can 'send Orders to London for the making of their Wedding Cloaths' (404). For the truly poor maid, cleanliness may testify to virtue, but for Arabella hygiene is transcendent and translates into a capacity to move effortlessly up the social ladder and to have the clothes that match her skin given to her. In this sense, cleanliness is the agent of nature within a hierarchical class order always seeking to restore itself, with Christian charity providing the means to ensure that happens for Arabella.

Arabella's beauty is also defined by whiteness. Like her cleanliness, her whiteness possesses an irrepressible social energy, mediating her relationships and restoring her to the social place of her birth. While on the road, Arabella darkens her skin with a dye made of walnut shells: 'she bruis'd the outward green Shells of a Wallnut or two, and smear'd her lovely Face, Hands, and part of her Arms, with the Juice; [...] she sigh'd and wept, to think to what base Extremities she was now likely to be reduc'd! That she shou'd be forced to stain that Skin which Heaven had made so pure and white!' (397). In this, she displays the knowledge of beautifying physic that would also allow her to be 'the fair Physitian' with a 'secret' that cures the eyes of the Kindlys' infant daughter (398). *Arts Master-piece: Or, the Beautifying Part of Physic,* a collection of cosmetic recipes printed in 1660, includes with more common recipes to make the face fair (or appropriately red) a recipe for 'Waters that black the Face':

With Chymical Instruments extract a most clear water, from green Walnut-shells and Gaules; with which if you wet the face or hands, they grow black by degrees, like to an Aethiopian; which if afterwards you would restore to their former whiteness, you must distil Vineger, Juice of Lemmons and Colophonia, and washing with that will take off the blackness.[72]

Eighteen Books Of the Secrets of Art & Nature also by Johann Wecker (1660) has a very similar recipe: 'From the green shells of Walnuts, the Chymists in France draw a pure water; if you wash your hands and face with this, you will be black as a Gypsie by degrees.'[73] In these two recipes, the cultural referent for blackness is ethnic difference, the gypsy and the Ethiopian. In *The Wandring Beauty*, the walnut-dyed skin marks a lower-class identity that will match the clothes of the Welsh husband-man's daughter. The daughters of Welsh husbandmen are not, in Behn's telling, white but have skin like gypsies and Ethiopians. Neither does the Kindlys' maid have Peregrina's brand of fair skin. Her beauty fills the maid with wonder, as she reports that Peregrina is a 'sweet and cleanly Bed-fellow' and that 'she never saw nor felt so white, so smooth, and soft a Skin' (397). Peregrina's white skin, along with her medical knowl-edge, is a sign of her birth and her distinction from lower class women, whatever clothes she wears. Like her cleanliness, this whiteness is irre-pressible. Despite the application of walnut juice, long-distance outdoor travel and unfamiliar domestic labour, her fairness returns not through the application of lemon juice but from its own natural force.

The Wandring Beauty confers moral and political significance on white skin. Aligning whiteness, like cleanliness, with virtue, Peregrina grants an existential meaning to her darkened face: 'if my Disobedience to my Parents had not stain'd my Conscience worse, this needed not to have been done' (397). The narrative does not actually require Peregrina to reform, for her rebellion against the patriarchal family order is well compensated, first by the re-establishment of her elite social position within a family more accommodating of female agency and then by the repentance of her own family. Yet, if Peregrina's darkness is wayward and lower class, her white skin becomes morally and socially superior. It is also the result of politics. Arabella Fairname is the daughter of a gentleman, Sir Francis Fairname, 'a True Church-Man, [and] a great Loyalist' (393) – that is to say, a member of the Church of England loyal to hereditary monarchy, to Charles II and even perhaps to James II and his descendants, given Behn's attention to the Jacobite cause in other works. Sir Francis is a Tory, surely. Arabella's whiteness is not just a mark of the privilege of birth but also of her political allegiances.

Behn's narrative is directly connected to Stuart politics. Its struc-ture follows the narrative example of another famous fair wanderer, Charles II. *The Wandring Beauty* was dedicated to his son-in-law, Edward Radcliffe, 2nd Earl of Derwentwater; the Earl was the husband of Lady Mary Tudor, the illegitimate daughter of Charles II and Mary Davies, an actress. The 2nd Earl's father had been elevated by James II, and he was himself the father of a Jacobite army officer.[74] Behn had relied on stories of the execution of Charles I published with the Restoration when she narrated the death of Oronooko.[75] *The Wandring Beauty* runs parallel to and draws upon several of the motifs found in narrative accounts of Charles II's escape from the Parliamentarians at Worcester in 1651 published in the 1660s and 1680s: *Englands Triumph: A More Exact History of His Majesties Escape after the Battle of Worcester* (1660), *An Exact Narrative and Relation of His Most Sacred Majesties Escape from Worcester on the third of September, 1651* (1660), John Danvers's, *The Royal Oake, or, an Historical Description of The Royal Progress* (1660), Charles Hammond's, *London's Triumphant Holiday* (1660), and Henry Jones's ballad, 'The Royal Patient Traveller' (1660), as well as Thomas Blount's, *Boscobel: or the Compleat History of His Sacred Majesties Most Miraculous Preservation after the Battle of Worcester* (1660, 1662, 1680). These texts, although more complex in their plotting, follow the same narrative pattern as Behn's tale. There is an initial crisis – an illegitimate usurpation of the hero's position, which causes him to flee. Arabella's father undermines the daughter's autonomy in her marriage choice, while Parliament prevented the ascent of Charles II to the throne. Although Arabella is alone in her wandering, while Charles is accompanied by a band of loyal aristocrats, Charles, very like Arabella, journeys from one friendly and charitable household to another – peregrinations that illustrate how England adheres to the wanderer's values. In his wandering, again very like Arabella, Charles is forced to change clothes with his inferiors. The 1660 *An Exact Narrative and Relation of his Most Sacred Majesties Escape from Worcester on the third of September, 1651* describes Charles's disguise at some length. He received from Squire Gifford, 'his best Cloaths', a 'Jump and Breeches of Green course Cloth and a Doe skin Leather Doublet'; from Humphrey Pendrill the miller, an old grey hat; from Edward Martin, a 'Hurden or Noggen shirt' of 'the coarsest of the Hemp' and from William Creswell, his shoes. He is, after a haircut, 'A la mode the Woodman', although he needs more instruction in assuming this country guise because his natural nobility seems inevitably to reveal itself: 'They had much adoe all that day to teach and fashion his Majesty to their Country guise, and to order his steps and straight body to a lobbing jobsons gate.'[76] A Mistress Lane helps him to further conceal his identity by sending him a 'parcel of leaves of Walnuts, boyled in Spring Water, to colour his Majesties hands, and alter the hue and whitenesse of his Skin in those places that were most obvious to the eye'.[77] In *Boscobel: or the Compleat History of His Sacred Majesties Most Miraculous Preservation* (1680), which lists the same wardrobe, Charles first blackens his face with soot from the chimney, but because 'His hands not appearing sufficiently discoloured, suitable to his other disguise Mrs. Woolf provided Walnut-tree leaves, as the readiest expedient for that purpose'.[78] Another catalogue of the King's appearance observes, in addition to his country wardrobe, 'his face and hands made of a reechy complexion, by the help of Walnut-tree leaves'.[79] Like Arabella, he must have clothes that match his skin colour to be fully in disguise. His male subjects charitably provide him with clothes, while his female subjects use their knowledge of medicine in his service, with the walnut juice and, in *Englands Triumph* and *An Exact Narrative,* by cutting the blisters on his feet and providing ease.[80] The King receives the help of women who, like Arabella, are skilled in physic. Finally, each journey ends in restoration. Charles escapes to France, where he is greeted as a king, an ending that prefigures the true Restoration he would have at the time the texts were published. Arabella is restored to her class position and to a marriage of her choice. In the stories about Charles II, fairness is a sign of privilege. It marks his natural authority, his aristocracy and his power, but for Arabella fairness is a sign of class that provides her with safety and agency. Their skin is white because they are upper class within a natural order that recognizes the merits of hierarchy; to masquerade as a lower-class person, they must become dark.

Behn is politicizing fairness to offer a vision of a social order in which white women – and only well-born English women are white – might have the kind of freedom to elude authority in the realm of marriage afforded a defeated king in the Civil War. In forced marriage, women's agency is usurped. *The Wandring Beauty* is certainly critical of forced marriage, as Susan Staves indicates in one of the few references to *The Wandring Beauty* in *The Cambridge Companion to Aphra Behn.* Yet Staves sees the utopianism of the plot as Behn's assessment that such good fortune is not generally available to 'real women'.[81] Frederick M. Link's equally brief assessment that *The Wandring Beauty* has a 'masque-like quality' is perhaps apposite (if unexplained).[82] Like the masque, *The Wandring Beauty* mystifies fair beauty in support of a Stuart political vision. Whiteness embodies both the privilege of class and of historical loyalty to the crown. The purpose of whiteness is not merely sexual conquest. No good comes from men, like Richland and Prayfast, who find Arabella's beauty 'Resistless' (393). Prayfast's attraction is directly attributed to her skin: 'the Chaplain himself, cou'd not hold out against her Charms. For her Skin had long since recover'd its Native Whiteness' (399). But his proposal of marriage is entirely lacking in merit, for although he is socially inferior to Arabella, he drops her when he learns the story of low birth that she told Kindly. The incident articulates the clergyman's place outside of the gentry, in that he fails to recognize her true origins, which are intuitively recognized by a gentleman of her own station. In the story, fair beauty is a force of nature within a culture where nature is defined by class hierarchy and a king; white skin possesses a privilege supported by royal authority. While the masque used the visual and narrative forms of drama, and the recipe collection displays the authorizing strategies inherent to collecting, *The Wandring Beauty* employs narrative to attach to white skin a providential, historical power that allows the elite woman freedom to wander and agency to choose.

Conclusion

Translated into English at the beginning of the Stuart period, Thomas Buoni's *Problemes of Beautie* (1606) addresses the problem of why upper-class women are more beautiful than other women. His answer is that not only does the 'delicate and exquisite' diet available to them make the complexion more beautiful, but aristocratic women also have noble natures, 'high thoughts, and honourable imaginations' that make them gentle in aspect; the mind depends on the body, the wit on the body's complexion, and so because the 'bodily parts being in women of high lin[e]age, most exquisitely perfect, it must necessarily follow, that even by nature they prove admirable, in the gifts of the minde'.[83] Nature gives elite women beauty which improves their minds, as well as high thoughts that make them beautiful. This is the problem of beauty that I have been discussing: fair beauty is not just a traditional literary aesthetic but whiteness, a structure of privilege. White, Homi Bhabha says, is 'a primer, a base color that regulates all others, a norm that spectacularly or stealthily underlies powerful social values'. It 'naturalizes the claim to social power and epistemological privilege', while '[t]he critique of whiteness [...] attempts to displace the normativity of the white position by seeing it as a strategy of authority rather than an authentic or essential "identity"'.[84] In *Salmacida Spolia, The Queens Closet Opened* and *The Wandring Beauty* fair beauty is being naturalized as a claim to social power and epistemological privilege, authorized by the strategies of authority unique to each literary form. With the machinery of court drama, *Salmacida Spolia* authorizes fair beauty as a metaphor for civility, order and national health in an England organized by class. *The Queens Closet Opened* authorizes fair beauty as health through the strategies of authority inherent to medical culture, to the social struggle between monarchs and physicians over knowledge processes in which the Queen necessarily triumphs within the particular context of the Interregnum. *The Wandring Beauty* authorizes fair beauty as a sign of social class and female autonomy in marriage through a narrative construction of fair beauty as a providential agent that ensures history will allow the well-born white English girl to occupy her class position and choose a young, rich gentleman for a husband.

All of these texts are constructing knowledge about fair beauty through the contiguous early modern contexts of health and politics and thereby conferring on whiteness a privilege that is also deeply divisive. To become the rational and true, whiteness stands in opposition to dark skin, which in *Salmacida Spolia* represents chaotic barbarism, in *The Queens Closet Opened* is a sign of ill health and in *The Wandring Beauty* signifies wayward virtue, inferior status and non-Englishness. In linking whiteness to freedom, the masque requires obedience from the good citizens, while Behn's fiction expects the acquiescent charity of a nation that recognizes the merits of a fair name. Whiteness divides women from each other and requires lower-class women, such as the Kindlys' maid, to accept that the white-skinned woman who controls her space is wonderful in her whiteness. Whiteness colonizes the definitions of health and social legitimacy for upper-class English people. As Anne McClintock insists, 'race, gender, and class are not distinct realms of experience, existing in splendid isolation from each other [...] Rather they come into existence *in and through* relation to each other – if in contradictory and conflicted ways.'[85] Far from transcendent, whiteness is coming into being here through political ideology, class conflict and gendered insistence. Elite white women do not possess all the privileges of white men. In these texts, particularly in *The Wandring Beauty,* the privilege of fair beauty is attached to women's vulnerability within a patriarchal culture, to being marriageable pawns in property alliances, to being legally invisible, to being impoverished by inheritance laws, to being attacked and silenced and regarded as ignorant. Although the risk of discussing whiteness is to re-centre a historically dominant discourse, whiteness should not be allowed to be merely normative. These texts are telling stories about women's history and in the process constructing a history of privilege that is a legacy for white feminists still learning to deconstruct that privilege.

Part Two: Clothes

3
The Greatness in Good Clothes: Fashioning Subjectivity in Mary Wroth's *Urania* and Margaret Spencer's Account Book (BL Additional MS 62092)

Despite the long-standing and often derogatory connection of women to fashion, we still know little of how women in seventeenth-century England regarded their clothes.[1] Research into historical patterns of female consumption – a field that often encompasses dress – has been more interested in the eighteenth century, probably because of the dramatic rise in consumer goods in that period.[2] Costume historians and literary scholars have instigated analyses of pre-eighteenth century English clothing, but their approaches, through the materials of dress and cross-dressing respectively, have not necessarily been conducive to understanding how women actually inhabited their clothes. Recent studies have, however, begun to redress this. Ann Jones and Peter Stallybrass's *Renaissance Clothing and the Materials of Memory* (2000), the essays on clothing in *Material London* (2000), Susan Vincent's *Dressing the Elite: Clothes in Early Modern England* (2003) and Roze Hentschell's *The Culture of Cloth in Early Modern England: Textual Constructions of a National Identity* (2008) for instance, pursue issues of economics, memory, nationalism and politics in the history of fashion.[3] Yet, while these works are mindful of gender, they attend to only limited evidence produced by early modern women themselves.[4]

The manuscript archive of women's account books and their printed imaginative texts, therefore, constitutes a rich vein of seventeenth-century resources that we have only just begun to mine.[5] Mary Wroth's *The Countess of Montgomery's Urania* (1621) is a prose romance persistently attentive to the social functions of dress, and Margaret Spencer's account book (c.1610–1613) documents her personal expenses.[6] Together, these texts detail the production, acquisition, wear and exchange of clothing. Wroth's *Urania* is renowned for its examination of the inward, but for some of Wroth's elite characters, that interiority is contingent upon the exterior world of dress, where clothes also serve a social function.[7] This chapter will focus on the tale of Nereana, a psychological and erotic quest narrative that turns on the loss and restoration of clothing. While Mary Wroth is, by now, renowned as an early modern writer, Margaret Spencer – one of seven siblings and the daughter of Robert, 1st Baron Spencer of Wormleighton (d.1627) and Margaret Willoughby (d.1597) – remains little known.[8] The account book, primarily in Margaret Spencer's own hand, catalogues her income and expenses between August 1610 and July 1613, ending some four months before she died, unmarried, on 6 December 1613, likely no more than 24 years of age (and very probably younger).[9] With family seats in Wormleighton and Althorp, Robert Spencer had only recently risen to the ranks of the nobility, having been created Baron Spencer of Wormleighton in 1600. The Spencer family had accumulated wealth through agricultural pursuits, especially sheep-breeding, and at the accession of James I, the baron was said to be the richest man in England.[10] An anonymous poem addressed to his three surviving sons (William, Richard and Edward Spencer) – *The Muses Thankfulnesse, or A Funeral Elegie, Consecrated to the perpetuall memory of the late All Honourable, and All-Noble Lord, Robert, Baron Spencer, of Wormleighton, &c.* – seems bent on defending the Baron from the charge that he is an impostor to his rank, a man whose wealth does not match his blood.[11] Yet the status of the Spencer family rises still further when William, Lord Spencer (the first baron's heir) marries Penelope Wriothsley (the daughter of Henry, 3rd Earl of Southampton, Shakespeare's patron) and their son becomes an earl, Henry, 1st Earl of Sunderland, 3rd Baron Spencer.[12] Edmund Spenser, in *Colin Clouts Come Home Again,* claimed a connection to this Spencer family, praising Elizabeth, Anne and Alice Spencer (Margaret's great-aunts), 'the noble familie:/Of which I meanest boast my selfe to be'.[13] Robert Spencer himself hosted Queen Anne and Prince Henry, an occasion for which Ben Jonson wrote a masque, *A Particular Entertainment of the Queen and Prince, their Highness at Althrope,* performed on 25 June 1603, 'as they came first into the Kingdome'.[14] Like Mary Wroth, Margaret Spencer was part of a literate, elite social context, and her account book precisely tabulates expenditures on items of clothing for herself and for gifts for members of her family, as well as related expenses for sewing, mending, laundry and transportation. While revealing little of the writer's emotional life, the manuscript documents connections among clothes, wealth, status and social relationships.[15]

Together these two texts create a richly textured picture of early modern women's dress. Margaret Spencer's account book is a fascinating, yet almost totally unexamined, record of the complex material, social and economic conditions in which one young early modern woman acquired and gave clothing. When her account entries are placed against the broader culture of seventeenth-century accounting, mercantilism and textile and clothing production, the account book laces the role of the clothing of one relatively wealthy early modern woman into a series of hierarchical social relationships in which she occupies both the subordinate and superior positions. Thus, even in the absence of affective discourse from its compiler, the account book speaks to the issue of subjectivity in its articulation of Spencer's social position. If subjectivity is, as Elizabeth Hanson defines it, 'the placeholder for human consciousness within discourse and material relations', when Margaret Spencer's account book tallies the economic and social circumstances of her clothes, it is documenting part of the material relations that constitute her subjectivity.[16] Here Pierre Bourdieu's notion of enculturation is useful, for he argues that all societies seek to 'deculturate' and 'reculturate [...] through seemingly insignificant details of dress, bearing, physical and verbal manners' because 'treating the body as a memory, they entrust to it in abbreviated and practical, i.e. mnemonic, form the fundamental principles of the arbitrary content of the culture'.[17] In Spencer's text, as well as Wroth's, clothes document 'the content of culture' and incorporate the wearer into a cultural system in which she possesses a social identity that is intertwined with her affective opportunities. Indeed, in early modern England, clothes were assumed to be active in fashioning not just the body and a social identity but inward states as well. Wroth's imaginative work may more effusively inscribe the world inside the gown, may write out specific emotional processes around clothing only suggested in Spencer's manuscript, but both texts suggest a version of female subjectivity constituted by dress; for each, dress is weighted with social significance which, in turn, informs the wearer's subjectivity.

In addition, this chapter argues that Wroth's representation of female subjectivity, a frequent focus in studies of her work, is informed by the material conditions and ideological constructions of dress. While the relationship between clothing and early modern subjectivity has already been observed by Ann Jones and Peter Stallybrass, as well as Daniel Roche, this connection has not factored into Wroth studies. Daniel Roche, writing about seventeenth-century France, draws attention to the Erasmian notion of dress that underpins many conduct books: 'Clothing was the "body's body, and from [it] one may infer the state of a man's character"'; clothes 'revealed "the harmony of the inner and outer man"'.[18] Jones and Stallybrass take this relationship still further, contending that clothes produce, as well as reveal, subjectivity: '"[f]ashion" can be *deeply* put on" or, in other words, that clothes permeate the wearer, fashioning him or her within. [...] Clothes, like sorrow, inscribe themselves upon a person who comes into being through that inscription.'[19] This chapter will press this notion of the productivity of clothing again to explore its applicability to women. Conduct books for women, for instance, forge a specifically female subjectivity through the materials of dress in just this way, and Mary Wroth represents female subjectivity both within and against this deterministic ideological framework. Applying this historically and culturally specific model to one of Wroth's female contemporaries, I conclude with an investigation of the material culture of clothing evidenced in Margaret Spencer's account book to query the version of female subjectivity that might be cast from the specific circumstances of her clothes.

How Clothes Make the Woman

Conduct books for women work in the Erasmian mode and presuppose a relationship between outward and inward states: clothes both reveal and create the woman. When Juan Luis Vives prohibits women from dressing in 'mannes rayment, elles let her thynke she hath the mans stomacke', he presumes that clothes produce a woman's affective and moral position.[20] Richard Brathwait, too, envisages a mutually constituting interweaving of clothes and self. 'So use the outward', he recommends 'that you darken not the inward; so dispose of the inward that it may rectifie the outward'.[21] Giovanni Bruto's *The Necessarie, Fit, and Convenient Education of a Yong Gentlewoman* similarly advises, 'how much more agreeable & of greater valour those vertues are that adorn the minde, than all the jewels which decke and beautifie the body, and most commonly make women more proud and hautie'.[22] Just as clothes can 'darken' the inward, a bejewelled appearance, not merely evidence of pride, actually produces that state. Here, clothes not only signal a woman's inwardness but also actively engender it.

Yet, a special difficulty arises when these assumptions about women's clothing confront parallel cultural dictates that employ garments in articulating class, rather than gender, hierarchies. Indeed, according to Susan Vincent, the utility of clothes in showing and maintaining class structure was the more immediate concern of English sumptuary laws. While there were debates around masculinizing or effeminizing dress, the laws – from the 1533 statute to the repeal of sumptuary law

in 1604 – were concerned primarily with class; even after acts and proclamations regulating apparel were no longer issued, the belief that the
'abuse of apparel' caused confusion of degree contributed to an understanding that a '"correct" social usage' of clothing would order a hierarchical society.[23] Because conduct books for women have a substantial
interest in maintaining female subordination within a gender hierarchy,
they have difficulty acknowledging the signs of class in the discourse
of female dress. To do so would require the admission that elite women
have access to a form of power from which many men, including the
conduct book writers themselves, are excluded by virtue of their lower
social rank.

Conduct books typically address the relationship between class and
dress only within an exclusively feminine social context – or not at all.
The Necessarie, Fit, and Convenient Education of a Yong Gentlewoman does
recognize the utility of clothing in announcing social status but allows
this function only within hierarchical relationships among women: a
woman should dress like her equals, without envy and without 'surpassing them in costly apparell', and she should shun familiarity with
servants.[24] Tellingly, when the text insists that adorning the mind is
more important than dressing the body, the virtues of the mind are
specifically not 'learning & humane Arts' but 'honestie & true vertue'.
As a result, the woman beautifying herself in this 'more comely and a
better ornament' is wearing little more than female subordination.[25]
Other conduct books likewise elide the conflict between gender and
class by discussing dress not as material but as metaphor. Vives, whose
work is actually addressed to a princess, nevertheless castigates those
ladies who insist upon dressing according to the prerogatives of class.
To their purported avowal that they 'must do some thynge for our byrth
and gentyl bloud, and possessions', he retorts, 'what are thou, that soo
sayest: a christen or a pagane?' He reminds them of the proverb: 'The
ornament of a woman is nat gold, but conditions.'[26] Richard Brathwait,
similarly rejecting ornament, calls for a return to the time when 'the
onely flower to be loved of women, was a native red, which was shamefastnesse'.[27] Dod and Cleaver's *Godly Forme of Houshold Government*,
after vilifying the wearing of 'gorgeous and sumptuous apparell, or
broidered haire trimmed with gold', likewise recommends instead sober
apparel, 'garnished and decked inwardly with vertues of their minds;
as with gentlenesse, meeknesse, quietnesse, and chastitie'.[28] These
figurative deployments of dress as virtue facilitate a turn to the inward
that erases the problem of class from the formation of the subordinate
female subject. Even in insisting that clothes make the woman, even

in maintaining that they actively produce her moral and affective self, the authors concede neither the currency of class nor the conservative utility of elite clothing within a class-based hierarchical social structure. Only by refusing to delineate concrete dictums about what to wear, and thereby neglecting the way that clothes make visible the class structure, can conduct books ensure that women inwardly understand their gendered subordination. Elite women's clothes inevitably produce a conflict between a gender hierarchy that insists upon female subordination and a class structure that insists that the upper-class woman reveal some status and authority in the expense of her dress. For women themselves, however, this conflict is rich in possibility, the more so precisely because of the notion that clothes can produce inward states: elite female clothes, destabilizing gender hierarchies, dress the inward with a version of elite female subjectivity more powerful than simply meek.

A 'Princesse without a Country, cloathes, or servants' in the *Urania*

Mary Wroth's *Urania* is certainly aware of this ideological framework, both employing and questioning its timbers. Her work, too, elucidates a productive, reciprocal relationship between the inward and the outward, but she, unlike her male conduct-book-writing compatriots, celebrates the prospect that elite dress may produce an insubordinate version of femininity. Not just the restrictive lexicon of conduct books, the language of inward fashioning is imaginatively useful to Wroth. She develops this perspective in her analysis of Nereana's clothes, which begins, but does not end, with the observation that clothes reveal the woman. When Nereana first appears at Pamphilia's court, her clothes announce her feelings. She is dressed all in tawny, as are the ten knights, pages and servants who accompany her. The tawny colour articulates Nereana's erotic attachment to Steriamus, who had earlier dressed in that colour and with whom she is in love, despite his own unreciprocated attachment to Pamphilia.[29] The tawny colour also indicates her feelings of abandonment and misery, for Steriamus does not love her, and her presence at Pamphilia's court is but the first stage in her quest to find him. The emotional symbolism of the tawny dress is culturally recognizable, for others in the romance – as in other contemporary poems – wear the colour to show the same emotion.[30]

Importantly, however, this very subjective revelation is tied to an announcement of class status. The tawny colour of Nereana's gown echoes through the bodies of those in her entourage, and their clothes, by providing evidence of her elite social position, further amplify and authorize her claim to her affective identity as a scorned lover. Class authorizes emotional expression, and clothes provide both evidence of status and, for Nereana, the materials with which the emotional text can be written. Nereana's strategy for dressing is like that of Antissia and Dalinea, for when Antissia dresses in mourning, so, too, do her servants (396). The mourning Dalinea is 'attended on with numbers of Knights and Ladies likewise in that habit' (241). In affording her characters the use of this affective livery, Wroth recasts the practice of wearing mourning livery in early modern England. David Cressy, drawing attention to the way that the mourning garb of servants articulates subordination, observes, '[w]earing black was a mark of dependency as well as respect'.[31] Moreover, the livery of servants enhanced the identity of the master, for as Jones and Stallybrass argue, 'livery came to mean not just clothing, but *marked* clothing, which incorporated retainers and servants into the social body of their master or mistress'.[32] For Wroth, such social and affective dynamics within the wearing of livery serve a specifically romantic cause: the authorization and revelation of female desire.

Yet her rationale for the use of livery is distinct from that suggested by Jones and Stallybrass. They tie the disappearance of livery to the emergence of the concept of the individual, the 'conceptual system in which a person is prior to his or her wardrobe'.[33] For Nereana and other elite female characters dress reveals emotions in a way that illustrates how aristocratic female characters have a subjectivity prior to their wardrobes; they dress to reveal their feelings. Yet this subjectivity specifically depends on the privilege the elite woman has to compel evidence of her social identity from liveried servants. She can express herself in her clothes – she is prior to her clothes – but only because her servants aid her in articulating her affective self. Her individuality, such as it is, remains socially contingent, dependent on a social context that legitimates the erasure of the separate emotional identity of servants and retainers. Because Nereana can compel her servants to eschew their own identities for hers, their bodies serve her by authorizing her expression of affect with evidence of her aristocratic power. In Wroth's version, the aristocratic woman's gown is a form of affective discourse; yet that dress is most authoritative when it is enhanced by the repetition of its signifiers through the garb of servants who reveal her power. She can afford, create and compel the meaning of their clothes.

When Wroth allows clothes to become affective costuming, she insists that the elite woman underwrite her articulate female subjectivity with the subjection of those of lower rank. Scholarly examinations of expressions of female subjectivity in Wroth's romance have not taken up this social dynamic, however. Exceptionally, Kim F. Hall has shown how the *Urania* 'uses the language of beauty to reinforce distinctions in class', particularly in terms of race; she argues that European women, not exempt from the colonial project, frequently negotiate a position of power against '"foreign" women coded as a threat to an already insecure, secondary position'.[34] Nereana, similarly, is negotiating a position of power against others, not through race but through class – through the subordination of her servants, whose own emotional identities are rendered insignificant. Yet, too often, critics are simply laudatory or solicitous in their approach to Wroth's representation of female subjectivity. Looking at Nereana, Akiko Kusunoki, for instance, sympathetically observes only that Nereana illustrates 'the uncontrollable quality of female desire, which is considered as madness if a woman fails in her performance of masking it under conventional behavior'.[35] Studies which focus on Wroth's literary formations of subjectivity, as Jacqueline T. Miller does with her study of rhetoric, Nona Fienberg of Petrarch and Amelia Zurcher Sandy of the pastoral tend to examine the gendered formation of subjectivity within patriarchal discourse, while obscuring the workings of class.[36] Heather L. Weidemann, who actually draws attention to the relationship of appearance and identity in the *Urania,* argues that 'appearances often point to a subjective female identity which is hidden but nonetheless authentic'.[37] For her, Wroth's version of female subjectivity is autonomous and independent of material conditions. Yet, Wroth's combination of affective female dress with livery supplies a more socially contingent and elitist construct. Clothes signal status, and that social identity affords Nereana the ability to claim an affective identity.

Still, Nereana's behaviour in love is illegitimate within the system of cultural values established in Wroth's romance – not, I should add, in subordinating her servants but in her inability to govern herself. Nereana's tale is a political parable about the dangers of the unbounded, public pursuit of unreciprocated love by a woman who should rule herself and her country. She must learn self-governance to regain political power, and Wroth employs clothes to instruct Nereana in this lesson, a methodology that presupposes that clothes produce – and not only reveal – the moral subject. Elaine Beilin has discussed Nereana's story, describing it as a 'draconian narrative of the ruler corrected and redeemed', in which Nereana must learn self-control and to abjure absolutism.[38] The political ideology of absolutism evinces an indecorous female subject who, unable to rule herself, also fails to recognize her place within gendered and political social relationships. Although, according to Pamphilia herself, Nereana is a woman of 'great beauty, high birth, rich possessions, absolute command, and what is most, matchlesse love, and loyaltie' (194), she is not welcomed into Pamphilia's social circle. Nereana's failing is a 'pride-fild heart' (194), a manifestation, it seems, of overweening political power; she is 'absolute Lady of that Iland [Stalamine]' (192) and a Princess 'borne absolute' (193). The absolutism that makes Nereana proud also makes her 'subject' to her passions (193); she 'despis[es] any passion but love should dare to thinke of ruling in her' (195). This desire for Steriamus signals her unfitness for rule. The tawny gown she wears is revealing affect deemed excessive, for desire rules Nereana, and her tawny dress is, in this unusual sense, inappropriately revealing.

Clothes are, furthermore, integral to her redemption. Nereana's emotional state changes when she gets separated from her clothes and her entourage. After departing the court to continue her pursuit of Steriamus, Nereana immediately gets lost in a forest, and, without her servants, she is captured by Alanius and tied to a tree because he believes her to be the nymph he loves. Already bereft of her liveried companions, Nereana is also stripped of her clothes, and thus of her social authority. Alanius explicitly acts on the assumption that clothing fashions within, for he believes that her gown 'made her unwilling to abide with him' (197). Thus, in an attempt to make Nereana love him, Alanius undoes her hair and leaves her nothing but a 'little petticoate of carnation tafatie' and green silk stockings, rolled down to look like buskins; her smock sleeves are rolled to her elbows, her neck bared, her head and arms adorned with garlands and her chest with a wreath (197–8). Alanius's expressed aim is to transform Nereana into a wood nymph, and he assumes that if he changes her clothes, he will be able to fashion her heart to be amenable to him. Wroth at first allows Nereana to resist this paradigm, however, for Nereana's pride remains intact, despite the violent re-costuming. Even garbed as a parodic imitation of a nymph, she valiantly reminds herself of her class identity: 'thine owne royall spirit shall never leave thee' (199). In this scene, Wroth is alive to the tenuous hold that early modern women have on their property and considers how this legal reality might make it difficult for women to control their feelings: if clothing fashions within, female subjectivity can be commanded by anyone who controls their clothes.[39] Wroth instead allows a subjectivity prior to clothes, with which Nereana can resist Alanius's attempt to compel her love. He controls her body and her clothes, but he cannot control her heart. Nereana inhabits a fashion system where clothes can forge subjective identities, but Wroth allows fissures within this system in order to place female subjectivity beyond the material world sometimes forcefully controlled by men.

Yet clothes remain powerful instruments with which to sound social authority, and when Nereana is stripped of her clothes and denuded of her social identity, this does ultimately have a deleterious effect on her identity. Wroth is plain that the woman travelling with neither her liveried servants nor her clothes is vulnerable to misrecognition, but the woman with these resources has some privilege. Juan Luis Vives, too, is aware of this circumstance, for he issues the reminder that 'Plutarchus sayth, that it is a custome in Egipte, that women should weare no showes, bycause they shuld abyde at home.' 'Lykewyse', Vives adds, 'if thou take from women sylke, and cloth of gold, & sylver, pretious stones, and gemmes, thou shalte the more easily kepe them at home.'[40] When Nereana's expensive garb is taken from her, she, too, is disempowered. She becomes, according to Wroth's narrator, a 'sportfull exercise of Fortune, a Princesse without a Country, cloathes, or servants, a Lady that must tell her selfe to be one' (334). Dressed only in a carnation taffeta petticoat, Nereana is not identifiably a lady, the most immediate consequence of which is that her words are not understood or believed. Even though the taffeta of her petticoat is expensive, foreign and appropriate for a princess's undergarments, the relative unclothing in her appearance creates dissonance in her claim that she is royal. When the knight Philarchos sees Nereana, he reads her prideful speech against her near nakedness and believes her to be merely a mad woman. Thus, in addition to authorizing the expression of affect and desire, in addition to enabling travel, clothes create the conditions in which female speech can register meaningfully.

Nereana, however, is finally unable to resist her diminished dress and changes inwardly. Being deprived of expensive clothes and her liveried servants, along with subsistence on a diet of berries, herbs, roots and goat's milk, results in psychological transformation, and Nereana becomes more self-effacing: 'I am humbled, and my former fault looks more odious to me' (335). Confirming the productivity of clothing, the humility that wearing only a petticoat has created immediately dissipates when she is rescued and once again changes her clothes. '[W]hen she had her greatnes againe in good clothes put about her', Wroth's narrator recounts, 'she began to grow to her wonted accustomed humours' (335). Good clothes, like humble garb, are psychologically productive. When Nereana puts them on she puts on greatness, too. Good clothes reproduce her pride. With this, Wroth's narrative seems to bear out the fears of conduct book writers, as she concedes that gorgeous apparel can deck the mind with virtues at some distance from meek, feminine subordination.

Nereana's insubordination is not of the appropriate kind for Wroth, however, and she will not allow Nereana simply to continue in these 'accustomed humours'. She ultimately learns self-governance after a final trial, being enclosed in a tower by her sister: she is made a 'poore, imagined distracted creature where she was absolute Princesse; little Justice was in this, yet she as a woman must suffer' (495). This trial tests Nereana's politics, for Wroth's narrator explicitly figures confinement in a tower as an antidote to her previous absolutism. But the subjection she endures is also, the narrator resignedly offers, a likely consequence of being a woman, as if it were the lot of women generally to endure constraints like the tower, a claim that further highlights how clothes enabled movement against these gendered restrictions. The resolution to the tale comes when one of the subjects of Stalamine, 'a great man welbeloved', is moved to urge his fellow citizens to offer restitution to Nereana. For her part, 'by her poore living, and neglect' she changes for the final time, and her reform is marked once again in her dress: 'so staid an habitation of gravity' (496). This is the rhetorical turn to metaphors of dress so common in conduct books, but Nereana's gravitas is hardly virtuous submissiveness. Rather, gravity suits her for power because it is evidence of her self-control, a sign that she is no longer subject to love. Nereana, having abandoned both her psychological pride and her political absolutism, proves 'an excellent Governess, and brave Lady, being able to overrule her old passions, and by them to judge how to favour, licence, and curb others, and this experience, though late, is most profitable to Princes' (496). Divested of pride and her tawny gown, Nereana rids herself of a political liability and the story ends with promises of future psychological and social stability.

In Wroth's narrative, clothes reveal inward states, but clothes also create them. In the first instance, when clothes articulate female affect, Wroth resorts to the supplemental significance of class, also substantiated by dress, to confirm the authority of women to travel and to be heard and understood. Conversely, when Wroth explores how clothes produce inward states, she is attentive to the fragility of women's attachment to their property and to the possibilities for psychological harm that could arise if clothes are imposed upon women or taken from them. Yet, while she allows Nereana to resist a man who wishes to impose his desires on her through his control of her clothes, Nereana cannot ultimately defy the humility that comes from wearing humble clothes. In the end, Wroth insists that Nereana not only be great because she wears good clothes but that she learn a version of female subjectivity in which erotic desire does not create female subjection. The self-governing woman also rules her state. To this end, Wroth insists that Nereana possess both the clothes and inward attributes of a queen.

Inwardness and Economics in Margaret Spencer's Account Book

While Mary Wroth's romance illustrates the social and psychological functions of dress in the generic terms of fiction, Margaret Spencer's manuscript does so in the forms of accounting. Spencer's work, too, draws attention to how a hierarchical society is woven into clothes and to how clothes might be lived by women in early modern England. By placing the theoretical model of clothed subjectivity, which Wroth's romance provides, within the material culture of early modern dress, the remainder of this chapter will explore how Spencer's account book scripts a version of elite female subjectivity. The manuscript documents personal expenses, listing payments for many goods and services, from books, paper, ink and quills, and lessons in playing the virginals and dancing, to a 'picktooth cass & picketooth' and 'a payer of pistalls' (fols. 8, 17). Margaret Spencer's largest category of expense, however, is clothes, which over the three year period comes to about £105 18s 4d. Including garments, shoes and accessories, as well as related expenses, such as the materials and labour that produce, mend, remake, clean and transport them, clothing costs amount to nearly 86 per cent of the money she receives. Even if Margaret Spencer does not explicitly record the affective significance of her clothes, the account book reveals the spending of a young woman within a hierarchical society that includes both family and kinship relations, as well as service and commercial ones. Through these records of economic, social and affective transactions, Margaret Spencer's manuscript becomes its own kind of narrative of subjectivity in a culture where, in the words of Jones and Stallybrass, 'fashion fashions, because what can be worn can be worn deeply'.[41]

It seems plain that Margaret Spencer produces the account book at the behest of her father, who acts as auditor. This is evident from the appearance of Robert Spencer's signature with a notation attesting to the date, the delivery of the account by Margaret, and the sum for the period in question, as well as Margaret's addresses to him in some entries ('mony I received of yr Lo[rdship]' (fol. 1)) and his correction to her sums (he alters her addition on fol. 23v).[42] While he is not always with her, as indicated by the occasional vicarious delivery of funds, the account book enables his watchful eye; he learns from its pages how she spends her time, as well as her money. Her father may also be training her in accounting's practices and habits of thought to fit her to future duties in household management – thus, not to watch over her own resources but his, as well as those of a potential future husband. Amanda Vickery and Amy Louise Erikson have celebrated this kind of female labour, arguing that accounting was, by the late seventeenth century at least, a recognized component of effective housewifery.[43] If we take Vickery's point that later women's account books 'catalogue the regime of the mistress housekeeper', for '[a] lady's work was managerial', Margaret Spencer is being taught how to manage a house that is, actually, a business in itself.[44] Indeed, Mary Spencer, Margaret's grandmother and Robert's mother, audited many of his household accounts for the years between 1599 and 1602 (British Library, Additional MS 25080). She supervises and accounts for domestic expenses ranging from the purchase of food, clothing and household labour to agricultural expenses such as cutting down trees, the repair of a windmill and the shoeing of horses.[45] Yet while Vickery and Erikson quite rightly point to the intellectual agency and administrative responsibility required in household management, women's accounting skills were still constructed as a contribution to the patriarchal social order. When Dod and Cleaver, for instance, place money management within the purview of the mistress, they insist that the wife's fiscal responsibility confirm her subordination: 'One point of subjection is, to be content with such apparell and outward port as her husbands estate can allow her'; contributing to the economic gain of husbands, women should not 'wring from their husbands more then he can well cut out from his revenues, or gettings'.[46] Even *Advice to the Women and Maidens of London* (1678), written by 'one of that sex', advocates accounting for women, in part, on the grounds that a woman's book-keeping benefits her husband, for the man whose wife keeps his accounts is not beholden to servants.[47]

Nevertheless, it was certainly possible to imagine more autonomous moral and intellectual results for the female account-keeper in early modern England. Even if fiscal prudence does serve the patriarchal household economy, when Margaret Spencer produces an account that proves she does not spend more than she has, she need not only be verifying her prudence for her father.[48] Accounting is an acknowledged intellectual accomplishment, with tangible economic benefits for women. In the 1670s, Bathsua Makin's *An Essay to Revive the Antient*

Education of Women (1673) defended women's study of mathematics: 'The Mathematicks require as much seriousness as any Art or Science, yet some Women have attained an extraordinary knowledge in these also.'[49] *Advice to the Women and Maidens of London* adds several more benefits of accounting for women: 'whereby, either single, or married, they may know their Estates, carry on their Trades, and avoid the Danger of a helpless and forlorn Condition, incident to Widows'.[50] Knowing her husband's business will keep the wife from ruin when he dies. When the author recounts how her parents taught her arithmetic as a young woman, she remarks that it 'set my brains at work, Yet there was much delight in seeing the end, and how each question produced a fair answer and informed me of things I knew not'. Beyond this, when her father teaches her accounting, the end is even more affirming: 'shee that is so well versed in this as to keep the accounts of her Cash right and dayly entred in a book fair without blotting, will soon be fit for greater undertakings'.[51] Thus, the ability to keep accounts, in addition to facilitating women's economic stability, provides intellectual pleasure and, most importantly, proof of female capacity. She shows she is fit for 'greater undertakings'. In having his daughter account for herself, Robert Spencer is surveying her activities and fitting her for household management, but he is also providing her with an opportunity to demonstrate her intellectual facility and to secure her own economic future. If her manuscript calculates her intellectual and spiritual capacity, as well as her expenditures, the responsibility that she has for her own clothes is not a merely trivial concern with 'frippery', but the occasion to substantiate a moral, intellectual and affective female subject.

The references to clothes in Margaret Spencer's account book also denote a version of female inwardness that extends beyond chaste, gendered subjection to encompass economic and social status. Her clothes and the means by which she acquires them allow her to understand herself against others whose labour she buys. This function of clothes is like the deployment of livery in Mary Wroth's romance, but in Spencer's account book the process of elevating the woman specifically depends on wealth, as well as class, to create subordinating relationships that set her above many men, as well as women. There are hints of Spencer's own productive labours. The purchases of a 'workinge frame' (fol. 1*v*) and 'canvices to work in' (fol. 9) and a 'silver thimbell' (fol. 21*v*) suggest that Margaret did do needlework, as do listings for silk, which, although not specifically marked for her own needlework, could also have been purchased for that reason. Yet Margaret Spencer is plainly a consumer of the labour of others. She pays for needlework and sewing, as well as the dying of fabrics. She also purchases a great many items ready-made. These include shoes, gloves, stockings and garters, collars and cuffs, hats and hair fashions, purses, farthingales and bodices. She employs the services of a tailor and hatter, for mending and changing her clothes. According to Margaret Spufford, tailors were commonly responsible for the production of larger items, with a more substantial ready-made clothing industry growing up only after 1660, but Margaret Spencer obviously purchases many of the smaller items, as well.[52] She also pays for laundry and its implements; she buys laundry tools – an iron to starch bands, a rounding block and a setting stick – and she pays for 18 weeks of washing, as well as for starching, starch and gum to starch bands. Rather than conforming to early modern ideals of the nearly self-sufficient household economy, valued by both Gervase Markham (amongst other early modern writers) and feminist scholars – albeit for different reasons – Margaret Spencer is a consumer of goods.[53] As such, her acquisition of clothing places her in a position of economic privilege in relation to those whose labour she buys. The very processes of clothing production and acquisition, as much as clothing's appearance, substantiate social power, particularly in Margaret Spencer's relationship to other women. Alice C. Clark shows that the work of spinning wool, linen, flax and silk was the monopoly of female labourers, who were paid only a subsistence wage for their efforts: 'except in the most skilled branches of the woollen industry, spinning was a pauper trade, a "sweated industry," which did not provide its workers with the means for keeping themselves and their families in a state of efficiency but left them to some extent dependent on other sources for their maintenance'.[54] More recently, Beverly Lemire has similarly argued that '[i]ssues of gender, of sexually specific patterns of work and patterns of trade, defined and constrained experiences; [...] From the outset, female sweated labour provided the foundation on which the clothing industry was built.'[55] For Margaret Spencer, the processes of clothing production and acquisition establish her economic difference from the labourers, especially female workers, whose efforts allow her to get dressed; as for Wroth's characters, the assertion of the upper-class woman's identity in clothing is contingent upon the subordination of others.

The historically specific means by which Margaret Spencer acquires her clothes also document the far-flung geographic connections of her clothes. In Wroth's romance, the aristocratic woman's clothes enabled the questing female traveller; in the account book Margaret Spencer herself travels regularly and transports her clothes, as well, in the three year period. She goes most often to London (fols. 13, 14, 24) and to locations connected to members of her family, such as Mereworth (fols. 5, 8) and Buston, in Kent (fols. 12, 14v); Althorp, in Northamptonshire (fols. 2, 3, 4, 15, 16, 25); Wormleighton (fol. 4) in Warwickshire and Penley (fols. 14v, 25v) in Hertfordshire. She provides evidence that she visited other houses and attended a christening, as well.[56]

Margaret Spencer's clothes themselves traverse space in ways that substantiate her economic and social power. Certainly, she could have acquired some goods from chapmen, for, according to Margaret Spufford, they frequently sold stockings and gloves, coifs, caps, hoods, bands, handkerchiefs and neckcloths, in addition to haberdashery items like needles and pins, buttons, thread, ribbons, tape, inkle, combs and pocket looking glasses.[57] Spencer's account book is replete with these goods, and they could have been more locally produced.[58] Yet, she also purchased goods from distant places, with her access to wealth and her social connections enabling their transportation. Some purchases are strictly economic transactions, while others depend on social relationships and kinship. She appears to make vicarious purchases through carriers; one brings her bodices to London and back, while another transports a white gown and farthingale.[59] Joan Thirsk in her book on the development of consumer society argues that by the late sixteenth century, the upper ranks, the gentry, yeoman and merchants had an 'almost encyclopedic body of knowledge [...] about where the best markets were to be found for different types of goods, and gentlemen or their servants, not to mention merchants, travelled long distances in search of their special needs'.[60] Such purchases may show Margaret Spencer's own knowledge of the marketplace, as well as the economic clout that enables her to employ carriers. Her contact with the servants of others, who transport her, as well as her clothes, further embodies her social position, substantiating her privilege, not on monetary but social grounds. Sir Francis Fane's man (fol. 8), Sir Semar Knightly's man (fol. 15), and the servants of three cousins bring her items such as plumes, gloves, and a ruff. The transportation provided by other men's servants is akin to the social favours that effect her own mobility, favours that she acknowledges with token payments, seemingly in the form of tips, or vails, to the coachmen of the acquaintances who gave her the gifts.[61] Susan E. Whyman argues that, like gift-giving, visiting in a coach is a 'symbolic activit[y] that stabilized social relationships'; the coach 'provided a prestigious place from which to view the not-so-privileged world'; it 'expressed urban values, like market competition, social mobility and conspicuous display'; it 'became a badge of membership in society'; it was a part of the patronage system; it reunited families. Furthermore, the coaches of the Verneys, the family at the centre of her study, were frequently at the disposal of women and gave them the power to 'grant the gift of independence, if only for a day'.[62] In Margaret Spencer's case, not only does her own travel mark her independence and her elite social position, but so too does the acquisition of her clothes, which is part of the same system of social relationships as that documented in coaches. Beyond their transportation, clothes function as gifts that articulate these social distinctions. While she gives money to her own nurse, the nurses of the children of others, poor women and men, maids and various other servants (chamberlain, butler, cook, groom), musicians and a chandler 'for his presentt of payers' (fol. 15), she gives articles of clothing to family members, and 'nurse kempe' who receives a 'blake cipars hatband' (fol. 6); she gives a fan and a 'payer of vellvett gallocias' to 'my La: le: despencer' (fol. 9, 11*v*), a purse to 'my La: fane' (fol. 9), and a 'payer of vellvitt slipars' to 'my brother Anderson' for New Year's gifts (fol. 21). As part of a gift economy, clothes themselves affirm and reveal elite connections and emotional attachments.

The social meanings of Spencer's clothes, acquired through economic and social relations, inform the way clothes could be imagined to create a self; in Spencer's case, clothes instantiate a female subject who is not merely subordinate. If 'fashion fashions', Margaret Spencer is a woman of the world, defined wholly neither by obedience nor privacy. She is, her account book suggests, a woman who inhabits the private sphere of family life in rather complex ways. Her 'home' and family are not confined to a single place nor entirely distinct from the marketplace, and her place within that family is not only that of the obedient daughter but also of the mistress of servants and friend and relative of aristocratic men and women.

Margaret Spencer's account book also documents, as Kim F. Hall observed of characters in Wroth's romance, a version of subjectivity informed by the emerging context of colonialism. Not just obtaining garments geographically marked through their manufacture outside the home, Margaret Spencer possesses clothes created from fabric that comes from still further abroad. She acquires pieces that are identifiably foreign, both explicitly in their style and implicitly in their cloth. Spencer distinguishes a chain, cuffs, a ruff and a petticoat as French, and a handkerchief, falling bands, cuffs and pearls as Italian. Even if such notations do not necessarily indicate the material origins of a piece, for an Italian ruff could be made in England, Margaret Spencer connects her clothes and their additional cost to non-English ideas about style. More materially, most of the fabrics she buys are not English, either. The English cloth industry, probably the largest employer outside the agricultural industry, produced both traditional worsteds and the new draperies.[63] Thus, with the exception of her purchases of 'bayes',[64] canvas and fustian, which doubtless had English origins, the textiles that Margaret Spencer wears originate abroad. She buys silks (such as satin, taffeta, tiffany and double tiffany and sarsenet), which came from Italy and Spain in the sixteenth century, and with the founding of four European East India Companies, from China, as well as Turkey.[65] She purchases linens (such as cambric, lawn and holland), which were probably from Northern France or Flanders, for the English industry then produced only coarse linen.[66] One of her costliest purchases is a calico gown, the components of which include '12 yardes of whitt calycoe' brought to her by 'Mtr dorman Sr. Francis fanes man' (fol. 8). This fabric, at 6s/yard, costs less than the taffeta and lawn she also buys, yet more than most other textiles.[67] If the fabric is not significantly more expensive, it is exotic, and it is only for the calico gown that Spencer compiles a record of all constituent elements, which, she says, amount to £6 4d, for goods and labour. Calico would become extremely popular by the late seventeenth century, but in 1610 it was an elite consumer good.[68] Although Philip Lawson's history of the East India Company proposes that the company began to diversify its business to include spices other than pepper, as well as indigo, calicoes and silk, only in the 1620s and 1630s, Beverly Lemire provides evidence that even in the sixteenth century English elites had access to Indian textiles.[69] Margaret Spencer's calico gown provides evidence of her social power, for the purchase of calico positions her in the midst of a controversy. Thomas Mun's *A Discourse of Trade, from England unto the East Indies* (1621) defends the calico trade, 'into which the English lately made an entrance'; Mun proposes that while it may not be 'profitable', 'in respect they [calicoes] are the manifacture of Infidells, and in great part the weare of Christans', trading in calico benefits England because it abates the cost of cambric, holland and other sorts of linen that are brought into the country; the calico trade also impairs the business of the Turks, a logic which affirms the wearing of calico on the grounds of faith.[70] Margaret Spencer's calico gown, then, seems placed at the forefront of colonial exchange, as she acquires foreign textiles through the servant of one of the most elite of her social relations documented in the account book, Sir Francis Fane.[71] The textile with the most distant origins explicitly brings the exotic and the elite into alignment. This connection between textiles and social power is also evident to Thomas Mun, who wrote that 'Tobacco, Cloth of gold and Silver, Lawnes, Cambricks, Gold and Silver lace, Velvets,

Sattens, Taffaeties and divers others manifactures, yearely brought into this Realme, for an infinite value' do devour English wealth: 'yet', he adds, 'the moderate use of all these wares hath ever suted well with the riches and Majestie of this Kingdome'.[72] To wear foreign riches, moderately, is to be well suited for rule.

Margaret Spencer's most expensive purchase of a single item is a hat, specifically 'a whitt bever hatt and hatt band', for which she pays £3 (fol. 14). This, too, is almost certainly a product of colonial trade. According to Murray G. Lawson, the beaver hat is the 'luxury demand which influenced the fur trade most in the seventeenth and eighteenth centuries'; from when it came into general favour in the early seventeenth century, the demand for beaver fur was at the centre of the European presence in North America.[73] Because beavers had been extinct in England since the mid-fifteenth century, the fur was definitely from abroad. It could have come from the New England coast, the focus of the English fur trade in the early seventeenth century (the Hudson's Bay Company was not established until 1670). In 1611, the Earl of Southampton – the father-in-law of Margaret Spencer's elder brother – sent an expedition to the New England coast.[74] The beaver hat could also well have come from France, for the French controlled the beaver trade in what is now Canada, and France, furthermore, was a centre of the hat-making industry.[75] In any case, Margaret Spencer not only has a beaver hat, but she has a white beaver hat, presumably made from an albino beaver, an even more rare and costly animal.[76]

These purchases of textiles and fur set the discourse of class and wealth against that of female subordination. The calico, the French and Italianate styles, and the fur transgress the way in which early modern conduct books codified female chastity through the rejection of foreign fabrics and styles. As Roze Hentschell shows, 'foreign cloth is sinister in its power to undermine England's virtue and the symbolic rectitude of the domestic wool industry'.[77] Easily translating this economic imperative onto female behaviour, Richard Brathwait maligns '[o]utlandish' fashions for signifying chastity's absence.[78] For Margaret Spencer, however, the revelation of wealth and status outweighs such gendered dictates. Interestingly, her purchases of starch also work in this way. In 1610, the production and use of starch actually occasioned legal discussion at the highest levels, with the making of starch being prohibited, according to Joan Thirsk, because of concern about the frivolous consumption of wheat; a second proclamation, the result of recalcitrant enforcement, was issued the same year, and starch makers would not be licensed again until 1619.[79] Spencer transgresses attempts to constrain consumption. Beyond the way that the appearance of dress manifests social hierarchies in early modern England, the hierarchical labour relations, elite social connections and worldly attachments to trade in distant realms establish Margaret Spencer's clothes as a site of social and economic power. If clothes enculturate, Margaret Spencer wears a privileged, worldly form of culture; if the outward engenders the inward, as conduct book writers and Mary Wroth suppose, Spencer has access to an insubordinate version of female subjectivity.

Conclusion

Although we have learned much from Gail Kern Paster, Michael Schoenfeldt and Jonathan Sawday about the history of the subject and of relationships between bodies and selves in early modern England, it is important to recognize that human bodies are also usually dressed bodies.[80] It is through dress that men and women negotiate with the world. Through dress, the world understands them, deeming them acceptable, or not, and the wearer communicates about him or herself. The dressed person embodies an array of cultural meanings, in connection to literary texts (such as Nereana's pastoral garb), religious texts (religious habits and dictums on modesty) and aesthetics;[81] as Anne Hollander explains the latter, '[d]ress is a form of visual art, a creation of images with the visible self as its medium'.[82] Clothing is also a legal text made possible, or constrained, by sumptuary laws delimiting the wearing of fabric by class and by gender.[83] More materially, as a technological text, clothing provides evidence of changing processes of textile manufacture and clothing production, and in a world only embarking on the road to global capitalism, clothes could script nationality, even as the developing trade in exotic goods allowed the foreign to contribute to the way in which clothing displayed power.[84] Clothing is, too, an economic text, knitting the labour of spinners, weavers, drapers, clothiers and needleworkers together with the trading practices of early modern merchants in textiles and clothing, both new and used.[85] Finally, clothing is a text inflected with gender, not only in how clothing denotes the gender of the sexed body beneath the clothes, but also in how it is the end product of gendered processes of production. Clothing is the result and signifier of contests of power: among monarchs and subjects, aristocrats and commoners, aristocrats and merchants, rich and poor, colonizer and colonized, and men and women, among others. In a world where fashion fashions within, all of these contests contribute to the way in which the wearer can construct a subjective stance through the material culture of her social context.

Mary Wroth's romance and Margaret Spencer's account book illustrate these processes in play, although they do so in different generic terms. Mary Wroth's romance is written for an audience and, as such, both involves and reconfigures the historical conditions of dress; Margaret Spencer's account book is for herself and her father and does not reflect on itself. Yet, both the account book and the work of fiction show that class functions in the discourse of clothing not just at the level of textiles, styles and colours, as regulated by sumptuary laws, but also in the multiple social relationships that are forged through and around clothes. For both Wroth and Spencer, clothes can articulate a non-subordinate social position for the woman of means, the woman with servants whose liveries can perform and authorize her own identity and the woman with access to servants whose labour, in transporting her and her clothes, articulates her privilege. If Juan Luis Vives proposes a woman should not dress in a 'mannes rayment, elles let her thynke she hath the mans stomacke', one wonders what is produced inside the woman who wears clothes which plait together economic, social, national and mercantilist structures. In early modern England, women's interest in clothes is far from superficial; it is the material of subjectivity itself.

4
What Not to Wear: Children's Clothes and the Maternal Advice of Elizabeth Jocelin and Brilliana, Lady Harley

This chapter will explore how two early modern mothers, Elizabeth Jocelin (1596–1622) and Brilliana, Lady Harley (bap. 1598, d.1643) theorized the dress of their children. Elizabeth Jocelin's advice, written before her daughter's birth, was printed posthumously as *The Mothers Legacie, To her Unborne Child* in 1624, while Lady Harley's advice survives in the form of a small manuscript advice book and numerous letters to her son Edward (1624–1700). Children's dress assumed a prominent place in histories of childhood when Philippe Aries and Lawrence Stone influentially argued that the similarity of children's dress to that of adults indicated the absence of a concept of childhood and of parental affection in early modern England.[1] Although Linda Pollock, Patricia Crawford and Kenneth Charlton have conclusively refuted these claims and shown that parents cared for their children with love and with concern for their spiritual state, education, socialization and protection, they did not consider the function of children's clothing within this revisionist framework.[2] This chapter is an investigation of how two early modern mothers cared for their children through the provision of clothing and in advice which theoretically engages clothing's social functions. Scholarly interest in maternal advice was defined initially by the question of authorial strategies and, more recently, by that of women's political engagements.[3] In the latter vein, I will argue that maternal advice is a form of governance, a means to regulate dress and, contingently, to imagine the social order and the child's place within it as an English subject with intellectual, religious, class and kinship allegiances. Clothing was not an exclusively feminine concern, in spite of discourses of clothing that produced knowledge about clothing as if it were. Elizabeth Jocelin's maternal advice about clothes contemplates the utility of clothes in scripting social harmony and makes legible the workings of women's minds. For Lady Harley, clothing should inculcate in her son a religious and political identity, and her advice and provision of clothes requires her to become a scholarly mother and political actor. Resisting the trivialization of feminine knowledge, both mothers establish for their children pedagogies of dress that fashion citizens, as a humanist education should.

The Governance of Clothing

Maternal advice and clothing were two of a range of practices that comprised early modern motherhood, but neither issuing advice about dress nor taking care of clothes were exclusively female concerns. Literate women could educate their young sons and daughters enough to teach them to read, to recite the catechism and, in the case of girls, to undertake various vocational skills.[4] Practically, clothing was the early modern parent's second largest expense, costing less than food but more than education; Margaret Spufford has argued that even amongst the poorest segments of society, most children had some new clothes.[5] Mothers played a role in the acquisition of these clothes, if they did not necessarily make the clothes themselves as Gervase Markham suggested the good housewife should.[6] So for instance, under his mother's supervision while his father was in Ireland, young Philip Sidney acquired for wear at Oxford boot hose, black silk buttons and lace, a silk girdle, various coats, gloves, a crimson satin doublet, 'a shorte damaske gowne garded withe velvette and laid on withe lace' and a double taffeta coat; Lady Mary Sidney signed the accounts kept by Thomas Marshall, a servant.[7] At a lower social level, Anne Archer, of Coopersale, Theydon Gernon, Essex, a widow after 1615, acquired an array of goods for her children.[8] In addition to food, the necessities for farming and gardening, medical treatments, servants' wages, and stocks in the East India Company, Anne Archer's domestic account book, compiled between 1600 and 1629, documents the purchase for her children of shoes, bodices, petticoats, coats, needlework, suits of clothes, hose, garters, hats and dressings for hats, waistcoats and doublets, jerkins, bands and aprons, as well as books, paper, a penknife, schooling expenses and haircuts.[9] These women are not entirely exceptional. Linda Levy Peck contends that 'women at all social levels made consumption decisions for the household and some engaged in the retail trades. Despite the limitations of coverture, which, interpreted strictly, meant that women could not make contracts, over the course of the seventeenth century married women, who had no standing in common law, were allowed to buy increasing amounts of luxury goods to support their husband's and family's status.'[10] Even beyond luxury goods, materially, practically and economically, ensuring that children had appropriate clothing was one of motherhood's activities.

But early modern English men were at least as adept as women at purchasing clothing for a household in a world without mass production and few ready-made garments, where the consumer needed to possess knowledge of textile properties and quality, current fashions and garment construction. Men had more access to the commercial and public sphere. Sue Vincent provides ample evidence that men made sartorial decisions for themselves and members of their households.[11] For his son Thomas, Sir Henry Slingsby sent to London for a first suit of clothes, made by his own tailor, and Robert Cecil, the Earl of Salisbury bought a diverse range of luxury goods for his children from the merchants in the New Exchange.[12] Margaret Spencer's purchases, discussed in the previous chapter, were supervised by her father, as were, more distantly, those of Lady Anne Clifford, discussed in Chapter 6. Dressing children was not only the purview of women.

Beyond furnishing clothing for children to wear, parents also provided instruction about its meaning and social function. Neither was this exclusively women's work. Sue Vincent outlines clothing's social role: 'the way a person dressed had the potential power to determine placement in the social ranking. It could also affect the expression of personality, and even produce forms of differently gendered behavior. Clothing could both define and delimit the body, and order its relationship with the body politic.'[13] For children, the material changes in the clothes they could wear as they matured supplied a gradual education in these meanings. Early modern children, of course, dressed like their elders. After the age of seven, boys were breeched and dressed like men, and after swaddling girls were always dressed like women.[14] Beyond establishing gender difference, children's clothes inducted them into their class position. Elite toddlers had 'complicated wardrobes', and as children they were allowed to wear increasingly expensive fabrics until they were attired in what was appropriate to their parents' station, or to their ambitions.[15] The Lisle letters from the sixteenth century, including many letters by Honor (Basset) Plantagenet, Lady Lisle (1493x5–1566), document how that family used clothing to shape the social advancement of their children.[16]

Maternal advice about clothes emerges within a culture where fathers, monarchs and the church attempted discursively to constitute the meanings of clothing. Kenneth Charlton argues that the family worked in concert with other agencies, such as the church, the workplace, the marketplace and schools to communicate ideas about the world; similarly treating the family as a place for cultural lessons, Daniel Roche argues that linen specifically took on meaning 'through modes of use and upkeep, in the pedagogies of the clothed and the unclothed, the clean and the dirty'.[17] Alan Hunt's work on clothing and his notion of governance, informed by Foucault's, are useful in defining how the attempts at clothing regulation by legal and ecclesiastical institutions relate to those by family members. For him, governance is not merely the actions of a government but power 'exercised by any social institutions, organizations, professions and other social entities that do not necessarily share the constitutionalized attributes of governments'. 'Governance', according to Hunt, 'is exercised where a relatively persistent set of practices select and construct some social object that is acted on in such a way as to restrain, limit and direct the activities of the selected object of governance'.[18] In early modern England, clothes are an object of governance, discursively theorized by the legal institutions, by the church, by monarchs, by conduct book writers, by fathers and by mothers. Maternal advice is an act of governance, too, if that governance is constrained to the extent that women are themselves governed.

I want to consider at some length just how the law, the church and other institutionalized authorities approached the dress of young people in order to dispel the easy notion that mothers who wrote about what their children should wear were engaged in a typically feminine activity. In fact, pedagogies of dress developed by those with institutionalized power often excluded women from thinking and speaking authoritatively or legitimately about clothing. During the Tudor period, dress was regulated by a series of sumptuary laws, the last of which came into effect in 1553. The last act of apparel concerned the wearing of silk fabrics among the lower classes, while proclamations issued by Queen Elizabeth dealt with other facets of fashion – in 1562, the amounts and types of textiles that could be used in hosiery and double ruffs. Further proclamations in 1574, 1577, 1580, 1588 and 1597 considered foreign goods, extended regulations to women who had previously been excluded and lowered the minimum income needed to become eligible to wear velvet, satin and other silk clothes to include anyone who kept a great horse furnished for service in war.[19] In 1604, James I repealed the existing statutes and attempted to enable himself to regulate dress by proclamation alone. Not the result of a waning interest in the regulation of consumption, this repeal and the subsequent failure to enact further legislation were the result of constitutional conflict between King and

Parliament, rather than a reduction in anxieties about clothes, which persisted throughout the seventeenth century. Bills regulating dress were introduced in 1610, 1614, 1621, 1626 and 1628 and, according to Alan Hunt, 'foundered, not because sumptuary ideals were rejected, but rather because of failure to agree on what and whom should be restricted'.[20] In addition to legislating class and gender difference, the laws regulated the young. Queen Elizabeth's proclamations of 1574 and 1588 also made specific reference to the profligacy of young men who spent too much money on clothes.[21] Amanda Bailey highlights the fact that '[a]fter the servant and the apprentice, the third most consistent target of state and local sartorial legislation was the male student'; Elizabeth's proclamation of 1562 targeted the apparel of students at universities and Inns of Court, and she attempted to influence the dress of students at various other times, especially at Cambridge, while both Oxford and Cambridge sought to govern dress independent of royal administration.[22] Such regulatory efforts document the imagined dependence of order on clothes, which were meant accurately to testify to the subject's place within hierarchies of age, class and gender.

A wealth of sartorial advice by older men to younger men accompanied the legal attempts to regulate dress.[23] Advice to princes, to sons and to humanist-trained young gentlemen treated clothes as a form of property that forged and managed a young man's social power. Clothes needed to be attended to with an appropriately grave assessment of their social function. In *Basilikon Doron,* King James considers Prince Henry's dress at some length as a register of moral, political, national, gender and class principles. In his choices of clothing, the prince must be moderate, neither superfluous like a 'waister', nor base like a wretch, neither artificial like a courtesan, nor sluggish like a 'countrie-clown', neither light and vain like a 'Candie-souldier' and a young courtier, nor grave like a minister. In addition to following these modulations of moderate masculinity that eschew figures of excess, such as women, feminine men and the plebeian, he should be 'proper, cleanly, comely, and honest'. But he should not only be that, for his dress requires both gravitas and grandeur to signify the multiple facets of his monarchical role, that he is at once man, minister, lawyer and soldier, and not merely a layman, as 'Papistes and Anabaptistes' would have. Even as the King offers this advice, he reminds his son that a man's mind should not be occupied with matters of dress, for this will cause his judgement to be less admired. The young man should eschew feminine perfuming and preening, while still attending to his appearance in times of war, when he should be 'galliardest and bravest, both in cloathes and countenance'.[24] Prince Henry's clothes should reveal that he occupies a position of power.

Most conduct books are more concerned with the subordination of male English subjects within a class structure than King James is. In the previous chapter, I discussed conduct books for women which treated clothes not as a material discourse of power but a spiritual discourse of virtue requiring upper-class women to avoid the markers of class power. Conduct books for boys urge them not to undermine whatever class position they have with their clothes but to use them to maintain it. Quoting King James's recommendation of moderation, James Cleland's *Hero-paideia, or The Institution of a Young Noble Man* (1607) criticizes the young gentleman who purchases too many expensive clothes for contributing to the decay of English society. He shifts his wealth from land, a traditional and permanent source of power, to frippery that is easily destroyed:

> They have put their lands, which contained a great circuit, up into a little trunck, and hold it a point of policie to weare their lands upon their backes, that they maie see that noe wast be done by their Tennants. But alasse when they would spred abroad their gaie cloathes againe into a longe feild, or a pleasant parke, they are so shorte that they cannot reach one ridge length, & so are dubd Sir John Had-land, knights of Pennilesse bench.[25]

Sir Walter Raleigh adopts a similarly abstemious stance on sartorial expenditure in his pithy advice, contained in the one sentence that comprises the seventh chapter of *Sir Walter Raleighs Instructions to his Sonne and to Posterity*: 'Exceed not in the humour of ragges, and Bravery, for these will soone ware out of fashion, but Money in thy purse will ever be in fashion, and no man is esteemed for gay Garments, but by Fooles and women.'[26] Francis Osborne's *Advice to a Son* (1656) proposes that while his son should recognize that order depends on fitting a man's clothes to his estate, he should be the finest of his kind, for 'Next to Cloathes, a good Horse becomes a Gentleman': 'Weare your Cloathes neat; exceeding, rather then comming short of others of like fortune; a charge borne out by Acceptance where ever you come· Therefore spare all other wayes rather than prove defective in this.'[27] If a young man should not spend more than he has, he should always attend to his clothes because it will help him to gain social acceptance.

Thomas Elyot's *The Boke Named the Governour* draws out the social consequences of a boy's clothing. He reminds his readers that there is 'apparaile comely to every estate and degree: that whiche excedeth or

lackethe procureth reproche in a noble man specially'; Christian men
and they 'that be nat of the astate of princes' should 'shewe a moderation & constance in vesture that they diminish no p[ar]te of their majestie either with newe fa[n]glenesse or with over su[m]ptuous expe[n]ces',
although sometimes it is expedient that the noble man when meeting
strangers 'advaunte hym selfe to be both riche and honourable'.[28] For
Elyot, aristocracy must be made visible in textiles so that men can recognize each other. Beyond having sumptuous clothes, men of authority
also have a quality that can be named 'Majestie, whiche is the holle
proporcion and figure of noble astate and is proprelie a beautie or come-
lynesse in his countenance, language, & gesture apt to his dignite, and
acco[m]modate to time, place, & company'. Not unlike the whiteness
discussed in Chapter 2, the beauty that Elyot ascribes to men does not
require fine clothing, for even in great hardship, natural majesty still
reveals itself in the countenance.[29] Still, noble men should dress well
because it is proportionate to their estate.

   Beyond the law and conduct books, the other major source of pedagogies of dress was the church. Amongst several sermons about clothes,
those issued at the request of monarchs highlight the magnitude of
clothings' social function. Only occasionally are such sermons not
concerned with reinforcing class distinction and gender difference.
'A Caveat for Craftesmen and Clothiers', Thomas Carew's sermon on
the text of James 5, exceptionally, urges a living wage for workers in
the clothing industry, including women.[30] More typical is 'An Homyly
Against Excesse of Apparell' in the Elizabethan volume of homilies 'set
out by the authoritie of the Quenes Majestie' to be read in churches and
printed repeatedly in the sixteenth and seventeenth centures (in 1563,
1571, 1574, 1577, 1595, 1623, 1633, 1635, 1640 and 1650). Governed
by the principle of moderation, the sermon provides four rules for
dressing: Christians should use 'moderate temperance' to control the
flesh, avoid inordinate care for the things of the body to attend to those
of the spirit, be accountable to God for the good use of what He has
given and be content with one's appointed degree. A man should live
within the economic and social boundaries to which he has been born.
A woman should be subject to her husband and ornament herself only
with his virtues, for in decking herself with gay apparel to please a husband a woman only sets out his foolishness, vainly attempts to reform
what God has made and wastes her husband's 'stocke'. Unlike their
male counterparts, women need not dress according to their station.
They should use less apparel than the law allows them because it is not
beauty that causes a woman to be esteemed but her modesty.[31]

John Williams, Dean of Salisbury, preached *A Sermon of Apparell* before King James and Prince Charles on 22 February 1619. Published 'by his Majesties especiall Commandement by Robert Barker and John Bill, printers to the King', the sermon castigates women for vanity while supporting elaborate dress for elite men. In explicating the text of Matthew 11:8, 'they that wear soft clothing are in king's houses' the sermon justifies the wearing of luxurious clothes by 'men of place'. God, Williams argues, made the world of nature a school and endowed it with things pleasing to the sight to provide evidence of God; great men might wear good clothes, 'not for the cockering and cherishing of their bodie, but for the credit and countenance of their place and dignitie. And if any wanton eye shall play the Spider, and sucke the poyson of lust out of these Robes, which are borne but to gaine respect and reverence, they must know that [...] it is scandalum acceptum non datum, and the fault is in the glancing and not in the cloathing, saith Isidorus Pelusiota.'[32] These arguments are never extended to women, who are always to blame if they incite lust in those who regard them; their good clothes merely discredit them as vain and uppity. While powerful men can claim control of the meanings of their clothes, women cannot, nor should they.

These institutionalized pedagogies of male dress produce two conclusions. First, although these sorts of laws and proclamations usually did fail to regulate dress, the efforts themselves should not be dismissed as historically inconsequential. As Hunt argues, whether or not the attempts at regulation were effective, they emerged and changed with the historical circumstances to which they were responding, circumstances which retained a compelling influence on society. The law, the church and educational institutions took charge of clothing, producing about it not just laws but theological discourse on the sin of luxury, economic debates on the wasting of resources and national protectionism, and strident expositions on the problems of gender, class and urbanization. These historical circumstances, particularly increasing urbanization and the movement of unattached young people to cities, created a need for recognizability: for social status, rank and occupation to be visible in clothes.[33] What Foucault says of sex, one might also say of clothes: 'it called for management procedures; it had to be taken charge of by analytical discourses'.[34] Advice about dress is a management procedure.

And second, pedagogies of dress produce gender difference through knowledge about clothing. Obviously, clothes themselves produced gender difference and helped to secure elite masculinity; the young man should not spend beyond his means to ensure that he could maintain the position that he occupied by birth and then, by making himself visible as a political subject, as a man who knows his place, whatever that place may be relative to other men. Clothes were a visible manifestation of a man's beliefs about class, sexuality, political ideology, national identity, religion and the proper use of money. It is only within the realm of patriarchal stereotype that maternal advice about clothes is simply evidence of a feminine interest in fashion or tender affection. Nevertheless, early clothing discourse strategically constructs knowledge about clothing in precisely these terms. Men and women must speak and know the material socio-political discourse of clothing differently. King James' advice is typical on this account. Even as he advises his son fulsomely about what not to wear, he warns that if men appear to be too occupied with matters of dress, they will be effeminized and their authority undermined. Men must attentively and knowledgeably develop a wardrobe that serves their political interests and maintains their class identity, but they must also disavow the appearance of vestiary knowledge in order to secure their masculinity. This is not the same thing as being actually disinterested in or ignorant of clothes. It is rather a construction of masculinity that depends on dissimulation. Men must pretend not to know about clothes to be men. Susan Bordo sees this kind of disavowal in contemporary advertisements for American men's clothing, when ads represent men as ignorant of style: they are unaware their pants are nice until a woman points it out.[35] Even in early modern England when elite men wore ornamental garb not unlike women's – high heels, bows, velvet, lace and silk – they adopted an attitude of renunciation. They must know about clothing but dissimulate their understanding. What Thomas Goad said of Elizabeth Jocelin's education – 'Of all which knowledge shee was very sparing in her discourses, as possessing it rather to hide, than to boast of' – defines how men interact with clothes.[36] They possess it rather to hide than boast of, and if they speak – as they must to be educators, ministers and legislators – women serve as the placeholder for what their speech is not: foolish and vain. When women are presumed to know no more than dressing, and their knowledge is then characterized as foolish or duplicitous, knowledge of clothing constructs gender difference in the service of patriarchal control. The trivialization of sartorial thinking as effeminate within a culture that actually treats clothes quite seriously mystifies the social power of clothes as instruments of social recognition within a class-based social structure and produces sexual difference through knowledge of clothing's social functions; to be feminine is to be ignorant of the power of class. The trivialization of women's knowledge of clothes functions to situate them as the governed rather than governors.

The dominant discourse of dress delimits the space in which women can speak legitimately and ethically about clothing. The editors of *Resistance Through Rituals* use the idea of 'winning space' to explain how subcultures engage with dominant cultures through negotiation, even when 'the subordinate culture *experiences* itself in terms prescribed by the dominant culture'.[37] One way to win space is through 'situated solutions'. When a theoretical, abstract assessment is required, the dominant culture will provide the terms for understanding the situation, but 'in concrete social situations involving choice and action, the negotiated version – or subordinate value system – will provide the moral framework'.[38] In this respect, motherhood affords the concrete social situation through which to negotiate a pedaogy of dress. Mothers and fathers were practically responsible for children's clothing. For mothers, without other options, this concrete social situation provides a place to begin to challenge the dismissal of women's knowledge of clothing as foolish and vain and to disclose instead the sobriety, gravity and moderation of the female mind and to resist the theoretical patterns of dissimulation about gendered knowledge to speak as men did about clothes and their social and political functions.

Elizabeth Jocelin Against the 'Fashionists'

When Elizabeth Jocelin writes about dress in her maternal advice book, *The Mothers Legacie, To her Unborne Child* (1624) she is undertaking a task with far-reaching personal, social and political consequences and engaging with the genres of political advice to sons and of spiritual guidance found in devotions, prayers and sermons. Scholarly interest in her work has focused on the issues of female authority and subjectivity. Wendy Wall and Theresa Feroli saw her deathbed legacy as an exemplar for the problems of early modern female authorship, wherein death and self-erasure provide the means by which to inscribe a female self in print. Kristen Poole investigated how Jocelin, like other early modern female writers, manipulated distinctions between public and private to authorize her work. Most recently, Lucinda M. Becker has returned to Jocelin's work to suggest, still more explicitly than her predecessors, that it is Jocelin's deathbed justification of the work, rather than the maternal legacy itself, that is of interest; the actual guidance is 'conventional'.[39] Beyond its prefatory materials, the content of Jocelin's advice is worthy of more sustained attention: pedagogies of dress, for instance, do not conventionally consider women as serious contributors to sartorial education. *The Mothers Legacie* does so by following the liturgical model of a daily prayer cycle, found in the Book of Common Prayer and other popular prayer books. Setting 'one day for a pattern how I would haue thee spend all the days of thy life', the volume comprises 13 numbered passages, each supported with scriptural references, which order the day around the first principle, to 'Remember thy creator in the days of thy youth.'[40] Jocelin's work provides structure for the day, from morning meditation on God's mercy to evening prayers of thanksgiving and repentance. In between, she recommends repentance; the avoidance of pride upon getting dressed; a morning devoted to meditation, prayer, good studies and honest recreation; careful conversation at lunch; and the avoidance of the devil's snares, such as dishonesty, drunkenness and a sin impossible to name. The book concludes with chapters devoted to a child's duties to keep the Sabbath, honour one's parents and to love one's neighbour. As in prayer books for women, getting dressed is one of the diurnal activities requiring spiritual reflection.[41]

The Mothers Legacie, To her Unborne Child exists in three different versions: British Library Additional MS 27467, the holograph version; British Library Additional MS 4378, an altered copy by the Church of England clergyman Thomas Goad and supplemented by his 'Approbation'; and the printed text, published at Goad's behest in 1624 and reprinted in the seventeenth century in 1625, 1632, 1635, 1685, with other editions appearing in the eighteenth and nineteenth centuries. The seventeenth-century printed edition reproduces many of the emendations made by Goad to the holograph manuscript, but also corrects errors and omissions made by Goad and prints corrections Jocelin made to her manuscript.[42] Jean LeDrew Metcalfe and Sylvia Brown argue that the changes introduced by Goad diminish the value of female education, emphasize the wife's place within a patriarchal social order, moderate Jocelin's godly rhetoric and her sabbatarianism, and shift Jocelin's understanding of social relations to place more emphasis on hierarchy than affection.[43] This editorial interference also informs how Jocelin's advice about clothes appear in print, for Goad adds scriptural references and Latin quotations, changes punctuation, spelling and paragraphing, and, most importantly, alters some of her words.

From the very beginning, *The Mothers Legacie* contemplates how the material world, including clothes, education and status, will be allowed to affect the spiritual life of Jocelin's child when she or he is grown. Accurately, I think, Goad regards the legacy as Jocelin's response to material disenfranchisement. He writes in his 'approbation': 'Our lawes disable those, that are under Couert-baron, from disposing by Will and Testament any temporall estate. But no law prohibiteth any possessor of morall and spirituall riches, to impart them unto others, either in life by communicating, or in death, by bequeathing.'[44] As the daughter of Sir Richard Brooke (d.1632) and Joan Chaderton and the granddaughter of William Chaderton, the Bishop of Chester (1579–95) and Lincoln (1595–1608), Elizabeth Jocelin was an heiress. From her maternal grandfather, she inherited two estates in Huntingdonshire and an extensive education.[45] Goad outlines the accomplishments of her youth, her knowledge of 'Languages, History, and some Arts, so principally in studies of piety', and her study of morality, history, foreign languages and poetry. It is in this context that Goad insisted that she revealed in her writing and in her person only her humility: 'Of all which knowledge shee was very sparing in her discourses, as possessing it rather to hide, than to boast of'.[46] Jocelin herself emphasizes the importance of humility in the prefatory epistle to her husband, Torrell Jocelin. Her gender identity informs her ethic of humility, for she claims in the holograph manuscript that when she thought of writing, 'I was ashamed and durst not undertake it. but when I could finde no other means to express my motherly zeale I encouraged my selfe wth theas reasons[,] first that I wrote to a childe and though I weare but a woman yet to a childes iudgement: what I understood might serve for a foundation to better learning' (46, 48). Humility is also a Christian virtue which children should learn because it informs ideal social relations. If the child is a daughter, her husband can determine the extent of her education, but she should, in any case, learn to be humble: '[...] but howsoever though disposest of her educatyon I pray thee labor by all means to teache her <truly though> true humilitie though I as much desire it may bee ^as^ humble if it bee a son as a daughter[,] yet in a daughter I more feare that vice' (50). She asks Mr Jocelin, whether a boy or girl, to 'let not they servants give it any other title then the christen name till it have discretion to understand how to respect others: and I pray thee be not profuse in the expence of clothe for it[,] my [me] thinks it is a vayn delight in parents to bestow that cost upon one childe wch would serve too or three[,] if they have them not of theyr owne[,] pauper vbiq iacet' (52). Like titles, clothes structure social relationships; just as a child's name can instil in him a sense that he is superior to others, so too can clothes. Consequently, a child should not be given access to privilege without first learning respect for others. Through tempered clothing expenses, a child might then learn that the proper exercise of power requires humility. Charity, also essential to social relations, is likewise learned through clothes. With a Latin quotation from Ovid's *Fasti,* Jocelin suggests that parents resist using their wealth only to the benefit of their own offspring and to remember that the poor are always there. In the end, she places her gendered humility within a social fabric where class hierarchy is knitted together with humility; one may possess power and wealth, but respect and charity, not dominance and exploitation, should govern one's interactions with others.

When Jocelin arrives at questions of dress again, it is in the chapter on pride, in which she ponders what not to wear. If there are diverse sorts of pride, none, she tells her child, is more 'pestilent to th<i>e soule then this of apparell' (70). The advice continues by examining ideal human relations and what is beautiful. Jocelin's advice is a textual version of a mother's prayer for her child's physical and moral well-being. But within this devotional structure, her pedagogy of dress, like those of her contemporaries, is invested in a vision of what the social order should be. For Elizabeth Jocelin, this means being engaged with ideas of virtue, aesthetics and a gendered political order. Jocelin's pedagogy of dress first of all rejects monstrous clothing: 'is it not a monstrous thing to see a man whome god hathe created of an excellent form each part answeringe the due proportion of another should by a fantasticall habit make himselfe so vgly that one cannot find among all gods creatures any thinge like him' (70). Seventeenth-century fashionable clothing did sometimes enhance the size of particular parts of the body. The padded doublet and codpiece that emphasized the male torso, trunk hose that showed and elongated male legs, ruffs that dominated the face, bodices that lengthened the female torso, and farthingales that enlarged women's hips all changed the shape of the body in ways that inspired anxieties about monstrosity. This was, according to Sue Vincent, a common component of anti-fashion discourse. The farthingale, for instance, allowed women to take space that society might not be willing to concede.[47] For Amanda Bailey, the vitriol against the monstrous in men's clothing is an attack on the absence of moderation, on 'a devolution from a state of civilized manhood' to that which is feminine and unreasonable.[48] Phillip Stubbes in his *Anatomie of Abuses* expounds at length on the monstrous, a view that is grounded first of all in his view that the proper function of clothes is hierarchical. The gentry and magistery should wear rich attire – 'every one in their calling' – because fine clothes 'garnish and set foorth their birthes, dignities and estates' and, even more, 'strike a terrour and feare into the hearts of the people, to offend against their office and authority'; yet men's 'great Ruffes' and doublets and women's wire hair dressings, ruffs and doublets are all monstrous and connected to deformity, profligacy, gluttony, vanity and hermaphroditism.[49] An aesthetic question as much as an economic one, the proportions of clothing register differently than the quality of textiles. Just as wearing velvet can mark transgression in the subordinate, so too can the size and shape of a garment.

Jocelin then is not unique in her concern about the proportions of clothing. The terms in which she rejects the monstrous hint at her sense of the philosophical underpinnings of the complaint. The language of means and extremes, classical in origin, was found throughout early modern ecclesiastical, constitutional, medical and erotic discourse, influenced, for instance by Cicero's linking of the ideal gentleman to the proper measure, Aristotle's equation of virtue and moderation and Augustine's valuation of temperance.[50] Informed by Plato's philosophy, Peter Bembo contended in Castiglione's *The Book of the Courtier* that the beauty seen daily in the countenance is 'well proportioned and composed of a certain joyous harmony of various colours enhanced by light and shadow and by symmetry and clear definition'. The mind can be seized by desire for this beauty, recognize it is good and perceive truth.[51] Plato's Timaeus had argued, 'the world has been framed in the likeness of that which is apprehended by reason and mind and is unchangeable'.[52] If what is beautiful in the world of nature is created according to a fair and perfect original, the ideal possesses the quality of proportion. This way of thinking influenced aesthetic theories, such as Richard Haydocke's translation of Giovanni Paolo Lomazzo's *A Tracte Containing the Artes of Curious Painting*, which begins with an explication of proportion as an essential feature of beauty. Proportion is a 'measure of the partes', which not only defines beauty but encourages civil discipline, by stirring men's minds to piety, reverence and religion.[53] For Jocelin, proportion likewise adopts both aesthetic and ethical dimensions. If the form of one part answers the due proportion of another, the human body corresponds to a rational and proportionate idea. When sartorial choices reflect that divine order of harmony, proportion and symmetry, good people will look like each other.

So, in addition to shaping the physical body, proportion also shapes the body politic. A lack of proportion leads to singularity, the social problem of living apart from others, of being single not in a marital sense but existentially. Jocelin allows that if she has a daughter, she might have leave 'to follow modest fashions but not to be a beginner of fashion < > nor would I haue you follow it till it be generall so that in not dooinge as others doo you might appear more singular then wise' (72). Singularity is a kind of foolishness that can be avoided with wisdom, by following the biblical examples of service, prayer and chastity of Anna, Elizabeth (the mother of John the Baptist), Esther and Susanna; choosing clothes that fashion identity in communal and historical terms will preclude singularity's taint. Aesthetic questions have sociable dimensions. Sir Frederick in *The Book of the Courtier* takes the same stance: 'one should adapt oneself to the custom of the majority'; he would prefer clothes not to be extreme.[54] Jane Bridgeman argues that in the Italian Renaissance, for writers such as Castiglione, '[c]oncepts of beauty were thus influenced by strongly expressed social conventions and expressions of personal taste were clearly subordinated to the demands of etiquette.'[55] From Jocelin's point of view, while singularity may be an expression of personal taste, it is a form of extremity. It makes one person entirely unlike another, not resembling others in 'shape or face yet for his rationall soule' (70); singularity in dress is the consequence of pride, which is without reason. Reasonable people resemble each other because they resemble a rational ideal, while the singular are 'fashionists' (70) who, despite believing themselves unlike other men, are copying each other, as 'apish' in their fashions and behaviour (70). For Jocelin, morally appropriate clothing is defined by the immediate social context rather than an absolute assessment of what is right and wrong; the gold and ornament so important in conduct books for women go unmentioned. Her pedagogy of dress dresses people into connections with each other. It is only pride which makes one 'scorninge to bee like other men', pride which makes one like a Pharisee who believes oneself greater, wiser and more learned than all others (74). Proportionate clothing underpins a social cohesion that is at once conservative and flexible. Like her contemporaries, Jocelin does not advocate using clothes to advance one's social power, not even through being the grandest of one's kind, as Francis Osborne recommends. Yet her disavowal of social contest could be transformative. Those who have the ability to use clothes to impress with their expense and extravagant proportions will refuse to do so, abandoning the privilege of their position, humbly, for the sake of social harmony and cohesion.

Perhaps the most famously singular person in early modern England, incidentally, was Margaret Cavendish, Duchess of Newcastle. Her approach is strikingly different and worthy of a digression. Margaret Cavendish wrote in her memoir, printed in 1655 in *Natures Picture Drawn by Fancies Pencil*: 'I did dislike that should follow my Fashions, for I always took delight in a singularity, even in acoutrements of habits.'[56] Cavendish reflects on her singularity again in *New World, Called the Blazing World* (1666) when the Empress of the Blazing World asks the Duchess, who appears in her own fiction, why she is 'singular' in 'Accoutrements, Behaviour and Discourse'.[57] The Duchess admits she is 'extravagant', beyond what is 'usual and ordinary', but nevertheless, she tries to 'be as singular as I can; for it argues but a mean Nature to imitate others; and though I do not love to be imitated if I can possibly avoid it; yet rather then imitate others, I should chuse to be imitated by others; for my nature is such, that I had rather appear worse in singularity, then better in the Mode'.[58] While Cavendish herself values singularity because it is creative, she is criticized for it by others. John Evelyn records in his diary on 27 April 1667 an account of meeting the Duchess, 'in extravagant humour and dress, which was very singular'.[59] Jocelin is more like Cavendish's critics that Cavendish herself, but for both women singularity in fashion is a social question. For Cavendish, dressing differently reveals her original nature, while for Jocelin, dressing like others helps one to find a place and to create a society that is more humble, equitable and charitable – a Christian society, that is, in which women might have a better place.

Goad's alterations to Jocelin's manuscript for his print edition highlight the place of social connectedness in the mother's legacy, too, simply because he shifts emphasis from humble self-restraint and cohesion to social control. Jocelin's critique of reasonless, proud souls with 'apish fashions a[n]d apish behauiour' becomes, after Goad's intervention, a rejection of 'new fangled fashions, and apish behauior' (70, 71). With the repetition of 'apish', Jocelin presents imitation as the problem, a problem with how people irrationally relate to each other. Goad's substitution of 'new fangled' adds innovation to the mix. Apishness debases individuals and deforms relationships between people, but newfangled fashions are a problem just because they are new. Goad introduces an absolute regulation that Jocelin herself avoids; indeed, she says that one should be dressed in new fashions when everyone else is doing so. To refuse to adopt a fashion when it is general is to be singular. Jocelin's manuscript also claims that the fashionist is 'playinge the foole'; Goad amends this to 'playing the fantastiques' (70, 71), again enhancing the critique of fashion, as such. Not just unreasonable, the fantastic is a particular kind of dresser, someone, according to the OED, who is given to fanciful or showy dress, or, according to Thomas Overbury, 'An Improvident young Gallant'.[60] Together Goad's emendations impose on Jocelin's text a more strident, definitive rejection of fashion and a deeper investment in tradition.

Jocelin also considers the special problems that daughters have in getting dressed. Like sermons and legal assessments of dress, Jocelin regards girls as more tempted to fashion sins. Her assessment of the reason is different, however. Jocelin first attributes this failing to women's weakness but adds that, because of this weakness, girls are more likely to observe the social power attached to dress and to want to be commended and advanced through this route: 'thou art weaker and thy temptations to this vice greater for thou shalt see those whoo perhaps thou wilt thinke lesse able exallted far aboue thee in this [k]inde, and it may bee that thou wilt desire to be like them if not to outgoe them' (70). Women are the weaker sex in part because they are weak socially, a disenfranchisement for which clothes provide a remedy. Jocelin knows clothes as men do: clothes are a discourse of power. Yet she rejects using clothes to elevate a woman's position, less from anxieties about female power than from a concern for what ambitious dressing does to women's minds. Like Naomi Wolf in *The Beauty Myth*, Jocelin is critical of how attention to clothing hinders the pursuit of education and learning: 'when thou shall grow in years and have attayned no higher knowledge, then to dress thy selfe. when thou shalt see halfe prhapps all thy time spent and that of all thou hast sowed thou hast nothinge to reap but repentance' (70). Knowledge of clothing is dubious not in an absolute sense nor because it is feminine but because it absorbs a woman's time and prevents her from getting an education. Tellingly, Goad amends 'higher knowledge' in this passage to 'other knowledge' (71). While Jocelin's 'higher knowledge' leaves space for the kind of classical education she received, Goad's 'other' knowledge is imprecise and need not include anything much. Goad erases Jocelin's support for learning when she laments that no similar approbation meets 'a wise or learned or religious woman' as the well-dressed woman. He changes the word 'learned' (72) to 'honest' (73), performing precisely the denial of approbation for the learned woman that Jocelin is critiquing.

Jocelin's pedagogy of dress speaks about clothes with a kind complexity not often allowed to women's thinking about dress. She shares with her contemporaries common concerns for the use of resources, for how clothes explain social structures and for preventing female vanity. In her work, instruction in humility and avoiding pride, exercising moderation and charity, and wearing clothes that demonstrate both aesthetic and social proportion are meant to ensure that her unborn child will become faithful, virtuous and embedded in a community that fashions itself after an ideal created by God according to orderly, reasonable principles. Like her contemporaries, she emphasizes the need for female humility, but she also establishes that virtue within a vision of a spiritualized social order where the powerful too must eschew privilege and practise humility. Jocelin can also be distinguished from her contemporaries by her attention to the place of women's minds in the pedagogy of dress: knowledge of clothing should not hinder female education. Her pedagogy of dress offers both a devotional aid and a political assessment of the problems of a gender and class order. Pursuing a form of governance, Elizabeth Jocelin seeks not to overturn the traditional class order but to make it a more respectful, humble Christian community, where people love their neighbours as themselves, the final duty she insists upon, within a community grounded in humility where women's minds and moral agency can become legible.

Brilliana, Lady Harley, and the 'Garment of Holiness'

The 375 surviving letters of Brilliana, Lady Harley include many written between 1638 and 1643 to her eldest son Edward Harley, then between the ages of 14 and 19. During this period, he was at Magdalen College, Oxford, at Lincoln's Inn in London and in the Parliamentary army, while she, for a remarkable six week period that began in July 1643, endured a Royalist siege of her household, Brampton Bryan Castle, shortly before her death.[61] Like the maternal advice books printed in the seventeenth century, the letters offer instruction in spiritual and moral matters, including reading, dress and social conduct.[62] Because Lady Harley's epistolary advice is not to an unborn child, she fits him with clothes appropriate to his class, education and career, which requires knowledge of the masculine institutionalized educational and political structures in which he actually lives. Although mothers might teach their sons to read and provide early spiritual training, maternal instruction of upper-class boys did not typically extend past breeching when boys were removed from maternal care to be educated by other men.[63] In Lady Harley's case, clothes maintain her involvement in her son's education. Her letters about his clothing are frequently accompanied by the clothes themselves, and so together both practice and theory work to educate him in his religio-political identity as a Harley

Lady Harley's letters to Ned are one component of a culture of advice she lived with him. She wrote a short advice book, which survives in Edward Harley's manuscript correspondence (British Library, Additional MS 70118).[64] Since, Lady Harley reminds Edward, it was her practice 'offten to put you in minde of thos things which tende to your Cheefest good', she has composed her advice in writing because they are no longer together.[65] The advice book is small, its six pages folded in half and bound at the fold with a string. The front cover has a dedication, 'for my Deare sonne Edward Harley'.[66] Trusting to God that her words will speak to his heart when he is without the guiding presence of his parents, Lady Harley advises Ned about how to interact with other men, what to respect in them and how to recognize true friends: 'you knowe in fruts it is not their excelency to be an Apell, or a plume, but to be of such a kinde of Apell or plume which is excelent, that gaines the Esteme, so amounge Men, the Esteme of them is as they are Religious and wise, and good Men, and not that they are meere Men'.[67] By analogy, men should not be respected simply because of their type, but because faith makes them excellent in their kind. Yet esteem even for worthy men should not override conscience: 'For if Men Aproufe of you And your owne Contience Condeme you what peace can you have.'[68] The manuscript advice book does not specifically address Edward's clothes. It does, however, insist that he look like what he is, a man who serves God: 'Let your Toung, Eyes, hands and feete Be the Instruments by which you May Expres the good Affections of your Hart.'[69] Neither should he go into debt, for a 'Bororrwer is sarvant to the Lender' and so he should keep within his means.[70] The advice book also seeks to establish an ethical attitude towards class hierarchy, counterbalancing respect for privilege with an evaluation of one's faith. Edward should choose for friends men who are born of God, rather than men of nobility who, despite their 'Excelent parts of nature', abandon themselves to swearing, drunkenness, and the scorn of religion. God, she says, 'is no Respecter of persons If Nobell Men sinn Nobell Men Must be punished. kings shall Not be Exempted if they sinn They must be punisched in this Life and in that to Come'.[71] Class neither garners automatic respect, nor provides absolute authority for one to do as one wishes – even for a King. Still class is to be honoured when it is accompanied by faith: 'Allways Chuse the Best Company to be with Rather thos Above you then belowe you. Yet Dispise not your Inferiours.'[72] In admiring those who have a higher position but not despising those who have a lower, Edward will maintain the position to which he was born. Likewise, because secrets give power to those who know them, Edward should take care with regard to whom he reveals his mind, speaking frankly only to proven friends but being trustworthy to those who reveal their minds to him. Lady Harley's personal letters continue to develop these themes, addressing the practical concerns of dress while also putting into practice her views on class, obedience to God and the body's meanings.

Lady Harley's letters couple advice to political news (such as lists of soldiers on the King's side, the names of those in Herefordshire who favoured episcopacy and the movements of the Scottish army), to accounts of family happenings (such as marriages, births, deaths, illnesses, including her own, and the whereabouts of Edward's father) and to intellectual debate.[73] She sends Ned a copy of the seven articles against the Earl of Strafford, and she reports to Ned on the need for and receipt of ammunition and guns at Brampton Bryan Castle.[74] The transportation links that enable the sending of letters also make possible the transmission of clothing, food and books from Brampton Bryan Castle to Oxford or London and back. Johanna Harris has demonstrated how Brilliana, Lady Harley's letters show a range of reading, including Cicero and Seneca, Calvinist theology, and church and world history, and knowledge of Italian, French and Latin; Harley, Harris argues, used the epistolary form for spiritual and intellectual edification, to participate in Puritan intellectual culture and to foster community.[75] Lady Harley's identity as a reader is evident in a commonplace book she compiled before her marriage. Divided by religious topics, it collects in various categories (the attributes of God, of Christ, of the Holy Spirit, predestination, prayer, the sacraments, friendship and marriage, amongst others) passages from the Bible, William Perkins, Calvin, Musculus, Mr Cole, Seneca, William Gouge and more.[76] Like Elizabeth Jocelin, Lady Harley is relatively well educated, and she offers maternal advice about clothes as a godly reader and educated woman. She involves Edward in her reading, translating and sending to him the parts of Calvin's life of Luther that are not in *Foxe's Book of Martyrs* – an effort meant to assess the charge of ambition made against Luther.[77] She asks Ned to send her books, including Eusebius, and she comments after reading a book that Ned has sent her that the author 'sauours of the spirits from below'.[78] With a basket of apples for Ned, she sends *A Return of Prayer* (Thomas Goodwin's *The Returne of Prayers. A Treatise,* printed in 1636 and 1638) to her son's tutor. She could not find the place in the book she had wanted to show him when Perkins was with her, but sends it now so that he can judge it. She adds that she disagrees with Perkins' view of communal prayer, but if she respectfully differs with the Oxford scholar, she would yield, she says, 'upon good reson'.[79] Brilliana Harley can construct herself as a rational godly thinker and through her son engage scholars in debate. These letters are accompanied by gifts of turkey and kid pies, apples, a loin of veal, bacon, books – and clothes. Lady Harley's advice about clothes is concerned, like the rest of her instruction, with his identity as a specifically Puritan, rational, readerly member of the gentry.

Lady Harley's engagement with her son's clothing while he was a student functions in concert with the instruction of his tutor, Edward Perkins. Scrutiny of the morality of the clothing of young men was not exclusive to those of Puritan leanings. Archbishop Laud, in his turn as Chancellor of Oxford University between 1630 and 1641, regulated hair, clothes and the frequenting of alehouses by the students.[80] Yet for Lady Harley, Edward Perkins is a godly figure within a corrupt university: 'As they doo at Oxford, so they doo in all places, take liberty to invaye against Puretans.'[81] In her view, universities are a danger to the gentry on religious grounds, taking in 'ripe grapes' leaving 'sower ons behinde'; that Edward has a godly tutor she is thankful.[82] Inviting Perkins to visit Brampton Bryan, she tells Edward of her view that 'so good a man, and loveing you and useing you so kindely as you assure me he dous, I cannot but love and respect him; and that I cannot doo every one'.[83] Aligned by spiritual sympathies within an antagonistic culture, both Edward Perkins and Lady Harley attend to what Edward Harley wears. She writes to Ned that she is glad that Perkins has 'made you hamsome cloths, and I desire you should goo hamsomely'.[84] Edward Perkins himself wrote to Ned about his laundry, telling him in 1641 that 'The laundresse did soe diappoint me who it seem [edge of manuscript cut off] hath had some of your linnen in her keeping ever since you went that I am contrary to my purpose enforced to deferr the sending of your trunke, by the next you shall receive every thing according to youre appoyntment.'[85] Although the Oxford scholar is responsible for his pupil's clothes, Lady Harley is the ultimate authority. She adds in another letter:

> I like the stufe for your cloths well; but the cullor of thos for euery day I doo not like so well; but the silke chamlet I like very well, both cullor and stuf. Let your stokens be allways of the same culler of your cloths, and I hope you now weare Spanisch leather shouwes. If your tutor dous not intend to bye you silke stokens to weare with your silke shute send me word, and I will, if pleas God, bestow a peare on you.[86]

Lady Harley watches over the colour and material in the textiles of his clothes and the leather of his shoes, all features that mark status. Although she disapproves of the colour of his everyday clothes, she approves of his wearing silk 'chamlet' (a type of fabric) and improves his silk suit by ensuring he has silk stockings. Even though the university is a place of religious contest, Edward Harley should dress in fabrics – silk and non-English leather – that reveal he is a gentleman.

In the later letters, after Ned has left school and begun his military career, Lady Harley continues to be concerned about his clothes. Eventually, her sartorial provisions for her son are circumscribed by the Civil War, when the political tensions of life within a Royalist county make it difficult for Lady Harley to send Ned clothes. After the siege of Brampton Bryan commences in July 1643, there are only three more letters, one in August, another in September and the last on 9 October 1643, only shortly before her death on 29 October 1643. That letter, addressed for the first time to 'my deare sonne Colonell Harley', congratulates Ned on being made responsible for a regiment of men and explains that she has taken a great cold which has made her very ill. Even as she feels threatened by troops in February of that year, she sends Ned his linens.[87] It is with a report on 11 February 1641/2 that her brother is one of the 63 lords who voted against the bishops that she tells Ned that she has sent his father, with a box of books for Ned, two pairs of riding stockings, pies and two cheeses.[88] In May 1640, she asks Ned to send her a shirt for her to take his measure by; in July 1640, she sends him a cape and in June 1641, handkerchiefs.[89] In May and June of 1642, she mentions repeatedly her troubled efforts to send him more shirts; with the last of these shirts, she sends more handkerchiefs and powder for Ned's hair.[90] In these circumstances, the material care of a wife and mother, for clothes and for food, not only supports the military and political efforts of men but it signals her own loyalties to her family and their class and political identity. At Brampton Bryan without her husband or eldest son, she is the de facto head of a household in an unfriendly environment.[91] She tells Ned in June of 1642 that at Ludlow 'they seet up a May pole, and a thinge like a head upon it, and so they did at Croft, and gathered a greate many about it, and shot at it in derision of roundheads'.[92] Even though she wrote many times to her husband asking that she be allowed to remove the household to London, when she receives permission to do so in September 1643, she refused to leave: 'heather to God has made me (though an unworthy on) an Instrument to keepe possestion of your howes that it has not fallen into the hands of spoylers, and to keepe to geather a handfull of ... such as feared the Lord togeather so that his word has yet had an [lidcing?] in thens paits'. She asks only that Ned be allowed to come to the house: 'I thinke he would doo his Cuntry servis and himself good in healpeing to keepe what I hope shall be his, and in maintening the Ghuspill in this place.'[93] In his absence, she carries on, maintaining the house and the gospel herself. Shortly after the siege she dies, 'being weakned', according to one sympathetic observer, 'with Sufferings of the

Barbarous Usage of those Enemies'.[94] Lady Harley's provision of clothes
and advice about them function politically and adjust the boundaries
of maternity to include political, religious and spiritual dimensions.
When Edward was at Oxford, she continued her role as teacher through
his clothes – clothes that his tutor also had to cope with – and when
Edward was in the Parliamentary army, the provision of clothing was a
component of her own role as warrior. Working on behalf of her family
and their political allegiances, she sends linens to ensure the status and
health of her husband and son, whose concerns she shares.

Lady Harley's maternal advice on clothing is both aided and complicated by her husband's authority in matters of dress. Despite his other
commitments, Robert Harley attended to the clothing of his family. Just
as the tutor's work is not set apart from the world of clothing, neither
is the politician father's. Robert Harley was often the source of clothes
for his wife and family, for he was frequently in London while she
remained at Brampton Bryan Castle. In 1626, she wrote to him asking
for 3½ yards of ash coloured damask for a waistcoat and then for 6 yards
of yellow fabric and another 6 yards of white 'Bustine' (a cotton fabric)
to make coats for Ned and Robin (her second son Robert); she reports
when she acquired cloth to make Ned and Robin shirts and aprons, and
she asks in an undated letter, probably from the 1620s, that he give her
sisters money to buy her a gown – 'I will not it have a cost above 4 or
5 shillings a yard' – and she thanks him for the stockings and garters
he has already bought, in addition to Robin's whittels (a child's napkin
or petticoat).[95] She asks her husband not to send down silk grogram, an
instruction that suggests this was his plan, and she thanks him for the
'very fine wascott' that he sent her, while sending him a doublet and
hose.[96] In June 1643, during a period in which Brampton Bryan Castle
was under constant attack, she wrote to Robert Harley to ask if he will let
their daughter Brill make her a 'plaine Blacke silke Gowne of as cheepe
a stufe as it is posciball without lase, for I Can not send to any towne
for any thinge'; she explains that she has worked out a way to have it
delivered to her.[97] This request seemingly needs to be repeated, for in a
marginal note to a long letter in September of 1643 explaining the situation at Brampton Castle, she reminds him that she had asked for a gown
some time ago: 'I desire it may be silke chepe made up plaine.' Lady
Vere's measurements, she says, will serve.[98] Robert Harley has substantial
control over the clothing of his family because he has access to London's
markets. He even knows, it seems, Lady Vere's measurements.

When Lady Harley writes to advise Ned on his dress, she reinforces
her husband's authority in sartorial questions. A letter of 14 December

1638 repeatedly uses the refrain 'dear Ned', includes advice on keeping the fast and exercising and concludes by noting that neither Robert Harley nor anyone in the household knows she writes. She first shifts the significance of dress to a spiritual plane: 'Be confident, he is the beest Master, and will giue the best waiges, and they weare the beest liuery, the garment of holynes, a clotheing which neuer shall weare out, but is renwed euery day.' Ned is God's servant, a position that elevates and connects him; he wears the best livery with his faith, whatever else he puts on. When Lady Harley considers Sir Robert Harley's role in determining what he wears, she focuses more on the virtues of plain clothes:

> Dear Ned, it is very well doun, that you submite to your fathers desire in your clothes; and that is a happy temper, both to be contented with plaine clothes, and in the weareing of better clothes, not to thinke one selfe the better for them, nor to be trubelled if you be in plane clothes, and see others of your rancke in better. Seneque had not goot that victory ouer himselfe; for in his cuntry howes he liued priuetly, yet he complaines that when he came to the courte, he founde a tickeling desire to like them at court.[99]

In this letter, Lady Harley asserts for her son an identity separate from his clothes. He should wear fine clothes just as he wears plain clothes: neither should affect his inward state because he has been dressed by God. To use Mary Wroth's phrase, he should not be swayed by the greatness in good clothes to imagine himself anything other than what he is: a Christian gentleman. Lady Harley's reference to Seneca – an author she cites in other letters and whose work is extracted in her commonplace book – acknowledges the temptation to assert social standing, but stoically he should resist.[100]

Lady Harley confers on him a clothing conscience. In his 'Character' of a Puritan, Robert Harley wrote that the Puritan 'Honors & obeyes his sup[er]iors as children should theyr parents in the Lorde, not for feare but fo[r] science sake'.[101] If children should obey their parents for 'science' sake, for knowledge and conscience, Edward should have an ethical undcistanding of his father's instructions in dress.[102] This is what Brilliana Harley provides. The vision of selfhood that Lady Harley presents her son depends on filial bonds but insists upon conscientious autonomy with respect to other men. J. T. Cliffe and Anne Laurence each argue that Puritans were concerned about how clothes balanced the competing demands of social distinction, marked in display, and faith, which necessitate avoiding extravagance.[103] Even more, Lady Harley wants Edward Harley to understand himself. He is a Christian gentleman: 'And this I say to you, not to make you proude or consaited of your self, but that you should knowe yourself, and so not to be put out of your self, when you are in better company then ordineray.'[104] And he should dress accordingly. After Ned had left university, she wrote to him that 'I could wisch your father would make you another shute of cloths, for one shute is to littell.'[105] But class is less important than faith to his identity. He should not be put out of himself by his circumstances. This is the driving principle of the political energies that compel her to resist Royalist enemies, even with organized violence. Not disputing the hereditary status of Charles I, she did dispute the legality of his actions. She wrote in a July 1643 letter to Sir William Vavasour, whose troops were stationed outside her castle and who was asking her to surrender it to his control, that she is loyal to the King because she cannot believe that the King would have her take soldiers into her house.[106] When the King writes personally to say that she should leave, she responds by saying that she and her household have never rebelled against the King and that she holds her house by the law of the land.[107] In this vein, Lady Harley develops a pedagogy of dress that balances respect for social authority with conscience, being respectful to God but allowing that men are all but men, most worthy of respect when they are virtuous.

Conclusion

Maternal advice about clothing challenges how we imagine early modern motherhood. Ensuring that a child has appropriate things to wear seems like a commonplace component of parenting, and it is. But in early modern England clothes were complex social documents, so significant in fact that monarchs, the church and an array of scholars and other powerful men issued instructions on what English men and women should wear. Clothing had aesthetic, moral, spiritual and political attributes, and consequently the kinds of clothes children could wear placed them within the religious, social and political beliefs of the family, in addition to identifying their class and gender roles. Pedagogies of dress were attempts at governance, at negotiating with and for positions of power. Elizabeth Jocelin and Brilliana Harley suggest that maternal pedagogies of dress were negotiated with their husbands. Jocelin addresses a portion of her advice directly to her husband to put into effect when the child is born, whereas Brilliana Harley, whose advice is for a teenage son, must consider her husband's control of economic resources, his access to markets for clothes, her location and his own competing paternal advice about what Edward Harley should wear. Maternal authority in these questions is far from complete. Nevertheless, they do negotiate a space for their advice through the practical work of motherhood. In developing their own pedagogies of dress, turning maternal labour to theory they contest the trivialization of feminine sartorial knowledge. Like their contemporaries, they consider how clothing placed children in society, but they offer their children social contexts of their own imagining, drawn out from their religious beliefs. For Elizabeth Jocelin, hierarchies of class should be crossed with humility to facilitate social harmony, while Brilliana, Lady Harley urges her son to evaluate a man's faith against his class position, a stance that renders class less than deserving of automatic respect. When Sir Walter Raleigh wrote that 'no Man is esteemed for gay Garments, but by Fooles and women' he suggested that women's understanding of clothes is driven by surfaces. Brilliana Harley and Elizabeth Jocelin treat clothes, even fine clothes, as the outcome of ethical inquiry and spiritual understanding.

Part Three: Hair

5
The Culture of the Head: Hair in Mary Wroth's *Urania* and Margaret Cavendish's 'Assaulted and Pursued Chastity'

Hair is not a popular subject in early modern studies. It might figure in the scholarly analysis of race in early modern England, given the significance of hair to contemporary studies of race, but it rarely does, for work there tends to focus on skin colour.[1] Histories of hair, while useful, tend to be cursory in providing only catalogues of fashionable hairstyles with more substantial critical analyses beginning only with the eighteenth century.[2] Yet, seventeenth-century hair does have a story to tell. 'Hair is', says Geraldine Biddle-Perry, 'one of the most powerful symbols of our individual and collective identities'.[3] Hair is also central to the construction of 'hierarchies of femininity'.[4] As Patricia Hill Collins explains, 'Race, gender, and sexuality converge on this issue of evaluating beauty'; while white women are objectified by being judged for their beauty, their 'White skin and straight hair simultaneously privilege them in a system that elevates whiteness over blackness'.[5] This chapter looks at two stories that forge a vision of female identity dependant on the construction of hair as a visceral instrument of privilege. *The Countess of Montgomery's Urania* (1621) by Lady Mary Wroth and 'Assaulted and Pursued Chastity', printed in *Natures Picture Drawn by Fancies Pencil* (1656, 1671), by Margaret Cavendish, Duchess of Newcastle make thick, soft and slightly curled long hair an upper-class attribute that can be used powerfully by women. Mary Wroth's *The Countess of Montgomery's Urania* tells the story of Leonius, a prince with aristocratic hair who dresses as a woman to win his beloved shepherdess Veralinda, whose own natural hair foreshadows the revelation that she is a princess. 'Assaulted and Pursued Chastity' recounts the adventures of a friendless gentlewoman in exile who dons male disguise and the name Travellia to escape a life of prostitution and in her travels comes to rule a people utterly awed by her hair. These two tales demonstrate

115

Noliwe M. Rooks's argument that 'like history and literature, hair, even in what is presumed to be its "natural" state, is shaped by culturally determined creative and re-creative acts to form and further particular ends'.[6] Giving a cultural shape to the natural hair of upper-class English women, Cavendish and Wroth construct hair's privilege with structures of class and race assembled from aesthetics and medical theories of hair's physiology; in each case, their representations of hair reinforce hierarchies of class and race to challenge women's subordinate position within patriarchal culture.

The hair stories of Lady Mary Wroth and Margaret Cavendish, Duchess of Newcastle particularly draw attention to the signs of race and class because cross-dressing throws them into relief, eliminating hair's reliability as a sign of sexual difference. Studies of cross-dressing have typically treated hair as little more than a subsidiary of the analysis of clothes, if hair is mentioned at all. Ann Jones and Peter Stallybrass, exceptionally, briefly discuss the use of theatrical wigs as prosthetic devices that perform sexual difference.[7] Indeed, hair was metaphorically likened to apparel; the hair of Milton's Eve is a veil, on the authority of Scripture, while William Prynne refers to men's long hair as 'the very Badge, and Livery of the World'.[8] As Johannes Endres writes, hair in the eighteenth century and before is 'part of the human body's "clothing"'.[9] But hair, unlike clothes, was a physiological attribute, an outcome of the body's humoural balance. It was a sign of blood and thus of origins, of culture, race and nation. For each writer, hair affords evidence of the workings of nature, while also providing a medium for art. Hairstyles document a knowledge of aesthetics, while hair length, proven malleable, reveals the art of producing gender. Both Wroth and Cavendish treat hair as an absolutely reliable sign of class origins, but Cavendish accords imperial power to a woman's long hair while Wroth uses a man's long hair to illustrate the cultural value of women's art.

The Culture of Natural Hair

Hair has, of course, its standard literary motifs in early modern England: the attractive maid whose beauty is confirmed, in part, by her fair hair; the seductress whose hair weaves a destructive net of enchantment; the attractive young man without a beard and his older, more masculine counterpart who has one; and the women and men who show their distress, madness or sexuality in their disordered, loosened and wild hair. From the black wires on the head of Shakespeare's Dark Lady to the 'modest wantons, wanton modesty' of the gold threads blazoned on the head of his Lucrece, from Sir Andrew Aguecheek's hair, which will not curl by nature but hangs like 'flax on a distaff' that some housewife should spin, to Aaron's 'fleece of woolly hair' that uncurls, not as a vene-real sign, but because 'Blood and revenge are hammering' in his head, from the 'sable silvered' beard of the ghost of the King of Denmark to the ornaments of Benedick's cheek that stuff a tennis ball and the 'smooth' female body that the tamed shrew Kate considers a sign of women's weakness, hair flits through Shakespeare's work, denoting conformity to prevailing standards of beauty, or neglect of them, sexual allure or cor-ruption, health or sickness, virtue or vice, youth or age.[10]

Similarly, the hair of Milton's characters attains thoroughgoing moral significance. Satan's hair shakes 'pestilence and war', while Adam's 'hya-cinthine locks/Round from his parted forelock manly hung/Clust'ring, but not beneath his shoulders broad' and Eve, 'as a veil down to the slender waist/Her unadornèd golden tresses wore/Dishevelled, but in wanton ringlets waved/As the vine curls her tendrils, which implied/Subjection.'[11] Adam's precisely coiffed locks and Eve's more 'dishevelled' mane connote their gender difference and their respective places in hierarchical relationships with each other, nature and God. Their hair embodies the relative value of art and nature and shows a marked pref-erence for the natural – the unadorned tresses, the likening to vines and hyacinths – and, some have said, prefigures Eve's unwillingness to be subjected. Milton loads the same weight onto Samson's locks, whose story hangs on Dalila's trim. God, Milton says, gave Samson strength in his hair better to show the power of God because hair is weak: 'Where strength can least abide, though all thy hairs/Were bristles ranged like those that ridge the back/Of chafed wild boars, or ruffled porcupines.'[12] Hair breaks under tension, and it does not make a man strong. Milton broaches the notion that a man's hair might signify patriarchal domi-nance, and turns from it. Hair is too weak. But it clearly is of some consequence.[13] In early modern England, the length, colour, texture and curl of the hair on a man or woman's head registers meaning in complex ways, defining moral posture, gender and racial difference, class status, physiological vitality and social conformity.

So first, a caveat: this chapter is about natural hair. Although both Wroth's and Cavendish's characters are incognito, costumed as a forest nymph and a boy, their hair is their own and it is this which provides the narrative crux in both stories. Wigs and other forms of false hair inspire a different set of questions.[14] Early modern men and women did wear false hair. Margaret Spencer, discussed in Chapter 2, purchased 'frilled hayres', and the account book of Mary Evelyn, the wife of

John Evelyn, records the purchase of several pieces of hair: a 'fortop' of hair, a 'taping of Haire' and two 'tours of haire' – a tower being a high pile of curls and a foretop a piece of false hair arranged on the forehead.[15] William Prynne claimed that those who wore false hair acted 'of a vaine-glorious, and fantastique desire of singularitie, or differencing ourselves from others' and censure God's judgement of their natural hair.[16] False hair was also castigated as a sign of class ambition. A broadside ballad from the late seventeenth century entitled 'Advice to the Maidens of London, to Forsake their Fantastical Top-Knots' berates country girls who go to the city and unwisely spend their money on the fashionable hairstyle.[17] False hair disrupts the stability of hair's signifying power, undermining its ability to demarcate class difference. Wroth and Cavendish position their stories in relation to this imagined capacity in natural hair. Additionally, their cross-dressing stories focus on the hair on the head, rather than eyebrows, beards or body hair, for the possibility of Leonius's beard appearing and beardlessness of Travellia both pass unremarked.

Natural hair can function as a sign of the wearer's origins because it is of the blood. It is a signifier of order (or disorder) and health (or corruption). Thick, full, fair, long hair is a symptom of good health, of humoural balance, while baldness, excess hair and coarsely textured or exceptionally straight or curly hair reveal physical imbalances in heat or moisture, which can have both environmental and cultural causes. The anatomy in Thomas Vicary's *The English Man's Treasure* defines the hair first as a consequence of the humours, as a 'superfluitie of members, made of the grosse fume or smoake passing out of the viscoues matter, thickned to the forme of hair'; in this vein, the hair's colour can make known the complexion of the brain, but it can also influence that complexion by defending the brain from too much heat or cold and allowing the brain to release its 'fumosities' – in addition to making the shape of the head more beautiful.[18] Helkiah Crooke's *Mikrokosmographia* offers a similar, but more extended, Galenic explanation of hair's function. Hairs, he says, are 'bodyes engendred out of a superflouous excrement of the third concoction, torrified by the natural heate'; that is to say, hair is produced by heat from the body's superfluous moisture, from 'sooty, thicke and earthy vapour' in temperate – neither too moist nor too dry – places on the body. Hair on the head is the longest on the body 'because the Brain affordeth a great deale of clammy moysture', but hair allows the body to balance itself, for hair opens the pores, 'for the better breathing or thrusting out of exhalations'. The texture of hair (its hardness or softness, its thickness or thinness), its plenitude, length, curliness and colour are all a consequence of the body's humoural disposition. If the body is dry, the hair will not grow long or it will curl wildly and the roots will go 'awry', whereas baldness is a consequence of coldness.[19] Rembert Dodoen's *A Niewe Herball, or Historie of Plants* (1578) recommends plants that will prevent hair from falling out of the head, restore hair that has fallen out and cause hair to fall out.[20] Baldness, for instance, is cured with hot and dry plants such as sowbread, aloe, cresses, garlic and rose, as well as myrtle (which is, exceptionally, dry and cold).[21] Similarly, John Parkinson recommends for making hair grow where it naturally should an application of 'Cremor Tartari', which purges humours, and he theorizes that hair falls out because of an excess of cold and wet humours.[22] Situated at the body's pores where the environment can reach the body's inner cavities, hair at once mediates between internal physiology and the external environment and embodies the body's balance, its complexion. The appropriately temperate body will produce soft, thick hair that is only a little curly.

The body's physiological complexion extends to an explanation for the beauty and racial attributes of hair. Nicholas Culpeper's translation of Galen links health and moderation to beauty, even, unlike most, precisely defining the hair's best colour: 'The Indications of a Moderate Temperature according to the whol Habit of the Body are, a mixed colour in the Face of red and white, as though the Lilly and the Rose strove for Superiority, the Hair yellow, and moderately curling.'[23] This view of physiology underpins representations of people from other presumptively less moderate countries. '[T]he haire curleth by reason of the drinesse of the temper; and therefore all Black-Moores have curled or crisped haire', according to Crooke.[24] Because geography fundamentally affects the humoural disposition of the body, Crooke contends:

> those that inhabit a hotte and dry country, have hard, blacke, dry curled and brittle hair, and of small growth, as the Egyptians, Arabians and Indians: contrariwise those that inhabit in a moyst and cold climate have soft haires which grow moderatly, are small or fine, straight and reddish, as the Illirians, Germans, Sarmatians and all the coast of Scythia, as Galen sayth. But such as inhabit a temperate tract betweene these, have hayre of greater growth, exceeding strong and somewhat blacke, moderately thicke, neither altogether curled, nor altogether straight.[25]

A moderate climate produces people of a moderate disposition with moderate hair, neither altogether curled nor altogether straight.

If hair was imagined to grow according to nature's beckoning, it was also wildly open to the manipulations of art, with scissors, colouring agents and instruments that change the curl of the hair and the size and shape of the head. In early modern England, barbers, female medical practitioners and servants seem to have been responsible for haircare, as well as the hair's owner. The Barber-Surgeons Company was incorporated in 1540, with barbers being banned from any surgery except the extraction of teeth; the barber described in Robert Greene's *A Quip for an Upstart Courtier* offers Italian, Spanish, French and English haircuts and curls and provides a variety of methods for trimming the beard.[26] A Norwich barber studied by Margaret Pelling included curling irons in his instruments, in addition to razors and a barber's basin, surely an indication of a more decorative approach to hairdressing.[27] Barbers were primarily male, although there may have been female barbers practising in London after the Restoration as cutters of men's hair; Wendy Cooper locates the beginnings of public hair salons for women in the twentieth century.[28] But some women in the later seventeenth century did advertise their hairdressing skills. One described in a printed handbill her services in prognostication and hair treatments: 'She hath a most rare and easie Art in shaping the Eye-brow, and in making low-Foreheads high, taking the Hair off so that it shall never come again, she hath also an Art to cause the Hair to grow thick and to colour it to what colour they please, and to continue so.'[29] Another woman, who promised to visit ladies in their homes, advertised her skills at cutting and curling 'Gentlemens, Gentlewomens, and Childrens Hair'; she also sold 'a fine Pomatum, which is mixt with Ingredients of her own making, that if the Hair be never so Thin, it makes it grow Thick; and if Short, it makes it grow Long'.[30] For aristocratic ladies, it seems quite likely that maids dressed their hair, although an elderly Anne Clifford reports on having a male servant cut off her hair – an event which will be discussed in the next chapter.

Whomever the hairdresser – the hair's owner, a professional or a servant – hair is a visceral medium for art. It is a covering for the head and the brain, and it is also itself covered, the setting for hats, jewels, flowers, crowns, ribbons and garlands. Richard Corson's *Fashions in Hair: The First Five Thousand Years* illustrates in pictures the art of seventeenth-century hair. Men's hair might be bobbed or long – a choice possibly made according to political principles – as well as straight or curly, smoothed down or loose, combed forward or back, or decorated with a single long lock at the side (a lovelock). Before the Restoration, Corson argues, it was not fashionable for men to wear wigs because observers might assume the wearer had lost his own hair due to disease. Women dressed their hair over pads, rolls, or frames, although the height of these dressings diminished after 1615; they wore fringes at the forehead, curls at the temples, or had their hair done up in twists, braids or chignons or left it hanging loose in curls or 'frizzed'.[31]

Significantly, hairstyles themselves could be polemically defined as natural. Despite the fact that anything done to the hair might technically be artificial, even combing and washing, a considerable body of seventeenth-century prose was dedicated to defining some forms of intervention as natural and others as artificial. The invective was grounded in Scriptural injunctions ordaining hair as woman's covering and banning long hair on men. Aligning God's law with nature, polemicists regarded hair as natural when it met this Scriptural test. In *The Loathesomnesse of Longe Haire* (1654), Thomas Hall explains the link between hair length and nature:

> by Nature here is meant, the light and dictate of right reason in the understanding, informing men by its common notions and instinct, what is good, and to be done, or what is evill, and to be avoyded. 'Tis that order and naturall inclination which God hath put in the Creature: And thus Nature it selfe is said to condemne long haire, as being contrary to that order, and naturall principles of decency and honesty, which God hath implanted in man.[32]

Hair length is a moral imperative that defines the natural as ethically good and the unnatural as immoral and deeply threatening to the social order. John Bulwer claims in his *Anthropometamorphosis,* a history of 'abused nature', that the purpose of 'Cosmeticall Physic' is 'that whatsoever is according to Nature, that it is to preserve in the Body, and so consequently to cherish and maintaine the native Beautie thereof'.[33] When cosmetical physic – the beautifying physic discussed in the first chapter – defined the ethics of hairdressing, it became natural to preserve the hair but unnatural for women to cut it or for men to let their hair grow: 'in every sexe Nature hath placed some note of difference, and the judgment of Nature is no way ambiguous.'[34] In this formulation, gender difference relies on the art of hairdressing, but that artifice is redefined as natural.

Hairdressing possesses a double social threat. Hairdressing can test a patriarchal social order. Thomas Hall argues that the Bible condemns long hair on men (1 Cor. 11:14; Ezek. 44:20) because hair is a type of visceral rhetoric; there should be a statement of 'Antithesis and

Opposition [...] betweene the haire of men and women'.[35] Women's hairstyles can also incite a disregard for female chastity. *A Looking-Glasse for Women* (1644) inveighs against female hairdressing for all of its ten pages, seeing decoration of the hair as a form of identification with the world, as lightness, vanity and pride, a provocation of lust and a type of nakedness.[36] Likewise, short hair on women marks a dangerous sexual propensity. The haircut features prominently on the title page of *Hic Mulier* (1620), where a figure in a mask (possibly a woman in a vizard and male dress) brandishes a large pair of shears above the head of a seated woman. Citing Scriptural precedent, the tract asks rhetorically: 'The longe hayre of a woman is the ornament of her sexe, and bashfull shamefastnesse her chiefe honour: the long haire of a man, the vizard for a theevish or murderous disposition: and will you cut off that beauty, to weare the others villany?'[37] In cutting her hair, the woman descends from the 'glory of a faire large hayre, to the shame of most ruffianly short lockes' – as if having 'large' hair were the natural state of woman and short hair the natural state of men, instead of being effects introduced by the use or avoidance of scissors.[38] *Hic Mulier* proclaims short haircuts on women 'barbarous' and 'monstrous' because they are unchaste: 'Shee that hath given kisses to have her hayre shorne, will give her honestie to have her upper parts put into a French doublet.'[39] In the same year, John Chamberlain wrote to Sir Dudley Carleton of how the Bishop of London, at the command of King James, had called together all his clergy to 'inveigh vehemently against the insolencie of our women', which expressed itself in their masculine dress and 'theyre haire cut short or shorne'. 'The truth is', he concludes, 'the world is very much out of order'; his solution is to restore women to patriarchal control, deciding how they should do their hair.[40] On the other hand, long hair on men can signal incivility and a lack of discipline. As Thomas Hall contends, the wearing of long hair is 'against the modest, civill, and commendable custome of our own Nation, till lately that we began to follow the French, and Spaniards, who yet are known Papists and Idolaters'. Even worse, long hair on men is the fashion of the 'barbarous', of the Virginians in America who worship the devil.[41] Hall advances a link between long hair and Catholic heresy when he claims that long hair on men is 'contrary to the civill, laudable custome of our land since the Reformation'. Formerly the ancient Britons worshipped the devil, held wives in common and had long hair, but since the Reformation, the days of Queen Elizabeth and the Stuart kings, 'a modest Tonsure hath been used' – not the extreme tonsure of the Catholic monks and nuns who shaved their heads but a moderate, Protestant hairstyle.[42]

Implicit in these claims about gender, of course, is the second threat posed by hairdressing – that to the nation. Writers present it as natural that English men and women style their hair differently to the men and women of other nations; gendered anxieties overlap with anxieties about ethnic and religious difference. When men and women adopt hairstyles of the non-Protestant, non-English others, hair fails to reveal the supposed inward difference of the English Protestant. Indeed, it is on this note that William Prynne begins *The Unlovelinesse of Lovelockes* (1628), a work ostensibly against the wearing of lovelocks but actually an extended polemic on hairstyling, whether alterations in the length, or 'curious, nice, and artificiall Embroyderies, Curlings, Textures, Colourings, Powdrings, or compositions of the Haire'.[43] England is, he says, becoming like Africa in producing strange fashions every moment. Historical precedent proves that 'the nourishing, use, and wearing of these unlovely Love-lockes, was common among Idolatrous Infidels, and Vaine, Effeminate, Barbarous, Uncivill, and Lascivious Pagans, whose Custome, Guise, and Gracelesse fashions, no Christians are to imitate'.[44] Culturally imitative hairdressing has the power to bring about the downfall of England, a presumed paragon of Christian civility, for hair is the 'outward Culture of [the] head'. Prynne suggests that the English may surpass the 'Persians, Tartars, Indians, Turkes, and all the Pagan Nations' because they are Christian, but that superiority abates when the English don the styles of those same 'pagans'.[45] For John Bulwer, hairstyle demarcates civility and barbarism. He praises as honourable, men trimming their hair moderately, according to English custom 'which is the Rule of Decency' and avoiding being 'singular'. Irish men and women, on the other hand, grow their hair long and 'breed Lice and Dandro [...] who as they are a Nation estranged from any humane excellency, scarce acknowledge any other use of their Haire then to wipe their hands, from the fat and dirt of their meales'.[46] When they imitate the hair styles of the Japanese, Persians, Indians, Africans, Tartarians, Europeans and Native Americans, the English 'seem to vie deformities with the most Barbarous Nations; so approving their affected shapes, that wee are in a manner unciviliz'd by them'.[47] Foreign hairstyles are contrary to nature, which is in Bulwer's vision orderly, hierarchical and committed to defining national and gender difference according to English custom.

Both natural hair and hairstyles are signs of culture and identity. Natural hair is a visible sign of the body's disposition, and it stands at the body's borders to regulate the complexion, controlling how the environment affects the body and the body's ability to order and rebalance itself. Hairstyles, likewise, distill social regulation, to the extent that conformity in style is defined as natural rather than artificial. Hairstyles are constantly used to mark differences of religion, nation and gender, and debate about hair often confuses the categories of art and nature in order to articulate a vision of nature that places the white, English, if not European, male at the apex of that order, as nature's most moderate, rational and faithful embodiment of nature's ideals. When constructed in didactic writing, hairdressing and hair are properly visible signs of cultural identity, revealing one's race – one's origins and one's blood. In this context, hairdressing is fundamentally a communal art; it aims to avoid singularity and properly signals one's place within a community of people who dress their hair in similar, even traditionally agreed upon, forms.

'Compositions of the Hair' in the *Urania*

In *The Countess of Montgomery's Urania*, the love story of Veralinda, an apparent shepherdess, and Leonius, the younger son of the King of Naples and Amphilanthus's brother, is also a hair story. The narrative echoes the adventures of the eponymous Urania, who like Veralinda had been displaced from the elite family of her birth to be raised as a shepherdess. The two discover their true aristocratic origins together, in a scene replete with the appearance of Apollo, a magic rod that awakens Pamphilia and Amphilanthus, vanishing chairs and a pillar of gold from which hangs a book containing the stories of their births. Veralinda is the daughter of the King of Frigia and his second wife but she lives as a shepherdess because the casting of her nativity at her birth predicted that she would rule a great people. Her step-brothers grew jealous and plotted her death but were thwarted by the would-be murderer who took his reward and the baby into Arcadia, where he left her with the shepherd. At the heart of the question of Veralinda's identity is that of her race, as John Florio used the term in his 1598 dictionary, *A World of Words*: 'a kind, a brood, a blood, a stock, a pedigree'.[48] Veralinda's race, her blood and her pedigree, make her worthy of Leonius, and he of her. As Ania Loomba explains, 'All over Europe, the nobility were often understood as a "race" distinct from ordinary folk, and colonial relations drew heavily upon pre-existing notions of class difference, although they also restructured the relationships between classes within Europe.'[49] Veralinda's hair stakes out the former territory of nobility, whereas Travellia's hair draws on class to structure colonial relations. Veralinda's hair is like that of Leonius, even when she is dressed as a shepherdess. The purpose of the narrative is to see her re-clothed in garb that matches her hair.

The story of Veralinda and Leonius is one of several in *The Countess of Montgomery's Urania* to develop the theory that hair is a reliable sign of class identity. Giving class a physiological basis, aristocratic characters have the same natural hair: slightly curled, thick and, often but not always, blonde. Colour is secondary to hair's texture, softness, curl and abundance, the qualities that allow hair to function as a physiological sign of race, of origin, and most specifically of the class of one's birth. For Steriamus and Selarinus, hair is one of the blessings of nature: 'their haire which never had been cut, hung long, yet longer much it must have been, had not the daintie naturall curling somewhat shortned it, which as the wind mov'd, the curles so pretily plaid, as the Sunne-beames in the water'.[50] Their soft, naturally curling hair contradicts the humble goatskin apparel they wear as shepherds, and the two, of course, turn out to be sons of the King of Albania. Similarly, the hair of a forester humbly dressed in green belies his seeming humility: 'his haire was thick, somthing long and curld, the Sunne had made it some-thing yellower, then it naturally was, as if he would have it nearer his owne beames, so much hee loved the Lad, and used to hold him neare' (341); the hair of his beloved, a forest nymph, is 'not so white or yel-low as others, but of a dainty, and love-like browne, shining like gold, upon blacke' (342). Physically and socially favoured by nature, the curly-haired blonde forester is actually the third son of an Earl, and the nymph, the daughter of a lord. Parselius, the son of the King and Queen of Morea, likewise has curly hair, for it 'delicatly and naturally curling made rings, every one of which were able to wed a heart to it selfe' (123–4). Worthy, if sometimes imperfect, lovers all, these men have both elite status and social virtue, as able governors, martial knights and pleasing lovers.

Conversely, low status and vice are marked in coarse, unruly, straight hair. Both the facial hair and the hair on the head of a dwarf in thrall to the King of Stromboli signify the severity of his abjection for he has no facial hair to distinguish him from a woman except a wart with hairs in it. The hair on his head, once black, is now 'grisled, yet still kept the nat-urall stubbornnesse of it being but thin, and those few haires desirous to be seene stood staring, neither were they of any equall length, but like a horses maine, new taken from grasse' (137). His hair is thin, straight and tough. It stands up. It certainly does not hang down to be gently played with by the breeze. Three 'monsters' who show their lack of respect for authority and for women when they kidnap Pamphilia have similarly

coarse hair, 'of a browne red colour; and bristled' (119). Their unwor-
thiness for power and their lack of deference to women – their cultural
coarseness – are revealed in their bristly, unruly hair. Wroth's Pamphilia
and Melasinda have gently curling locks and a capacity to rule, unlike
Milton's Eve, whose curled hair shows her subjection, while the curled
hair of Wroth's men reveals an inward disposition to defer to the desires
of women. Because both men and women are beautiful when they have
soft, long, curled hair, natural hair does little to mark gender difference,
but it does function effectively to make plain both class hierarchy and
one's place in a community forged around women's agency. Sheila
Cavanagh contends that in the *Urania*, '[i]nstead of country of origin or
residence, [...] religion, love, and genealogy serve as prime determinants
of identity'.[51] Identiying characters along these lines, hair is an extraction of birth and feminist complexion.

  Wroth certainly raises the possibility that hair could be used to
deceive, that it might not be a transparent signifier, but those who
attempt trickery fail. Selarinus can initially trick Olixia Queen of Epirus
by sending her a head made to look like his own. Yet the head, the
narrator acknowledges, lacks a true resemblance: 'the haire of the same
colour, but so much wanting the cleare brightnesse, as a dead mans
haire will want of a living mans, the bloud as trickling downe out of
the vaines, some spinning, and so naturally was all done to the life,
as cunning could not performe more' (313). Because Selarinus's blood
does not run in the dead man's hair the illusion fails: at first sight the
Queen's court imagines the head is his, but they soon discover the
deceit. Rosindy is momentarily deceived in believing that his beloved
Meriana is dead because he sees her head with its distinctive hair held
on a pillar above the palace: 'the haire hanging in such length and deli-
cacie, as although it somewhat covered with the thicknesse of it, part
of the face, yet was that, too sure a knowledge to Rosindy of her losse,
making it appeare unto him, that none but that excellent Queene was
mistrisse of that excellent haire' (158). Rosindy is right that the hair is
Meriana's, but Meriana is not dead, for her captors have created a pillar
within which to hold the living lady. Rosindy's belief that the lady's hair
is a certain sign of her identity is not disappointed.

  Hair's reliability as a signifier of class functions even within non-
European contexts. Kim F. Hall has argued that the *Urania* 'uses the
language of beauty to reinforce distinctions of class. Thus we find racial
difference often subtends Wroth's emphasis on class differentiation [...]'.[52]
Although Hall is discussing the dark/light binary of skin colour, her claim
applies to hair as well. But Wroth's narrator does not even account for

the hair of the characters with black skin whom Hall discusses, not the 'black-moor' women nor Rodomandro, King of Tartaria and Pamphilia's eventual husband. Only their blackness matters with respect to the function they serve in the narrative. Handsome, black Rodomandro, for instance, becomes Pamphilia's husband, with his blackness providing, as Hall suggests, a 'visual cue that he will never win Pamphilia's love'.[53] But his hair is left out of the blazon. His sister's hair, on the other hand, is 'of a lovely light browne', a fit accompaniment to the Princess's skin 'of purest snowe'.[54] A Persian princess whose skin is so white as to make the Milky Way seem like dirt and snow appear as the black sea has hair of 'a dainty, light Browne'. Wroth's narrator registers the lady's status in the shine of her hair and its transcendence of the poet's linguistic powers: 'Her heair (alas, that I must barcly call that haire which the heavens envy for the richnes, and yett strive to immitate the bright luster of itt, when for ther greatest glory they desire to shine brightest, and hett but as gold upon black).'[55] The hair of aristocratic non-European foreigners is the same as their aristocratic European counterparts; it shines, it is delicate and it exceeds poetic language because of their shared position at the apex of an international class hierarchy.

Wroth is at odds with those of her countrymen who saw Tartarians and Persians as having hair as foreign as their culture. Early modern geographers and travellers took the view that Tartaria was inhabited by 'a fierce and cruell people', who, part Asian and part European and neither Christian nor Muslim but 'Gentiles', were 'of great stature, rude of behaviour'.[56] John Frampton says that the people of Tartar are 'of an evill shape', that the men lack beards and 'in the forepart of their heads they weare their hayre long like women of our countrey'.[57] *The Estates, Empires, and Principallities of the World*, translated from French to English by Edward Grimeston, declares Tartarian men to be 'of a meane stature, and have very broad brests and shouldiers; they have great gogle eyes, and thicke eyebrowes: they are broad faced, and have thinne beards with great mustachos: they commonly shave the backe part of their heads and let the other grow long, which they tie behind their eares';[58] *Anthropometamorphosis* repeats this assessment, citing his source.[59] Persian women, Thomas Herbert contends, have 'blacke and curling' haii, as well as black eyes, high noses, large mouths, thick lips and painted cheeks.[60] In Wroth's work, hair does not register these sorts of national difference, but instead makes visible an essentialized class identity that crosses national boundaries. Only those with the right kind of natural hair, the right class origins, can rule and be admitted to the circle of acquaintance with Pamphilia, Amphilanthus and their friends. Hair distinguishes those who come from a race of kings and queens from those who do not and those who accept the feminized courtly values that make female writing and rule possible from those who do not. A moderate texture and slight curl document the blood that runs in the person's veins not only to make the hair shine but to make him or her capable of governance. Assimilating elite foreigners into a European hair culture, Wroth's approach renders invisible the ethnic differences that might be marked in hair and consequently erases the potential for diversity in forms of beauty and in the creative variety of forms of expression that hair enables. Although non-Europeans can have privileged hair marking class origins, that hair derives from the thick, soft and slightly curled moderate hair she gives elite Europeans.

The story of Veralinda and Leonius relies on this aristocratic, cultural formation of natural hair, while also reconfiguring the function of hair-dressing in sexual difference. Veralinda's hair is thick, long and slightly curled: 'Sun-beame haire falling downe at the full length, which with a little fine, and naturall curling reched to the small of her leg, and the rich thicknesse spread it selfe over her shoulders' (432). Her hair is artfully coiffed in a natural way, with flowers rather than with jewels. While her grey gown has a white ruff that reveals the natural whiteness of her skin, 'as white and soft as Swannes downe on the breast', her hair is 'carelesly throwne up, neither tyde, nor untyde, but cast into a delightfull neglectivenes, some pretty flowers, and knots of ash-colour ribon, being here and there placed between the loose fastenings of her haire' (423). When it becomes the object of artful attention, hair is dressed with an art that hides itself. The tying up seems to be but neglectfulness. Not only does the natural curl of Veralinda's hair fore-shadow her true identity but so too does the aesthetic by which she styles her hair.

Wroth does not mention who labours to dress Veralinda's hair, but it is artfully arranged and Veralinda is credited with adopting the style. Ostensibly, it signifies her humble social place, for she dons the hairstyle of other of Wroth's pastoral figures. A forest maid dreamt of by Ollorandus, a prince of Bohemia, is 'apparelled in greene, her haire hanging carelesse, nothing holding it, but a delicate Garland, which she wore upon her head, made of Pansies, and Wood-binds' (78). But just as the purported artlessness of the forest maid's naturally beauti-ful hair is a prelude to the revelation of her true status, for she turns out to be Melasinda, Queen of Hungary, Veralinda's hair denotes her true aristocratic identity, as yet unknown even to herself. She has an innate respect for social hierarchy and an understanding of aristocratic aesthetics. She does not do her hair in the self-conscious elegance of Pamphilia. Knowing who she is, Pamphilia wears a crown of diamonds, and 'her haire (alas that plainely I must call that haire, which no earthly riches could value, nor heavenly resemblance counterfeit) was prettily intertwind betweene the Diamonds in many places, making them (though of the greatest value) appeare but like glasse set in gold' (169). Pamphilia's diamond hair decorations visibly mark her status, wealth and power and distinguish her from the shepherdesses. Even so, her hair is most beautiful because of its natural qualities. Her hair becomes gold, the thing to which it is compared, while also making diamonds seem as glass. Superseding metaphors, Pamphilia's natural hair surpasses the mere artifice of diamond jewellery. For Pamphilia, Veralinda and Melasinda, whether their hair is decorated with flowers or with jewels, their hair is most beautiful because of what nature has made it. The 'fine, and naturall curling' in Veralinda's hair is the work of nature – a seemingly superior kind of curl to that effected by art – but the 'delightful neglectiveness' of its arrangement with ribbons and flowers is a form of art that eschews itself.

For Veralinda, this aesthetic choice is linked to lineage. She has an innate knowledge of the aesthetic codes of the community to which she was born and truly belongs. Her hairstyling codes are influenced by the aesthetic theories of Baldesar Castiglione and by Wroth's uncle, Philip Sidney, who drew on the work of his Italian predecessor in developing an aesthetic. In *The Book of the Courtier,* Count Lodovico defines *sprezzatura* as a grace defined by 'a certain nonchalance which conceals all artistry and makes whatever one says or does seem uncontrived and effortless'. True art, he adds, is 'what does not seem to be art; and the most important thing is to conceal it, because if it is revealed this discredits a man completely and ruins his reputation'.[61] Although we have recognized Castiglione's marked influence on sixteenth-century verse, including Sidney's poetry, both applied a similar aesthetic to women's hair. Count Lodovico praises as graceful the woman who lets her hair 'fall casually and unarranged' and 'betray[s] no effort or anxiety to be beautiful'.[62] Sidney affixes this doctrine to hair in *The Countess of Pembroke's Arcadia (The New Arcadia)*. Like the hair of Wroth's Pamphilia and her Persian princess, the hair of Philoclea exceeds the poet's powers. Sidney's narrator professes that her hair is 'alas, too poor a word; why should I not rather call them her beams?'[63] Philoclea's hair is the perfection of Castiglione's theory: 'In the dressing of her hair and apparel, she might see neither a careful art nor an art of carelessness, but even left to a neglected chance, which yet could no more unperfect her perfections than a die any way cast could lose his squareness.'[64] Surpassing even artful neglectfulness, Philoclea's hair is the perfect union of art and nature, the art that emerges from nature so perfect the art is neglectfulness itself. The 'delightfull neglectivenes' of Veralinda's hair in Wroth's romance testifies to the shepherdess's innate understanding of aristocratic literary culture.

Leonius, too, has naturally beautiful hair and literary guidelines for his hairdo. Garbed like Diana in white buskins, Leonia has 'her haire tyd up, only some of the shortest, and about the temples curled, crowned with Roses and Hyacinths' (433). To dress like a woman, Leonius does not wear a wig, for his own hair is appropriate natural material for a feminine hairstyle. He has hair long enough to tie up and thick enough to leave some hairs loose to hang down. His hair curls, and when it is crowned with flowers, it is indistinguishable from female hair. Although the other shepherdesses observe that the nymph's 'fairenesse seemed more masculine, as fitted with her estate, yet full of grave, modest, and seemely bashfulnesse' (436), his performance of femininity is convincing, his masculinity attributed to his lower class. His male body functions effectively as feminine when gendered by the feminine art of hairdressing.

In this, Wroth is still reflecting on Sidney's romance. Dressing as a woman for the sake of love of Philoclea, Pyrocles becomes Zelmane, an Amazon.[65] Zelmane, too, has naturally beautiful hair. Musidorus observes of Zelmane:

> the hanging of her hair in fairest quantity, in locks, some curled and some as it were forgotten, with such a careless care and an art so hiding art that she seemed she would lay them for a pattern, whether nature simply, or nature helped by cunning be the more excellent; the rest whereof was drawn into a coronet of gold, richly set with pearl, and so joined all over with gold wires and covered with feathers of divers colours that it was not unlike to an helmet, such a glittering show it bare, and so bravely it was held up from the head.[66]

Zelmane's hair is thick, curly and artfully dressed carelessly. Physiologically, it does not embody sexual difference, and it need not mark gender difference. The hair of Zelmane and of Leonius has an inherent grace, a consequence of the elite identity they share with the women they love. Elite masculinity affords Leonius the physiology – the soft, curled hair – and the aesthetic knowledge – the ability to gracefully hide one's art – necessary convincingly to play a woman. Class and *sprezzatura*, in this sense, enable the cross-dressing man. If Sidney's Musidorus briefly shares William Prynne's anxieties about the transformative powers of hair, that by 'Crisping, Curling, Frouncing, Powdring, and nourishing of their Lockes' men are 'wholy degenerated and metamorphosed into women', the class of Pyrocles and Leonius anchors their masculinity in grace but allows them to perform femininity.[67]

Having won his beloved by rescuing her, Leonia is a convincing shepherdess because he is a prince. But Wroth's narrative also considers how he negotiates the chasm of rank that divides a shepherdess from a prince and overcomes the barrier to affective expression imposed by marshal masculinity. In this context, cross-dressing is emotionally enabling. Leonius had previously linked manhood and untidy hair as he 'rubd up his Haire, wiped his face, set on his most manly, yet amorous countenance' and expressed the view that 'women love not childish men, how much soever they commonly like lovelines, and the choicest beauties' (428). Leonius is in a bind. As he rubs up his hair, a manly gesture that signals his difference from children, he distinguishes his messy locks from the artfully dressed coiffure of a woman, but he also distances himself from the loveliness that women want. His masculine appearance is doubly constraining: first because women prefer beauties, not men with messy hair, and then because he must refrain from being excessively emotional. Weeping, no matter his adult sorrow at being separated from Veralinda, would be deemed childish. Masculine discipline functions here as a barrier to the consummation of heterosexual desire. Moreover, Leonius controls his feelings for Veralinda specifically to accord with her wish to respect the class difference between them. Wroth compares his feelings to 'Motes in the ayre', the swarming of bees and the fury of wasps, yet being like a fisherman,

> that in his net catcheth all that comes within it, yet pickes hee out the choicest, and appoints some to keepe, some to sell, some to give, and some to throw in againe, as not fit for keeping: so did he cull his severall passions, some he chose to present her withall, some to hold in himselfe, to please her withall, others not to be seene by her, he cast away into the floud of his forgetfulnesse, whence none should arise to give her distaste. (427)

Leonius practises a version of masculine self-mastery that depends not on mastering women but submission to their desires, but that self-control is restrictive. He cannot win Veralinda's love from this position because she requires of him deference to class hierarchy. An old man helpfully provides the solution to Leonius's dilemma, when he recommends a female disguise, which will 'make her unable to withstand so much pitty as must breed love, and that love if you then discreetly governe it, will procure your happinesse' (431). That is, dressed as a woman, Leonius can appeal to Veralinda's pity and so sigh out his passions without the taint of childishness. For women, it is appropriate to speak feelingly.

The rules governing male sighing are evident from the beginning of the romance, for Urania begins the whole tale by reprimanding Perissus for weeping about Limena, telling him to 'Leave these teares, and woman-like complaints' (15) and to take action to revenge her supposed death. Perissus resumes his armour and with it, his masculine identity, to prove himself worthy of Limena. Leonius takes another path to win Veralinda. He transforms 'woman-like complaints' into a productive expression of heterosexual male desire. As Leonia, he speaks woefully of his love and instantly wins Veralinda's friendship and sympathy, through which he wins her love, for because she is in love with Leonius, she sees in Leonia the 'memory of her love' (436). Companions in their woe, they pass their time at a fountain, unhappy only in the night that keeps them apart. The feminized social space produced by cross-dressing allows Leonia and Veralinda to gain emotional intimacy and a physical connection, kissing.

Providence appears to support this emotional intimacy between lovers, as well as heterosexual consummation between men and women of the same class, and intervenes to remove the barrier to the latter posed by Leonia's female identity. Veralinda's adopted father has a dream that he should send her to an island. When she follows his direction, she learns that she is a princess and that Leonia is a prince. Leonia blushingly reveals herself as Leonius, 'shewing that hee was ashamed of his habite, and yet that habite became that blush' (456). A viscerally feminine trait, the blush marks his face as physiologically indistinguishable from a woman's, just as his hair is. His femininity is productive and creative for him and appointed by 'Destiny' (456). Leonius's masculinity may first attract Veralinda's attention, when he rescues her from a bear, but his femininity allows them to be together. The martial codes of masculinity are affectively disabling, in so far as the expression of love and loss by a prince can only be equated with childishness and effeminacy. Cross-dressing liberates the male heterosexual lover from the gendered meanings of his body, which is not utterly different from a woman's. With respect to hair, gender difference is a work of art. Stephen Greenblatt comments in an essay on cross-dressing that '[m]ale

writers of the period regarded gender as an enduring sign of distinction, both in the sense of privilege and in the sense of differentiation'.[68]
In Wroth's narrative, hair marks a community of beautiful, privileged
people who share blood and aesthetic values, separate from those with
coarse hair, but the narrative does not reproduce masculinity as a form
of distinction. Rather, masculinity functions most effectively when it
can adapt to the feminine. Wroth is challenging a central proposition of
what constitutes natural hair: sexual difference. For many of her seventeenth-century contemporaries, male hair was naturally short, naturally
different that is from female hair. Wroth's construction of natural hair
does not distinguish between male and female hair – any difference
is the result of art – but between classes. Not causing the downfall of
civility and morality, as William Prynne would suggest, the erasure of
sexual difference enhances civility. Wroth's narrative calls into question
the inferiority of female nature, while also re-evaluating the respective
cultural values that trivialize female arts and venerate masculine self-
governance. Hairdressing produces love and the fulfillment of desire,
while masculine self-governance produces frustration that can only be
overcome by feminine art.

Margaret Cavendish and Imperial Hair

Margaret Cavendish's 'Assaulted and Pursued Chastity', a prose narrative printed in *Natures Picture Drawn by Fancies Pencil* (1656, 1671), also
links class, race and gender. Heavily invested in questions of beauty,
Natures Picture Drawn by Fancies Pencil, is a volume of narratives in prose
and verse. Book One, in verse, has a framing device that establishes that
a group of men and women have gathered at a fire on a cold winter
evening to tell stories to pass the time. It is striking just how often the
tales in both books deal with the trials of the attractive – or of those
absolutely not so; the appearance of the heroines goes only rarely
unremarked. Cavendish expresses some resignation about the tyranny
of normative aesthetics in *Sociable Letters,* where she writes, 'The Lady
C. E. ought not to be reproved for grieving for the loss of her Beauty,
for Beauty is the light of our Sex, which is Eclips'd in Middle age, and
Benighted in Old age, where-in our Sex sits in Melancholy Darkness [...]
The truth is, a young beautiful face is a Friend, when as an old withered
face is an Enemy, the one causes Love, the other Aversion.' The only
consolation she can offer is that it is better to be wrinkled than dead.[69]
Likewise, *Natures Picture* dwells on beauty, not because it mounts a
challenge to society's definition of what is beautiful but because it is

aware of the problems that beautiful women face within this patriarchal framework, including the inability of beauty to ensure absolute
economic security, the arbitrariness of male desire and the fragility of
looks that can be changed by disease and age. Like Wroth, Cavendish
is little interested in changing the definition of what is beautiful. What
Cavendish does do is explore how the beautiful upper-class woman can
move outside of the patriarchal sexual economy within a colonial context because of her hair.

The premise of 'Assaulted and Pursued Chastity' is that beauty
'betrays': 'for Young, Beautiful, and Virtuous Women, if they wander
alone, find very rude entertainment from the Masculine Sex'.[70] So it is
that when Miseria, a female exile (and seeming fugitive of the English
Civil War, like Cavendish herself) to the Kingdom of Security, decides to
return home to the Kingdom of Riches – the multitude having repented
of rebellion against the King – she is endangered by her appearance.
A storm forces her ship from its course, and she lands in the Kingdom
of Sensuality. Because she lacks friends or companions – her father died
in the war and her mother of grief – she decides to go into service,
but ends up in a brothel. Here, the lady becomes involved in a philosophical debate over nature's rationale for beauty. Reading 'Lectures
of Nature', her mistress contends that beauty is meant to be used, an
argument deployed in Shakespeare's Sonnet 2, Marvell's 'To His Coy
Mistress' and Milton's masque. Because nature made beauty to delight
her creatures or to procure more by procreation, it is a sin against
nature to be coy and reserved (397, 398). Miseria believes in natural
beauty but resists these lectures. Even if the bawd decks her in jewels
for the liaison she arranges with a prince known to be a seducer of virgins, the lady holds to her natural beauty and chastity, with her 'lovely
Features, exact Proportion, graceful Behaviour, with a sweet and modest
Countenance, […] more adorned thus, by Nature's dress, than those of
Art' (400). With the bawd's lectures, the *carpe diem* argument is exposed
for what it is: a reduction of women to the value of their looks, nature's
coin exchanged by men who want only to profit in pleasure.

Yet for all her natural beauty, Miseria soon comes to have a beauty
routine, one defined, as for Wroth's female characters, by carelessness.
The *sprezzatura* motif still had currency in the mid-seventeenth century
which, when applied to hair, Stephen Dobranski suggests, was frequently used to hint at 'promiscuous behaviour'.[71] Miseria is quite clear
on the chastity of her version of careless beauty. When she begins to
desire the Prince – despite his attempted rape from which she escaped
only to be captured and held by his aunt – she starts to 'look often in

the Glass, curl her Hair finely, wash her Face cleanly, set her Clothes handsomely, mask her self from the Sun; not considering why she did so' (414). The natural practices of beauty include washing the face, but not painting it, curling the hair but not covering it with a wig or with powder, and keeping herself white by protecting herself from the sun. Beautifying is careless to the degree that it is a consequence of unbidden, unconscious desire for the Prince, not of her sexual agency. She does not beautify to seduce or deceive, as beauty's critics claimed. When the Prince expresses his desire in his grooming he is more deliberate. He 'used Powdering, Perfuming, and rich Clothing' to woo her (414). The lady's natural beauty does not depend on an ascetic unwillingness to tend to her looks but on her aristocratic knowledge of aesthetics, chaste *sprezzatura* and innocent, artless artfulness.

The lady has more agency once she leaves the Kingdom of Sensuality. This, too, depends on her hair. Having already shot the Prince with a gun, Miseria escapes the still undisciplined Prince's next assault attempt, which occurs after his lusts become inflamed during a banquet, by cutting her hair, donning the clothes of a page and renaming herself Travellia. In this, Cavendish directly challenges the idea, from Milton's masque or Shakespeare's *Rape of Lucrece*, that beauty is weakly held. Disguised as a boy, Travellia protects herself best by taking to the sea. There she heals her master, using her feminine knowledge of medical skills (much like Behn's Arabella Fairname), and is adopted by him as a son. By cutting off her hair, Travellia displays a singular commitment to cross-dressing, for the tonsure is not immediately reversible. Arabella Stuart, by contrast, escaped arrest by wearing French hose over her petticoats and by putting on various articles of male attire, a doublet, a cloak and russet boots, as well as 'a man-lyke Perruque with long Locks over her Hair'.[72] Arabella Stuart maintains the intimate parts of her femininity, her petticoats and her hair, but Travellia does not. If Cavendish's Miseria reverses the example of Lucrece in attempting to kill the rapist rather than herself, Travellia protects her chastity by reversing the meaning of cross-dressing. Jean Howard argues that female to male cross-dressing was regarded as something akin to prostitution: 'cross-dressing, like other disruptions of the Renaissance semiotics of dress, opened a gap between the supposed reality of one's social station and sexual kind and the clothes that were to display that reality to the world'. Thus, when women dressed like men, '[t]hey became masterless women, and this threatened overthrow of hierarchy was discursively read as the eruption of uncontrolled sexuality'.[73] Short hair also was sexually corrupting in its confusion of sexual difference.

A Looking-Glasse for Women argues that a woman who cuts her hair makes herself a hermaphrodite, 'a woman downward in your apparell, and [...] a man upward in your Hat, and haire' – a sin aligned with immodesty and pride.[74] Cavendish challenges the association of female sexual corruption with bobbed locks and male clothes to offer an ironic critique of a culture where men endanger women most when they look as they should, like women. Yet she initially maintains a gender hierarchy. Although Travellia is able to inhabit a masculine identity, Travellia is not at first a masterless woman, having placed herself in the service of a sea captain who treats her as a son; she provides herself with a foster father and a new patriarchal social group.

Only when Travellia and the captain are shipwrecked in the Kingdom of Fancy does the need for that patriarchal governance disappear and Travellia emerge as autonomous and politically powerful. This further transformation, like the previous one, depends on her hair. The foreign context changes the rules, as gender hierarchy dissipates in the face of an ethnic contest. Held captive by a cannibalistic people and believing themselves about to become sacrifices to the gods, Travellia and the old captain devise a plan of escape. The plan relies on their gendered education, for the old man collects the materials to make gunpowder and two pistols, while Travellia, his purported son, draws on a lady's knowledge of fashion and beautifying. Travellia weaves himself a garment like green satin from grass, places buskins of flowers on his legs and a garland in his hair and creates sandals of the green fabric and flowers. Thus artfully arrayed like Wroth's shepherds, Travellia shows himself in these clothes, shoots the pistols and reveals his hair:

> his Hair (which was grown in that time, for he never discovered it, keeping it tyed up) untied, and let down, spread upon his back: But when the Priest (which came to fetch him forth) saw him thus drest, never seeing Hair before (for they had none but Wool, and very short, as Negroes have), was amazed at the sight; and not daring to touch him, went by him, guarding him (as the chief Sacrifice) to the place (434).

Travellia has the long thick hair of the European aristocratic woman. As a woman, she is of high birth, for her father was 'one of the Greatest and Noblest Subjects in the Kingdom' (409). As the hermaphrodite feared by conduct book writers, Travellia confronts *Hic Mulier's* antipathy to short hair by having long female hair on top and male clothes below. Marina Leslie argues that 'Travellia represents not an inversion of "proper" gender roles so much as a hermaphroditic combination of female and male, defensive and aggressive, vulnerable and powerful.[75] That hermaphroditic power, showing feminine hair with masculine clothes, becomes the basis of Travellia's absolute rule.

Cavendish translates to a colonial context the romance motif of the cross-dressed heroine who reveals her hair to spectacular effect. Michael Shapiro argues that scenes in which a cross-dressed heroine suddenly shows her hair are common in Renaissance romances and derived from classical sources; Clorinda in Tasso's *Jerusalem Delivered* (1581), Brandamante in *Orlando Furioso* (1516–1532) and Britomart in *The Faerie Queene* all dramatically reveal their hair.[76] In Cavendish's version, the revelation of the feminine hair does not signal the end of her male identity, however. Travellia tells the old man only much later that she is female. As a result, the beautiful, feminine hair functions in concert with the masculine clothes of a page to protect her from an eroticized gaze. In the Kingdom of Sensuality, Miseria's beauty had been read sexually, a gaze which only endangered her with commodification, attempted rape and imprisonment. In the Kingdom of Fancy, feminine hair, worn with masculine clothes, institutes a political relationship based on awe. Kathryn Schwarz argues that Travellia uses chastity as a sexual identity, which 'finally overrides questions of gender, the agency that invests it constructing a figure who, taken for a woman or for a man, cannot ultimately be taken in any conventional sense at all'.[77] But Travellia's hair makes femininity matter. It utterly impresses the inhabitants who have hair that is completely different.

In this, Cavendish is combining the romance motif of the spectacular revelation of long, female hair with scenes of colonial amazement commonly found in early modern travel narratives. These tend to focus more on the power of white skin to so amaze. Samuel Purchas, for instance, includes the report of Cadamosto, a Venetian, about his travels in Africa: 'The Negros came about Cadamosto, with wonder to see his apparell, and the whitenesse of his colour (never before had they seene any Christian) and some of them with spittle rubbed his skinne, to see whether his whitenesse were naturall, or no: which perceiving it to bee no tincture, they were out of measure astonished' – an astonishment that leads them to trade nine or 14 slaves for a single horse.[78] Thomas Herbert records such purported colonial wonder when two Englishmen go ashore in Sierra Leone: 'thousands of the Aethiopians flockt about them, extremely admiring their Colour, so passing along, they were often presented with Flowres, Fruits, Toddy, and like things'.[79] Aphra Behn's *Oroonoko*, however, uses hair to amaze when Behn reports that the naked, indigenous people of Surinam admired her glittering and rich clothes, taffeta cap, black feathers and short hair.[80] For Margaret Ferguson, Behn's hair shows the possibilities of cross-dressing: her escape from male/female, European/other binaries.[81] In Cavendish's tale of colonial wonderment, Travellia's long hair asserts the possibilities for power within the female body given the opportunity to escape from the gendered constructions of the body's meanings. Released from the context of heterosexual desire, she does not seduce the inhabitants, but awes them. The femininity and aristocracy of her hair allow her immediately to transcend the class structures of the foreign society. The King himself shares the priest's amazement and they all adore Travellia as a god, placing her at the very highest rung of their own social hierarchy. Her hair also legitimates her speech. It is when her audience is amazed by her hair that Travellia addresses them, claiming to be a messenger from their gods and then shooting the chief priest with her pistol, before silencing and starving the people, instructing them to fast, to avoid speaking and to obey only the old man and himself. Far from being a sign of subjection as conduct book writers suggested, a woman's long hair enables absolute imperial power. No mere Rapunzel, Travellia's long hair, not matched by her clothes, conquers a kingdom.

Cavendish sets the immediate dominance of Travellia's hair against the naturalized subjection of the inhabitants of the Kingdom of Fancy, a class-based society whose social ranks are marked in both hair and skin colour. The lower ranking are a deep purple colour, 'their Hair as white as Milk, and like Wool; their Lips thin, their Ears long, their Noses flat, yet sharp; their Teeth and Nails as black as Jet, and as shining; their Stature tall, and their Proportion big' (421). These purple people are highly deferential and take the new white arrivals immediately to the house of their governor, who, similarly respectful of hierarchy and uncertain of the newcomers' place in it, sends them along to the King. The status of the King and others of royal blood is also marked on their bodies, for they are a different colour to the rest: 'they were a perfect Orange-colour, their Hair coal-black, their Teeth and Nails as white as Milk; of a very great height, yet well shaped' (429–30). The royal people also have tattoos, their skins 'wrought, like the Britans' (432). The priests have their own hair styles, distinguished from the rest by being bald but for a tuft of hair at the crown (430). With these descriptions, Cavendish adopts the anthropological style of early modern travel writers to observe and record physical features and relative attractiveness.

According to Alexander Butchart, the early modern period saw a shift in anthropological ways of seeing, 'not by the semantic force of myth and legend but by the very bodies of people and things themselves'. A grid devised by the Royal Society in 1666 to organize a country's natural history epitomized this 'new knowledge' as a way of organizing a country's natural history. Of 'Natives and Strangers' one should observe 'their Stature, Shape, Colour, Features, Strength, Agility, Beauty (or want of it), Complexion, Hair, Dyet, Inclination, and Customs that seem not due to Education'.[82] These were, however, long-standing aspects of ethnographic description, if their form was not always so rationalized. Stephen Greenblatt notes the existence of a 'whole complex system of representation, verbal and visual, philosophical and aesthetic, intellectual and emotional, through which people in the late Middle Ages and the Renaissance apprehended, and thence possessed or discarded, the unfamiliar, the alien, the terrible, the desirable, and the hateful'.[83] Valerie Traub records how early modern maps represented racial and ethnic taxonomies and a domestic, heterosexual gender order.[84] And Sujata Iyengar observes too that from the first, English slave traders 'produce[d] tribal ethnographies that rapidly produce what [...] is already a version of racialism – a hierarchical ordering of human beings that depends on skin color and labor, especially slavery'.[85] Constance Relihan argues that fiction functions alongside such ethnographic texts, where 'observable data and received wisdom occupied the same space'.[86] A fictional text constructed from the ethnographic tradition of cataloguing, 'Assaulted and Pursued Chastity' represents hair as a component of knowledge about culture – about people, social structures of power and inter-cultural power relationships.

While the fantastic skin colours of Cavendish's orange and purple people secure their place in a land of fancy, since their colours fall outside the usual taxonomy of human hues, her characters possess a range of much less fantastic physical characteristics which were frequently accorded to non-European inhabitants of the world.[87] The black teeth of Cavendish's purple people are, according to Samuel Purchas, characteristic of the people of India – in Pegu and Cambaya – of Japan and of some inhabitants of the New World.[88] The tufted hair worn by the priests is reported by John Frampton to characterize the men of Tartar, who are 'of an evill shape' and beardless, 'in the forepart of their heads [...] weare their hayre long like the women of our country'.[89] John Bulwer's chapter on the hairstyles of various nations in *Anthropometamorphosis* attributes a tufted hairstyle to the 'Japonians', who believe it, he says, to be a great beauty to pluck out all the hair but of a bunch of hair, tied together, at the crown.[90] Thomas Herbert suggests that the woolly-haired Ethiopians shave their heads to create tufted hairstyles, too: 'some shave one side, and leave the other long and curled. A second shaves all off (one tuft, a top excepted) a third makes five tufts, the skull shaved betweene: others have a little haire before, bauld else-where, not unlike occasion.'[91]

More specifically, the straight and 'woolly' hair of the orange and purple people draws on contemporary representations of the inhabitants of the New World and Africa. As Iyengar observes, the purple people have typically African hair.[92] Cavendish's use of the word 'wool' is common in descriptions of the hair of Africans. In Thomas Herbert's account of his travels to Africa and Asia, the 'Savage Inhabitants' of the Cape of Good Hope, of a 'swarthy' dark colour with 'flat noses, and blubberd lips', have the hair of Cavendish's purple people: 'Their heads are long, their haire curld, and seeming rather wooll, then haire; tis blacke and knotty.'[93] Charles de Rochefort's *The History of the Caribby-Islands* (1658), published first in France and translated into English in 1666, describes the hardy African inhabitants of the island: 'They are all Negroes, and those who are of the brightest black are accounted the fairest: Most of them are flat-nos'd, and have thick lips, which goes among them for beauty [...] The hair of their heads is all frizl'd, so that they can hardly make use of Combs.'[94] The inhabitants of Guinea, according to Richard Blome, are 'of a Corpulent body, flat nosed, broad shouldered, white eyed and teeth'd, small eared, &c.', while Ethiopians are 'of a good stature, flat nosed, woolly haired, of a nimble spirit, and very jovial'.[95] The hair of Behn's African prince, Oroonoko, is distinguished from that of other Africans by not being 'frizzled' or 'woollen' but hair 'down to his shoulders, by the aids of art, which was by pulling it out with a quill and keeping it combed'.[96] The word 'wool' linked African hair to servility, even animality, and continued to be used in the eighteenth century in advertisements for runaway slaves and for slave auctions, where the wool justified enslavement. Dark-skinned and kinky-haired slaves were regarded as less beautiful and therefore less valuable, while the scientific community would also come to relegate the 'woolly'-haired people to the bottom of the evolutionary ladder.[97] Historically, for Africans themselves, hair was 'a complex language system [...] used to indicate a person's marital status, age, religion, ethnic identity, wealth and rank within the community'.[98] But for Cavendish, and for her European contemporaries, African hair is merely a marker of absolute subjection, even to other colonized subjects.

The black hair of Cavendish's higher ranked orange people is like the black-haired indigenous inhabitants of the New World, who were often said to have hair more like Europeans in texture, if not always in colour. The indigenous people in Aphra Behn's Surinam are nearly orange in colour ('reddish yellow'), and they have 'long black hair and the face painted in little specks or flowers here and there'. Blome describes the natives of Florida as 'an Olive-colour, great stature, but well proportioned; their hair is black, which they wear very long'. The native inhabitants of Canada (his name for much of eastern North America) have dark hair, 'never light or red'.[99] Kim F. Hall argues that early narratives of travel to Africa did not immediately dismiss the inhabitants as 'savage', but assessed them 'according to their projected malleability to Eurocentric forces'.[100] Travel writers came to see the natives of the New World as more civilized than Africans because they were perceived to be more malleable, a preference that makes itself visible in descriptions of their more European hair. William Strachey describes the hair of the natives of Virginia by distinguishing it from African hair: 'Their hair is black, gross, long, and thick; the men have no beards; their noses are broad, flat, and full at the end, great big lips, and wide mouths, yet nothing so unsightly as the Moors.'[101] So, too, for Richard Ligon, who writes in *A True and Exact History of the Island of Barbados* (1657) of his sense of the superiority of Native Americans to the African slaves. Not only are Natives more apt to learn than 'the Negroes', 'Indian' women 'are more of the shape of the European than the Negroes, their hair black and long, a great part whereof hangs down upon their backs as low as their haunches, with a large lock hanging over either breast, which seldom or never curls'.[102] Hair explains social structures. The straight, black hair of those brought to the island to be slaves marks them as superior to the African slaves but less worthy than the Europeans, whose more temperate, curlier hair is not so black. Margaret Cavendish's 'system of representation', her taxonomy of cultures, is a pastiche of references to travel literature by her contemporaries. She repeats and rearranges the purportedly authoritative observations of body parts by travel writers and geographies, works that are themselves not simply experimental but also historical, citing predecessors as if to prove what the travellers see. Her orange and purple people are less fanciful than a rearrangement of the already known that enables the production of new knowledge about women, who become capable of ruling such subjects. The consequences of this physiological pastiche are anything but uncontrolled.

Tony Ballantyne and Antoinette Burton argue for 'the centrality of bodies – raced, sexed, classed and ethnicized bodies – as sites through which imperial and colonial power was imagined and exercised'.[103] In 'Assaulted and Pursued Chastity', the Captain and Travellia attack the bodies of their subjects with a vegetarian diet of salad and water, being careful not actually to starve them, for excess hunger would make them prone to rebellion. Cavendish imagines the bodies of colonial subjects will be both submissive and adaptable to the inculcation of manners. Travellia lectures the natives on philosophy, with a discourse about souls and spirits, and forbids their 'Vain and Barbarous Customs, and Inhuman Ceremonies' (442). The people are converted, and the two continue to teach, to live in splendour, to have the love of the people and to be their law. When they weary of the honours afforded them, and because 'an humble and mean Cottage is better beloved by the Owner, than the bravest and stateliest Palace, if it be another's' (448), they decide to attempt to return home, after offering further instructions to the King to rule with love and peace and, to his people, to obey. They leave behind all of the country's riches, departing with only their own boat and enough to 'defray their charges in a time of necessity' (450). The two demand complete cultural change, but not the transfer of wealth. Although Travellia's freedom is short-lived, for she is soon captured by pirates, she then becomes a soldier and wins a battle against the Prince's powers, so that when she eventually marries him, the dynamics of their relationship are transformed. He has learned self-governance, and they determine that 'he should govern her, and she would govern the Kingdom' (512). The heterosexual marriage with which the narrative ends allows Travellia to become as politically powerful in her new homeland, the Kingdom of Amity, as she was in the Kingdom of Fancy. The temporary possibilities for fracturing patriarchal control available in a colonial context are also possible in a marriage where female political power splinters a husband's command.

Externalizing class, Cavendish's representation of hair reflects a desire for a stable social order based on class hierarchy and for English superiority. Historically, in England, aristocrats and commoners might share the same colour of hair and skin, even if outdoor work, malnutrition and sickness practically distinguished them. In England, a masquerade of class identity was possible, for people of low birth might be raised, through marriage, perhaps, or business, and become indistinguishable from those with status by birth. The physiological features of the people in the Kingdom of Fancy render such social movement impossible, for their origins are indelibly marked on their skin and in their hair. The story is also a fantasy of European superiority in cross-cultural contact, where aristocratic, European bodies induce awe and submission in those who encounter them. Returning to Anne McClintock's idea that race, class and sexual difference are coming into being in relation to each other, we can see Cavendish producing race through a hair story.[104] With the politically dominant and culturally transformative power of the hair of a woman from the Kingdom of Riches, Cavendish establishes that bodies can more surely and meaningfully articulate differences of culture, class and access to power than gender difference.

Conclusion

Beautiful hair is shaped as much by cultural ideas about power as by hairdressing. In early modern England, natural hair renders ideology visible. Hair is a sign of blood, of aristocratic kinship relations, of where one comes from. Hair might ensure social cohesion, not only through hairstyles developed on a shared understanding of social and aesthetic values but also because the physiology of the hair imagines an essentialized group identity. Hair also ensures social distinction, setting people apart from each other on the basis of class and ethnicity. Within this framework, Wroth posits the cross-dressed head as proof of the artifice of gender difference amongst the socially powerful. For Cavendish, on the other hand, female hair and boy's clothes combine to create a hermaphroditic figure capable of absolute political power. Both writers disentangle women's hair from its gendered meanings, from weakness and subordination. Cavendish gives Travellia 'a Masculine and Couragious Spirit in her' that enables her to win a war for the Queen she serves against the Prince who pines for her (476), while Wroth documents an affective weakness at the heart of masculinity that can be overcome with feminine hair. For both, hair is powerful, but not because it is seductive. These are not hair stories where female hair proves a temptation or a net that traps men with its erotic force; hair is not powerful because it is like Stella's locks, her 'day-nets' from which 'none scapes free'.[105] Through cross-dressing, Wroth and Cavendish change hair's story and re-imagine the context in which it can function. They write themselves into a history of class conflict and empire, challenging female subordination with powerful, essentialist constructions of class identity that provide the frame for imperial power. 'Everything I know about American history', Lisa Jones writes in *Bulletproof Diva: Tales of Race, Sex, and Hair,* 'I learned from looking at black people's hair. It's the perfect metaphor for the African experiment here: the price of the ticket (for a journey no one elected to take), the toll of slavery, and the costs of remaining. It's all in the hair.'[106] The history of empire is marked in English hair too. That history is written by medical texts, travel writing and in fiction that imagines long, thick, slightly curled hair as an ideal that is not only beautiful but privileged and politically active in rationalizing dominance.

6

An 'absolute Mistris of her Self': Anne Clifford and the Luxury of Hair

We know Anne Clifford, the Countess of Pembroke, Dorset and Montgomery (1590–1676), best as the diarist and formidable combatant in the lengthy inheritance dispute that ensued when her father, George Clifford, the Earl of Cumberland, bequeathed his estates to his brother, Francis Clifford, rather than to her.[1] We do not think of her as a woman who was concerned with beauty and appearances, perhaps because to do so would seem to diminish her intelligence and tenacity. Yet, it should be clear by this point in the book that in early modern England one's appearance was not necessarily a trivial matter. Hair was not inconsequential for Anne Clifford, either. It is a matter of record, documented by her in portraits, life-writing, account books and her chronicles of her family history. Hair becomes what Marina Warner calls a 'language of the self': 'like language, or the faculty of laughter, or the use of tools, the dressing of hair in itself constitutes a mark of the human. In the quest for identity, both personal and in its larger relation to society, hair can help.'[2] In the previous chapter I discussed how hair articulated gender, class and ethnic identity. Hair is also a visceral expression of history and ageing, and this chapter explores how Anne Clifford's use and rejection of hair's requisite beauty practices manifest her changing approaches to the ideology of luxury and the consumption of luxury goods – things that are characterized as refined, pleasing, comfortable, transient and superfluous.[3]

Although most contemporary feminist scholars approach hair through an analysis of race and gender, hair has also been treated as a register of the history of consumption, particularly with regard to the eighteenth century. In *Big Hair*, Grant McCracken observes that women in the 1770s wore their hair in elaborate, big, ornamented styles as a form of what Thorstein Veblen called 'surrogate consumption' to provide evidence of their husbands' wealth.[4] Louisa Cross also proposes that both men and women in eighteenth-century England adopted theatrical hairstyles – high hair, big wigs – to garner attention in the '"social theatre" of public life'.[5] Big hair and conspicuous consumption did not necessarily align so neatly in the seventeenth century; women's hair was simply not as lofty, and the use of luxury goods, while culturally significant, was governed by a different ethos. Linda Levy Peck argues that while the ethics of luxury were essential to understandings of the self, gender and social relationships, there were at least two ethical constructions of luxury and conspicuous consumption in the seventeenth century: some thought it moral to consume what was appropriate to one's status, while others maintained that morality demanded the rejection of luxury as an effeminate devaluation of one's status.[6] Woodruff D. Smith likewise posits two conflicting approaches in the period. Luxury consumption could be regarded as an expansive, positive economic force or as a sinful drain on resources to be avoided in favour of the moderation critical to civility and governance by gentlemen.[7] Suspicion of luxury was not unique to the period. Early modern thinkers wrote within a long tradition of Christian theologians who linked luxury to lechery, and so to sexual corruption and effeminacy.[8] Alan Hunt puts the point this way: 'Luxury is the feminine, and the feminine is not only in itself weak, but – as in the Samson myth – it undermines the masculine principle of self-sufficiency and hardiness.'[9] Samson brings us back to hair. If his can be a story of enfeebling luxury, it is also a hair story. Samson's long mane is not in the conventionally masculine early modern style, but Will Fisher's reading of Milton's Samson is useful in explaining one early modern link between hair and luxury. Milton, Fisher contends, establishes Samson's masculinity through an absence of ornament, associated more with 'bedeckt' Dalila.[10] The seventeenth-century discourse of luxury infiltrates the discussion of hair through the moralizing of ornament, a social contest around the just use of goods.

Hair is a placeholder for ethical behaviour with respect to consumption. Gustav Ungerer writes that in the Middle Ages women's hair was 'the stamp of lechery personified in Luxuria. It was seen as a trap set by Lechery to lock men in the lascivious embraces of flowing tresses.'[11] Early modern conduct books relied extensively for their tonsorial guidance for women on Biblical sources which characterized women's hair as a type of clothing subject to the same sumptuary laws as dress. Behind the dictum of 1 Corinthians 11:14 and 15 that men should have short hair and women long, discussed in the previous chapter, is the principle that women's 'hair is given her for a covering'; God gave women long hair as clothing to cover the corrupt female body to make her fit for the eyes of God. In addition to being long, women's hair should also be fashioned in a plain style and controlled. 1 Timothy 2:9 states that women should 'adorn themselves in modest apparel, with shamefacedness and sobriety; not with broided hair, or gold, or pearls, or costly array', and 1 Peter 3:3 couples the wife's subjection to the husband to avoiding 'outward adorning of plaiting the hair, and of wearing of gold, or of putting on of apparel'. Juan Luis Vives quotes these verses when he recommends that instead of braided, bejewelled or dyed hair, a woman should merely comb her hair 'cleanly; nor lette her not suffer her head to be full of scurfe', and wash her hair instead to keep it from stinking.[12] In addition to distinguishing her from men, a lady's hair should be evidence of a disciplined body that avoids the physiological excess of scurf and the sumptuary excess of ornament. *A Looking-Glasse for Women* (1644), a manual protesting the outward adorning of hair, contends that ornamenting hair with braids or curls is a form of unlawful attire – light, vain, proud, unseemly – such that even if women amongst those 'the Lord is so pleased to bestow this worldly wealth upon' might dress in the silver and gold appropriate to their rank, they may not 'weare their haire out'.[13] Hair is a sensitive register of chastity and obedience within a patriarchal family structure, but it is also a medium with which to display status. For the critics of hairdressing, it is by eschewing the latter ornamental function that the woman shows that she is under control. A woman must style her hair to manage the threat to patriarchal authority that her class might present. I discussed this conflict between class and gender hierarchies in Chapter 3. Hair can become still more challenging than luxurious clothing to male superiority because hair is a part of the body. Embodying class identity, loose hair is more sumptuous than silver, braided hair as luxurious as gold.

For seventeenth-century men, too, hair was subject to sumptuary regulation. The question is less of ornament than of length. The distinction between Cavalier and Roundhead was polemically based on hair (if not always so clearly demarcated in reality). The Cavalier, exemplified by Charles I, had long flowing locks, often including a lovelock to honour the object of his desire, and the Roundhead purportedly assumed a shorter style.[14] William Prynne's invective against the lovelock regards a man's hairstyle as an indication of his ideological perspective on the use of goods. He lists the sin of prodigality amongst his many complaints about lovelocks and long hair, along with effeminacy, foreignness and pride. Men who wear lovelocks 'cause a prodigall, vaine, and great expence, sufficient to relieve the wants, and miseries of many poore distressed Christians, who starve for want of succour and relief'; the only people taken up with 'Frizeling, Frouncing, Colouring, Powdring, or nice Composing of their Haire', he says, are 'Incontinent, Vaineglorious, Proud, Sloathfull, Carnall, or Luxurious persons: who are altogether prodigall, and carelesse of the Beautie, Culture, and Salvation of their Soules: who are Negligent, and Sloathfull in God['s] Service, and in the practice of all Holy dueties'.[15] Long hair signifies waste and selfish parsimony. The Roundhead, says *A New Anatomie, or Character of a Christian, or Round-head* (1645), is glorious in his financial prudence. He possesses inner 'Apparel more costly than Salomons in all his royaltie [...] Being like the Kings daughter all glorious within, though hee weare his worst side outmost'.[16] Concerned more with spiritual things, the Roundhead does not show himself to be the possessor of luxury goods. The visceral mark of that economic restraint is his short hair.

During the course of her long life, Anne Clifford's hair denoted first the legitimate possession of luxury goods suitable to her station as the daughter of the Earl and Countess of Cumberland and then her disciplined self-governance as the Baroness of Westmorland. It is possible to examine the shifts in Anne Clifford's understanding of her hair in portraits, in her life-writing and in her account books. Inscriptions in 'The Great Picture', a triptych commissioned by Clifford in 1646 and often attributed to Jan Van Belcamp, claim that the side portraits are of Lady Anne Clifford at the age of 15, the year of her father's death, and then as she is 'now Countess of Pembrooke', having inherited her father's property with the death of her cousin in 1643.[17] The portraits of the 15-year-old and 56-year-old Anne Clifford frame and refract the central panel which pictures the Countess of Cumberland, the Earl of Cumberland and Lady Anne's two older brothers, Francis and Robert, who died young. Additionally, her *Great Books of Record* (Cumbria Record Office Hothfield MS WD/Hoth/A988/10) and two of her account books – one kept between 1600 and 1602, when Clifford herself was a girl between the ages of 10 and 12 (Beinecke Library Osborn MS B27) and another for the years 1665 and 1667–1668 when she was a widow between the ages of 75 and 78 (Cumbria Record Office Hothfield MS WD/Hoth/A988/17) document Clifford's changing approaches to dressing her hair and herself. Anne Clifford's account books are, like her better known diary, a form of life writing. In chronicling some of the same events as the yearly summaries compiled for the *Great Books of Record,* even using the same language, Anne Clifford's account books are a record of her life, her movements, her labour and the economics of her social life. The account book provides the script by which good social relations can be retained. The *Great Books of Record* are a collection of documents tracing the Clifford family history from the Norman Conquest onwards. Many of the records were preserved by Margaret Clifford and copied for her daughter by Roger Dodsworth, an antiquarian.[18] There are three volumes: Books I and II are legal documents, family trees and life histories of her male and female medieval and Tudor ancestors, while Book III continues that history into the present with Anne Clifford's own reflections on herself, her birth, her parents, her marriages and yearly summaries of events between 1650 and 1676. Like the legal records that precede it, the Countess of Pembroke's writing of her own life is proof, as the title page of Book I indicates, of 'the right title, which her only childe, the Lady Anne Clifford, now Countes of Pembroke, Dorsett & Montgomery had to the Inheritance of her ffather, and his Auncestors'.[19] The *Great Books of Record* are deeply teleological documents positioning the Countess as the natural end of their history. The summaries of the lives of her father's heir, Francis Clifford, 4th Earl of Cumberland, and Henry, the 5th Earl, are provided merely 'by way of digression'.[20] Together, these portraits, accounts and crafted historical documents provide a record of the state of Anne Clifford's hair throughout her life and of the function of that hair as a language of the self.

Lady Anne Clifford's Inheritance of Beauty

For Anne Clifford, to write history is not only to create and compile textual records of the past, as she does with the *Great Books of Record*. To record history is also to generate a visual account, as she does with the monuments she built to the memory of her parents: the life-size effigy of her mother built in her memory at Appleby Church, the alabaster monument for her father's grave, and the pillar which still stands on the location near Brougham Castle commemorating the occasion in 1616 when she last saw her mother alive.[21] 'The Great Picture' is the visual and textual record of the history of how Anne Clifford looked at two distinct historical moments and a testament to her family history and her reading. The textuality of this portrait distinguishes it from other Elizabethan and Jacobean pictures with which Clifford was familiar. Ann Jones and Peter Stallybrass point to portraits of her father and first husband – Nicholas Hilliard's painting of George Clifford, Earl of Cumberland, and Isaac Oliver's and William Larkin's pictures of Richard Sackville, 3rd Earl of Dorset – as examples of one approach to portraiture. These pictures are 'as much the portraits of clothes and jewels as of people – mnemonics to commemorate a particularly extravagant suit, a dazzling new fashion in ruffs, a costly necklace or jewel' that reveal 'a subject composed through textiles and jewels, fashioned by clothes'.[22] 'The Great Picture' likewise composes the subject through clothes – and hair – but the textiles and pearls are supplemented with texts that interpret and explain the image.

The dress and the hairstyle of the young Anne Clifford pictured in the left panel of the triptych recall elements of her mother's appearance. The picture draws attention to the richness of her clothing, from the headdress of jewels, to the open ruff of cut linen, to the sea-water green satin gown embroidered with orange flowers and owls down the front, around the bottom, and on the slashed sleeves.[23] The Countess of Cumberland has her hair drawn up, like her daughter's, with pearls at the back of the head, and she wears a dark coloured overdress embroidered in gold, over a satin petticoat, a ruff, and strings of pearls.[24] The eyes of the young Anne Clifford look out of the painting in the same direction as her mother's do in the central panel, although their bodies are positioned differently, to face towards each other. Their eyes, noses and mouths have a similar colour and shape, and identical, fashionable peaks of hair on their foreheads frame their faces. Anne Clifford considered the significance of these physiological similarities in the autobiographical section of the *Great Books of Record,* subtitled 'A summary of the records and a true memorial of the life of me':

> I was very happy in my first constitution both in mind and body, both for internal and external endowments, for never was there child more equally resembling both father and mother than myself. The colour of mine eyes were black like my father, and the form and aspect of them was quick and lively like my mother's; the hair of my head was brown and very thick, and so long that it reached to the calf of my legs when I stood upright, with a peak of hair on my forehead, and a dimple in my chin, like my father, full cheeks and round face like my mother, and an exquisite shape of body resembling my father. But now time and age hath long since ended all those beauties, which are to be compared to the grass of the field.[25]

This brown, thick, long hair – the very aristocratic hair discussed in the previous chapter – is visible in the portrait, piled up and decorated with pearls. Anne Clifford's hair is a matter of record, evidence that her blood is strong and her constitution balanced, as the possessors of such hair were thought to be.

1   Left-hand panel from 'The Great Picture' depicting Lady Anne, Countess of
Dorset, Pembroke and Montgomery (1590–1676) aged 15, 1646

Lady Anne Clifford records the details of her mother's appearance even beyond the visual image in the portrait. An inscription on the painting describes the Countess of Cumberland as 'a greate naturall witt and judgment, of a sweete disposition, truly religious and virtuous, and indowed with a large share of those 4 morrall virtues – Prudence, Justice, Fortitude, and Temporance'.[26] Anne Clifford's biography of her mother, her 'Records concerning the virtuous and Religious Lady, the Lady Margarett, Countesse Dowager of Cumberland' in the *Great Books of Record*, develops this character further. The Countess was 'from her very infancie, soe religious, devout, and conscientous, as the like hath scarce beene known. Besides, she was endowed with many excellent perfections both of body and mynd more then can be expressed by woords.'[27] Decking this catalogue of her inward virtues with a description of her external appearance, Clifford adds that her mother was 'naturally of a high Spiritt, though shee tempered it well by grace haveing a ^very^ well favoured face with sweete and quick gray eyes and of a comely personage. She was of a gracefull behaviour which she increased the more by her being civil and courteous to all sorts of people' – as well as having a discerning spirit, a great wit, and an excellent mind, well read in books in English.[28] This intelligence the mother conveyed to her daughter, for '[s]he did with singular care, and tendernesse of affection educate and bring upp her said most deare, and only daughter, the Lady Anne Clifford, Seazeninge her youth with the groundes of true religion and morall vertue, and all other qualities befitting her Birth'.[29] Clifford's representation of her mother's beauty mitigates the potential stigma of two aspects of her mother's life: that her father and mother did not live together for some years because of conflict between them and that her mother was engaged in legal disputes with her husband's heir over the inheritance of her daughter. The Countess's beauty is evidence that she is virtuous – a good woman despite her legal disputes – while her wit and judgement are revealed in the books on the shelf above her head.

In equating beauty and virtue, Anne Clifford recalls the Neoplatonic tradition articulated at the Elizabethan court in Thomas Hoby's transla-tion of Baldesar Castiglione's *Book of the Courtier*. This book stands on the shelves above the 15-year-old Anne Clifford's head in 'The Great Picture' as one of the books she read in her youth.[30] In Book 4 Peter Bembo rejects the charge that beautiful women can be cruel and wicked by defending the proposition that

> beauty springs from God and is like a circle, the centre of which is goodness. And so just as one cannot have circle without a centre,

so one cannot have beauty without goodness. In consequence, only rarely does an evil soul dwell in a beautiful body, and so outward beauty is a true sign of the inner goodness. This loveliness, indeed, is impressed upon the body in varying degrees as a token by which the soul can be recognized for what it is, just as with trees the beauty of the blossom testifies to the goodness of the fruit.[31]

For her daughter, the Countess of Cumberland's beauty is irrefutable evidence that her resistance, far from being shrewish or monstrous, is divinely sanctioned. Reinforcing this point, Anne Clifford provides an account of a 'great divyne' who thought it a great happiness that she was descended from such a woman, who, like gold, had been tried and clarified by unkindnesses.[32] In connecting her youthful appearance to her beautiful, good mother through their hair and face, as well as their books, Anne Clifford polemically articulates her maternal history of virtue, recognizing that critics might see her mother merely as a disobedient, litigious troublemaker.

Anne Clifford also links her appearance to her father's. In her 'Life of Me', the colour of her eyes, the dimple in her chin and the shape of her body she credits to the Earl of Cumberland. Depending on how one interprets her syntax, her hair might be like her father's, too. In the portrait, it is brown, thick and long enough to reach his shoulders. On the portrait itself, she records that the Earl is a 'man of many naturall perfections, of a great witt and judgment, of a strong body, and full of agillity, of a noble mind, not subject to prid nor arrogancy, a man generally beloved in this kingdom'.[33] The portrait of the Earl of Cumberland in 'The Great Picture' is based, according to Aileen Ribeiro, on a 1590 miniature by Nicholas Hilliard (National Maritime Museum MNTO 193), although his rich blue coat has been replaced in 'The Great Picture' by a plainer brown one.[34] The elaborate hat in the Hilliard portrait, topped with a towering feather and Elizabeth's glove, has similarly dwindled to a plain fabric hat. The armour he wears under the coat remains visible on his forearms and legs, as the armour that he wore when, as Knight of Pendragon Castle, he became the Queen's Champion in 1590, the year of Anne Clifford's birth.[35] The armour establishes the Earl of Cumberland's body as publicly heroic and strong, its shape even preserved for posterity in metal (another of the Earl's suits of armour survives, decorated with a Tudor Rose, the Fleur-de-lis and the letter E at the Metropolitan Museum of Art).[36] To have a body that resembles such a father is to have a body whose shape is precisely marked by English history and nobility, and with the portrait's change of clothes, by a discipline that eschews the luxurious trappings of feathers and blue velvet. With this portrait and her narratives of herself and of her parents in the *Great Books of Record*, Anne Clifford assesses her looks historically. Her appearance is an inheritance of virtue, intelligence and heroism, a self-construction that aligns with her overarching concern with paternal legitimacy, class status and resistance to patriarchal disinheritance. The daughter who was disinherited was beautiful and therefore good; she had inherited her father's looks, his blood and should inherit his land.

In addition to having long, thick hair, Lady Anne Clifford also has fashionable hair. The natural inheritance she has in the hair itself is supplemented with ornaments that document her wealth and access to luxury goods. Her hair may not be big, but it does register her consumption. In 'The Great Picture', her hair is up, seemingly over a roll, and wound about with a string of pearls. The image of Lady Anne's head used in 'The Great Picture' is very like that found in a line engraving by Robert White (NPG D13681), made from a 1603 portrait by an unknown artist. Here, too, she has her hair up, with small curls by her ears, and decorated with a string of pearls; in the engraving a large jewel hangs from the pearls, touching her forehead.

The account book kept for Lady Anne Clifford between the years 1600 and 1602, from almost the same period as that purportedly pictured in the portrait, suggests that the young Anne Clifford did wear her hair in this way when she was a girl. Her hairstyle is a component of her consumption of luxury goods. If the meaning of Lady Anne Clifford's hair is conferred by its status as a natural inheritance from her parents, it also has significance as a part of the body to be dressed, ornamented and cared for in fashionable and luxurious ways. From a shop in Cheapside where she also purchased three pairs of gloves and a dozen silk point roses, she purchased a hair brush for 7d (f.14), two combs for 3s (f.15), and a 'litle coombe bruishe' for 2d (f.32).[37] Her long, thick hair is cared for, controlled and laid over wires, for there are records of the purchase of a 'weyer for her la[dyshi]p head' at 2s 6d (f.13*v*), a 'hare wyer' at 5s (f.31), 12 yards of white tape for hair lacing at 5d (f.15*v*) and a 'heare rolle' at 15d (f.32*v*). Mistress Goodwin bought her a head bench, too, in addition to four pairs of white gloves and hair-coloured taffeta (f.32*v*). With these accessories, young Lady Anne dresses her hair in the styles fashionable for adult women in the early seventeenth century. The account also documents other fashionable head coverings. She pays 4d for the 'drawing of a coiffe', a close fitting cap (f.29), and then 5s for a wrought coif and

2   Anne, Countess of Pembroke (Lady Anne Clifford), 1603

forehead cloth and 9d for a 'peke', the front part of a headdress. Two
yards of bone lace, worth 6d, are 'to edg my La a coyffe & cross clothe'
(f.33), another name for a linen cloth worn on the forehead. Certainly
Clifford's own young daughter would wear elaborate head-dressings,
for she records in her diary on 14 May 1617 that Lady Margaret 'left

off many things from her head, the weather growing extreme hot'.[38] The coifs Lady Anne wears as a girl confine her hair chastely, but they are also luxury items, white, embroidered and edged in lace, which ornament her hair.

Anne Clifford's hairstyles and head-dressings are one component of a wardrobe defined by luxurious surfaces and enlargements. Her linen coifs are not unlike the expensive fabrics she purchases for her gowns – silk, velvet and metallic textiles, including 16 yards of white 'shagge' (£3 12s), a cloth of silk or worsted with a velvet nap on one side (f.27v). Robert Hunter, a tailor, is paid 7s 10d 'for to make my La Anne white ryban Sypres gowne' (f.32), cypress being a cloth of gold, a high-quality satin, or a light material like cobweb lawn.[39] A Captain Davies, perhaps the most prestigious carrier, 'came to my La with Indean clothes' (f.12v). Like Margaret Spencer, discussed in Chapter 3, Anne Clifford is the owner of exotic Indian textiles at a young age and at an early stage of their entry into England. The linens she wears – cobweb lawn, cambric and holland for ruffs, handkerchiefs, smocks and bands – is sometimes striped with silver; one under-petticoat is lined and has a fringe (f.28v). The gowns, already of expensive fabrics, are made the more luxurious by their trimmings, the quantities of lace and ribbon which include for one gown, lawn, lace, silvered pearl and silvered wire (f.14) and for another, 'silver lace & parls of my la Annes gown' (f.25v). A full £5 goes to the silk man for silver lace, ruffs of silver and silk to trim her laces, which appear to match the shoes of silver and spangles purchased at the same time (f.25). Besides pink ribbon, hair-coloured ribbon, straw-coloured ribbon, and narrow and broad tinsel ribbon (a satin ribbon interwoven with gold or silver thread), she buys an expensive braid ribbon (f.22v), as well as girdles (a kind of belt) – one of silver pearl (f.15) – gloves, jewellery, stockings and shoes. She purchases during the period of the account book 12 pairs of gloves, of kid leather, cut-fingered leather, white kid leather, and, most expensively, a pair 'turnd downe wth oreng tawney' at 16d (f.31v) and a pair made of dog skin that cost 2s (f.28). The wearing of jewellery is suggested by the purchase of silvered wire 'to stringe pearles' (f.31).

Even as a child, Anne Clifford participates in the culture of luxury. Between the ages of ten and 12 when the account book was compiled, Lady Anne Clifford wore velvet, silk, pearls, and silver – from silver pile for a dressing to silver textiles, silvered pearl for a girdle, silver wire, and silver shoes. Anne Clifford, like the children discussed in Chapter 4, donned the expensive clothes appropriate to her parents' station.[40] Clifford herself says as much when she recalls in her memoir of 1603 that she was much used then to go to Court, for there was, 'as much hope and expectation of me both for my person and my fortunes as of any other young lady whatsoever'.[41] It would be easy to read her clothes simply as decoration meant to ensure a good marriage, but Clifford seems retrospectively to see in her youth a hope for her fortune rooted in her identity as a Clifford. Her stylish hair, expensive textiles, and the many ornamentations that decorate both the clothes and her head are evidence of a collective attitude towards luxury goods and serve as visible signs of the place that she should achieve, a place that the nature of her hair – its thick, abundant riches – reveals her already to have. Her consumption as a child is not about her own desires so much as an entrenchment of her place within aristocratic kinship relations. Lady Anne Clifford is becoming a lady under the direction of and with the economic assistance of women, first of all her mother, and then her mother's kin, especially her aunt and great-aunt, as well as her maternal uncle who provides her with gifts of clothes, money and other tokens.

Secure in her social position, the clothes and hair of the young Lady Anne Clifford strike a balance between luxury and chastity. Her confined and controlled hair – laid over wires or worn under a coif – is a long-standing component of the public presentation of female chastity. As Thom Hecht writes, 'the socially conspicuous nature of head hair makes it a versatile example of embodied power: disciplined hair is a powerful representation of controlling authority on and off the body'; disciplined hair – Hecht's example is the nineteenth-century school-mistress's bun – shows 'women in control or in need of control'.[42] Yet within the historically specific circumstances Clifford inhabits, controlling and structuring with rolls was read by some merely as variations on the crimes of painting, immodest dress or excess consumption. Like *A Looking-Glasse for Women*, Philip Stubbes applies the biblical rejection of braiding to contemporary fashions for curls and rolls:

> the trimming and tricking of their heades, in laying out their hair to the shew, which of force must be curled, frizled and crisped, laide out (a world to see) on wreathes and borders, from one eare to an other. And least it should fall down it is underpropped with forks, wiers, and I can not tell what, rather like grim and sterne Monsters, then chaste Christian matrones. Then, on the edges of their bolstered hair (for it standeth crested round about their frontiers and hanging over their faces like pendices or vailes, with glasse windowes an every side) there is laide great wreathes of gold and silver, curiouslie wrought and cunning-applyed to the temples of the head.

Curling the hair, buying other hair and dying it, and ornaments like hoods, caps, hats and cawls, especially when they are made of velvet, silk, gold and silver, are all of a kind and prideful.[43] Even the linen cap can be critiqued. The linen head covering must mark cleanliness and propriety, for linen was, says, Daniel Roche, 'a substitute for washing the skin' and it 'conferred respectability', something which aristocratic women had more of because they could buy more linens of a better quality.[44] Yet Lady Anne's coif is not just clean but embroidered (f.31) – just as her other linens are striped in silver or embroidered. Like Behn's Arabella Fairname, she possesses a conspicuous cleanliness. Even worse for hairstyling's critics, the bolstered hair, the curl and the jewel as supplements to the head are ornamental; they employ the head in the display of luxury goods and they allow women to broach the frontiers of their own bodies. As *A Looking-Glasse for Women* puts it, the woman who covers her head with ornamented hair has 'but a seeming covering, and no reall covering, and it will appear that it is rather an uncovering as you use it, then a covering, in that you take it out of its proper place, to hang it down in another place'.[45] Ornamented hair is not subjected hair but hair that reveals both status and agency.

The meaning of the size of young Anne Clifford's bolstered hair might also be elucidated by the size of her clothes, for her hair props are a component of a wardrobe full of under props and stiffenings. She acquires two farthingales (f.11v, 16v), and soon after the second purchase, Mistress Taylor spends 2d on farthingale wire for 'dressing' (f.16v). Wires enlarge her linens, too, for she wears standing collars, supported by the rabato wires she buys. Farthingales were the particular focus of satirical attack for their size until their popularity waned in the second decade of the seventeenth century; they could be connected to popishness – one style originated in Spain – deformity, and deception linked to sexual autonomy, for the wearing of large hoops about the waist could hide a pregnancy or mitigate a case of pox.[46] Hugh Latimer yokes farthingales and hair rolls to luxury in his sermon on St. Stephen's Day, 1552 on the text of Luke 2: 6–7. He criticizes the 'jolly Damsell[s]' of Bethlehem who would not humble themselves to visit Mary in her stable to comfort her in childbirth because they would 'study nothing els but howe they shall devise fine raimentes', attending to their bracelets and farthingales while the poor suffered for lack of 'necessaries'. According to Latimer, Mary not only rejected the wearing of farthingales and 'fine geare' to be content with 'honest and single garmentes' but she also eschewed the 'laying out the hayres artificially' as tokens of pride to be avoided.[47] In these terms, bolstered hair signals a sinful mode of consumption – a lack of charity and a desire for more than one's share. For Thomas Carew, too, the farthingale is like the hair roll, an outward manifestation of inward taint. In a sermon printed in 1603 on the text of 1 Peter 3, he writes: 'The want of religion in many women is seene in their apparrell, their harts being as hollow as their verdugales, their mindes being as light as their feathers.'[48] '[M]any now a dayes', he says, 'will have other faces or complexions, other haire, and other bellies, then God hath made them'. Women who wear their hair 'set up a fore like a forehorse toppe' and 'weare monstrous vardugales which as is saide, were invented by a strumpet to cover a great belly, which requires more stuffe, and takes up more roome in meeting then some of them are worth and worthy of' both challenge the prevailing gender order.[49] Size matters. With enlarged hair and enlarged gowns, women spatially contest their subordination. These things are not immodest in the contemporary sense, a standard dependent on revelation of the body; indeed, they cover the body. Nevertheless, the underwires in the clothes and hair seem less to fortify and discipline Lady Anne Clifford to chaste womanhood than to introduce her to a fashionable, courtly and threatening femininity. *Pleasant Quips for the Upstart New-fangled Gentlewoman* (1595) laments 'These flaming heades, with staring haire/these wyers turnde, like hornes of Ram', 'These glittering caules, of golden plate', that make women like peacocks, and busks which allow women to go like Amazons, in 'armours stout:/Wherein like Gyants, Jove they flout'.[50] Ornaments are dangerous. Sue Vincent says of the bolstered fashions in this period that 'extremity of dress form was matched by the extremity of its surface appearance'.[51] So, too, with hair, even if hair at the beginning of the seventeenth century was not in its shape as extreme as the styles that would follow in the eighteenth century. Early seventeenth-century hair had an artificial shape and a surface appearance that coordinated with the aesthetics of elaborately ornamented, embroidered and bejewelled clothing (like the hair of Wroth's Pamphilia, discussed in the previous chapter). Even as a very young woman, clothes and hair accorded Lady Anne Clifford access to a discourse of class-based power. Her hair and clothes mark her participation in the elite world of fashion and, as such, in a world where she occupied a position of some social power – the subordinate position of the child in relation to her parents and kin but a powerful class position in relation to much of England.

One important point to make about her consumption, however, is that it functions within a social context that materially protects her chastity. If critics like Philip Stubbes might charge that hair such as hers provides evidence of a lack of chastity, she actually consumes luxury goods chastely. She does not shop for them, and in this, her chastity is secure. Karen Newman argues that '[i]n the early seventeenth century, woman became the target for contemporary ambivalence toward that process [of commodification]. She is represented in the discourses of Jacobean London as at once consumer and consumed – her supposed desire for goods is linked to her sexual availability.'[52] Lady Anne Clifford, however, did not usually go shopping herself. Although she buys with her own hands an ivory box to house a picture, a rebato wire and a girdle of silver pearl (f.15), more often, Mistress Taylor (Anne Taylor her governess) and servants, Grace, Mistress Carrington and Mistress Goodwin, purchase the items on her behalf at various shops and the Royal Exchange.[53] The employment of female servants in this way differentiates the femininity of mistress and servant. According to Laura Gowing, the Royal Exchange was built for men, for 'confident male strolling' and left women in an ambiguous position because at night it was a place for prostitutes and for mothers to abandon their illegitimate babies, and where, during the day, women might be verbally or physically accosted; thus, 'the rhetoric of enclosure and the identification of female mobility with sexual and economic disorder shaped female identities and women's use of space'.[54] When it is Grace, Mistress Goodwin and Mistress Carrington, rather than Lady Anne Clifford, who go to market, they must negotiate the sexualized terrain of shopping, securing Anne Clifford's chastity by exposing their own. If moralizers might regard her sumptuary practices as unchaste in their attachment to luxury, the social context of that consumption and the bodies of the servants who shop for her materially protect her chastity. Luxury goods distance and distinguish her from one group of people (the merchants and lower class female servants) even as they tie her to another, the kin and friends who provided for her.

The account books, the portraits and the historical chronicles create a record of young Lady Anne Clifford's hair as a luxury good. Although Mihoko Suzuki has argued that Clifford rejects her youthful improvident consumption later in life, this chapter resists that dichotomy.[55] The clothes she acquires are clearly luxurious, but that luxury is not treated as wasteful, not least because it is carefully accounted for and authorized. The account book is made under the authority of the Earl of Cumberland, to whom it is addressed (the Earl is addressed throughout as 'your Lordship'). Her mother trains her in the ways of accounting and in meeting her own obligations to trades people, to the poor, to her servants, and the servants of the friends and relations who bring her things, as suggested by evidence of payments. Rather, she treats her hair as an inheritance, a sign that she is an heir. Her hair is the concentrated, embodied version of her identity as a daughter, its natural qualities revealing her to be chaste, aristocratic and worthy of the luxury goods with which she ornaments her head.

'Mistris of her Self': The Baldness of the Baroness of Westmorland

When she is older, Anne Clifford's portraits, history writing and accounts change the meaning of her hair. Just as Anne Clifford does not script the hair of her youth according to her culture's dominant narrative where female hair is an alluring seductive net, she does not follow precisely the role of the older woman who should give up sexual desire and retire from a world that deemed women's primary social function to be reproduction. Neither when she looks back at her youth nor when she contemplates herself as an older woman does she represent the meaning of her hair in relation to a heterosexual economy of desire. Hair is the cynosure of ageing. Clifford wrote of ageing as the death of beauty when she concluded her assessment of her youthful appearance in her 'Life of Me' on a melancholic note: 'time and age hath long since ended those beauties, which are to be compared to the grass of the field'.[56] Her view of the dissipation of beauty is a common one, forming the basis of the *carpe diem* poems in the seventeenth century. Richard Steele's *Discourse Concerning Old Age* prosaically links old age to beauty's departure, too. In old age, 'the Carkass of the Man remains, but the Beauty is changed into wrinkles, and the Strength into weakness. They had a pleasant prospect in their Glass, but their Flesh hath bid them farewell, their Roses and Lillies are withered, and a wan duskishness hath taken possession: their Strength and Beauty are buried both together.'[57] Hair's function as a particular sign of old age is explained by Henry Cuff in *The Differences of the Ages of Man's Life* (1640), a book that appears in 'The Great Picture' as part of Anne Clifford's mature library.[58] Because hair is made of 'the putrifaction of that excrementall humour', hair on vigorous bodies is vigorous, while 'hoary-headednesse proceeds from a defect of heate'.[59] For Francis Bacon, however, if grey hair is a sign of old age, it is also, when unaccompanied by baldness, a sign of long life (as is hard hair, 'like bristles').[60] Like a diary or a picture, hair is a historical register. It records physiological change, it is both dead and living, and it is both an excrement and a manifestation of the inward complexion, of diminished heat and desire.[61] Yet, when Anne Clifford is older, her hair does not merely turn grey – if it does this, she does not mention it – but it disappears, first under coverings and then by being cut off. The remainder of this chapter will explore this intervention. Angela Rosenthal writes that 'the growing, grooming, cutting, shaving or losing of hair – on the body and head – were often associated with transformative life experiences, with rites and rituals, and with the marking of cultural difference'.[62] For Anne Clifford, Countess of Dorset, Pembroke and Montgomery and after 1645 the Baroness of Westmorland, the disappearance of her hair seems to be associated with her emerging autonomy. The end of her beauty does not bring about worthlessness and death, as *carpe diem* poems suggested it might, but a vigorous life as a baroness. She held this title through her father rather than her husbands, by whom she became a countess. It is her position as a baroness that is, for Mary Chan and Nancy E. Wright, what Anne Clifford's legal battles were all about; not merely wealth, 'Westmorland was, for Lady Anne, an attribute of her "self."'[63] Resisting an ornamental social function for women, the Baroness uses her bald, covered head as a signifier of social power, as she retrospectively does with hair for her youthful self. But in her old age that social power was constituted not through the display of luxury goods but in showing a self-disciplined control of them. Clifford's baldness covered by a cap comes to document her power according to a privately masculine, rather than feminine script. She eschews sartorial luxury and ornament in the name of self-discipline and natural legitimacy, which are both masculine and appropriate to widows. With her hair, she ultimately engages in a kind of physiological cross-dressing that forges her social control.

In 'The Great Picture', the panel with the figure of young Lady Anne Clifford hangs opposite a full-length portrait of her after her cousin, Henry Clifford, the son of her father's brother Francis, had died. In this right-hand panel, the Countess of Pembroke appears in a black gown made of satin and adorned with pearls, a tapestry hangs off the table, and a drapery with a large gold tassel decorates the wall behind her. The books, too, are numerous and well-bound. If her black gown is much plainer than the one she wore when she was young, it subtly exhibits signs of her aristocratic identity. The fabric shines, the sleeves are slashed, and the linen collar and cuffs, in addition to being large, are also edged in lace. As with the white linen she purchased in her youth, the many yards of linen she displays here must even more insistently be a sign of 'a refined and disciplined body'.[64] More white linen covers her forearms in fitted sleeves under her large cuffs. Signs of cleanliness and discipline mix with other signs of wealth, for beneath the collar run two strings of pearls, and a girdle, also of pearls, hangs from her waist.

3   Right-hand panel from 'The Great Picture' depicting Lady Anne Clifford, Countess of Dorset, Pembroke and Montgomery (1590–1676) in middle age, 1646

Finally, her head is draped in a black cloth revealing only a small curl at her forehead and a longer one that peaks out at the side of her face. In accord with changing styles, her hair is not enlarged with rolls, but the head covering is still not fashionable. Unlike the portraits of Queen Elizabeth, which provided an unchanging picture of beauty, this picture of Anne Clifford marks her age and her changed relationship to beauty culture. When I viewed 'The Great Picture' when it was on display at the Tate Gallery in London, one other visitor walked into the hall, took a look at the picture, declared Clifford ugly, and left – a comment that suggests one viewer's continued expectation that women in pictures should always be beautiful. For Anne Clifford herself, ageing is marked in her hair, its covering, and her clothes, the garb, according to Eileen Ribeiro, of a widow or an old woman.[65]

The very format of 'The Great Picture' represents Clifford as a widow. The iconography recalls paintings which represent what Elizabeth Honig calls 'the Good Widow ideal'; such portraits, exemplified in that of Mary Neville, Lady Dacre, depict the wife's role as preserver of her husband's memory by placing the widow beside a portrait of her deceased husband.[66] The title page of the 1631 edition of Richard Brathwait's *The English Gentlewoman* similarly imagines constancy with an engraving of a woman saying 'Fancy admits to change of choice' while pulling aside a drapery to reveal her husband's portrait. So does the Countess of Pembroke stand beside the pictures of her husbands, the Earl of Dorset and the Earl of Pembroke. Her clothes are the black garb of widowhood, the gown, like the portraits, a sign of wifely loyalty, as black marked both mourning and the rejection of fashion; in black, the wife is not sexually available.[67] But these were not the only meanings of the widow's black dress. Catherine de Médicis, according to Sheila ffolliott, used the garb of widowhood as an 'iconography of power', as she cast for herself an appearance that was appropriate to a woman while also being assertive and powerful, since black was also worn by sober and wise men.[68] When Allison Levy looks at the 'work of mourning' done by a widow's black dress in portraiture, including Catherine de Médicis's, she asks if widows might not appropriate the masculine meanings of black dress; if, generally, black on a woman signified only her mourning, on men, according to Castiglione, it 'signified grace, seriousness, respect and distinction'.[69] Clifford is interested in these meanings of black dress, too. Despite the portrait's clear suggestion of two husbands remembered and a widow's sober garb, in 1646 Clifford was not a widow. She was 56 – she would live for 30 more years – and married to the Earl of Pembroke, who would not die until 1650, four years after the painting's commission. George Williamson describes Anne Clifford in 'The Great Picture' as a 'stately, but masculine figure', which actually seems to be the point, if his use of the word 'but' suggests something regrettable.[70] The black dress and covered head are appropriate to a woman because they are the costume of a widow, but in portraits of many of her male contemporaries, such serious, sober attire expresses their power, gravitas, wisdom and virtue. Many of the male portraits from the 1640s in the collection of the National Portrait Gallery use black and white dress precisely in this way, whatever the political affiliation of the sitter.[71] Just as these portraits embrace moderation, the necessary virtue in the gentleman, 'The Great Picture' shows Anne Clifford to be in full possession of these virtues. She is like her father, who has in her image of him in 'The Great Picture' donned a plain brown tunic rather than a more extravagant blue one, the plain brown hat rather than the one ornamented with a feather.

In addition to signifying gravitas, black dress and white linen on men could ostentatiously eschew ostentatious display in the name of inherent, natural superiority. While male non-conformists adopted such a style in the name of rejecting class hierarchy, they did not hold a monopoly on the meaning of the outfit. The Earl of Carlisle commented earlier in the seventeenth century that the Earl of Arundel's black dress 'in his plain stuff, and trunk hose, and his beard in his teeth, [...] looks more like a nobleman than any of us'.[72] The Earl of Clarendon said, too, of Arundel's clothes: 'He wore and affected a Habit very different from that of the time, such as men had only beheld in the Pictures of the most considerable Men; all which drew the eyes of most, and the reverence of many towards him, as the Image, and Representative of the Primitive Nobility, and the Native Gravity of the Nobles, when they had been most Venerable.'[73] Henry Peacham, a tutor in the Arundel household, in addressing his *Compleat Gentleman* (1622) to the Earl of Arundel's youngest son, William Howard, similarly urges thrift, but not baseness or parsimony, in apparel; a prince may dress plainly without derogating from his position.[74] The great are so, not because of their external appearance, but because their power is natural. It is not those who

weare the Cloath of a Noble Personage, or have purchased an ill Coate at a good rate; no more than a Player upon the Stage, for wearing a Lords cast suit; since Nobility hangeth not upon the ayery esteeme of vulger opinion, but is indeed of it selfe essentiall and absolute. Beside, Nobility being inherent and Naturall, can have (as the Diamond) the lustre but onely from it selfe; Honours and Titles externally conferred, are but attendant upon desert, and are as apparell, and the Drapery to a beautifull body.[75]

Here, the beautiful body is the one with noble blood, not the one ornamented by expensive clothes. The artifice of fashion can actually obscure a man's natural, class-based power because it can be a symptom of a performance; not confident in his own inherent power, he plays to the crowd with a display of luxury that merely shows he cares about the opinion of those ostensibly beneath him.

Clifford was not unaware of this approach. If the portraits of her finely dressed husbands are fabulous examples of the opposite point of view, she also knew the Earl and Countess of Arundel, who were painted in black dress and white linen in a double portrait by Daniel Mytens circa 1618 (NPG 5292 and 5293); this portrait signals, according to David Howarth, how 'Lady Arundel pursued her interests independently and separately from her husband whenever she so chose.'[76] Anne Clifford certainly knew Alathea (Talbot) Howard, for Clifford dined with her and the Countess of Arundel visited Clifford as well, including once before a contentious visit to King James; Clifford records that the Countess was 'exceeding kind with me'.[77] Printed together in 1641 and dedicated to Philip Herbert, Earl of Pembroke and Montgomery, and Anne Clifford, the Countess of Pembroke, Richard Brathwait's conduct book duo, *The English Gentleman* and *The English Gentlewoman*, expresses a similarly ascetic approach to beauty and blood. The ideal lady recommended to the Countess's service should be neat, dress with more care than cost, and reject fashion that is fantastic and foreign; coming from a 'nobly vertuous family', '[h]er life must express the line from whence she came. [...] As the blood that streames through her veines was noble derived, so must it not by any action or affection drawne from the rule of her direction, become corrupted.'[78] For the Baroness of Westmorland, too, appearance can be historical, expressing the line from whence she comes. But she is not Brathwait's beautiful, chaste ornament to the power of an aristocratic family. She holds that power as a widow, a gentleman in a dress.

Widowhood is for Anne Clifford less a marital state than a state of mind, an identity that she inhabited long before she actually became a widow. Erin Campbell draws attention to how early modern pictures of older women are often pictures of '"unenduring" female beauty', which 'negotiated masculine anxiety, above all, fears about growing old, a state which posed a potential threat to male virility, creativity, and power in certain contexts'.[79] For Anne Clifford, unenduring beauty is to be announced, as she does in the *Great Books of Record* and in the parallel panels of 'The Great Picture'. She is not negotiating male virility but articulating her autonomy. Because it is a physiological part of her body, her covered hair visually situates her outside the patriarchal economy of reproduction.

'The Great Picture' was not the first to resist constructing Anne Clifford as the beautiful wife. In Anthony Van Dyck's 'Philip, 4th Earl of Pembroke, and his Family' (1636), she is the Earl's wife and has the curled hair and pretty exposed forearms common in portraits of wives, but she is withdrawn from the group. Compared to portraits of wives in family portraits in the period, the Countess of Pembroke's dress is more like that of Sir Thomas Browne in the portrait of the physician and author, than his wife Lady Dorothy Browne (NPG 2062 by Joan Carlile), more like that of William Fairfax, 3rd Viscount Fairfax of Emley, than his wife Elizabeth (NPG 754 by Gerard Soest) and more like that of Arthur Capel, 1st Baron Capel, than Elizabeth, Lady Capel (NPG 4759 by Cornelius Johnson). The ladies are all dressed in gowns that are lighter, more colourful and more revealing of the shoulders or forearms. Their hair is curled in fashionable styles, as well and covered, if at all, only with lace. The Countess of Pembroke folds her arms close to her body and looks straight out of the painting, turning neither her body nor her head nor making eye contact with any of the nine other people in the painting, who do interact with each other and are dressed in more colourful garb – the Earl's two daughters in blue and silvery white and the sons in shades of red, brown and orange. The Earl is a famously fashionable man, and his family reflects this. His wife wears black and sits apart from them and their aesthetic values. She explains her marriage to the Earl of Pembroke in the *Great Books of Record* through her relationship to beauty culture. She notes that after the death of Richard Sackville, the Earl of Dorset – her other spectacularly fashionable courtier husband – she contracted smallpox, 'so extreamly and violently that I was at death's door and little hope of life in me'; the disease 'did so martyr my face, that it confirmed more and more my mind never to marry again; though the Providence of God caused me after to alter that resolution'. That is to say, she married Philip Herbert, not because she is fair – not implicitly because she is desired by him, or desires him – but because God ministers to 'the crossing and disappointing the envy, malice and sinister practices of my enemies'.[80] Her martyred face is a sign of providence: if her beauty is gone and yet she marries, God must be interested in the state of her inheritance. That she is no longer pretty – a state marked in the 'The Great Picture' by the covered forearms and the covered head – is visible evidence of the legitimacy of her desire for her land; God is working through history to give it to her.

4   Philip Herbert (1534–1650), 4th Earl of Pembroke and his family

In widowhood, women were to eschew beauty practices, fashionable clothes, cosmetics and hairdressing. The widow's hair, in particular, provides the cultural script for female autonomy and, as Baroness Westmorland, Anne Clifford uses it to her own purposes. According to Juan Luis Vives, a widow should 'lette passe al that trimming and araying of her body, which whe[n] her husband lived, might seeme to be done for pleasure: but when he is dead, all her life and al her apparrel must bee disposed and ordered after his will, that is successour unto her husband, that is immortall God unto mortall man'.[81] A woman might beautify to please her husband, but in his absence, the pleasure is merely her own and therefore dangerous; beauty practices, from this perspective, are justified only by a patriarchal sexual economy. Yet by the same logic, the wife who refuses to be beautiful disrupts that economy in refusing her husband's pleasure. 'The Widow's Glass', a translation from Latin of a conduct book by Fulvius Androtius, a Jesuit, printed in 1621 with *The Treasure of Vowed Chastity* likewise links a widow's appearance to her sexuality, located on her head. For him, the uncovered head of a widow signals the absence of the cardinal female virtues of chastity and silence; the bad widow plaits her hair and adds 'frizeled tops', whereas the good widow's 'untrimmed head knoweth this to suffice, that it is covered'. To be a good widow, a woman should 'take heed of adorning or attyring her head with pearles, Jewells, or pretious carcanets, nor use frizeled hayre; for these be the true signs of hell-fire'. She should instead be virtuous to gain Christ, 'the spouse of the soul'.[82] Hairstyles that might be appropriate to married women are not appropriate for widows. Widows must be physically disciplined; they should 'bring their body into servitude, and subject the same to the spirit, thereby to be able to serve their second spouse Christ Jesus, in their sacred and spirituall Marriage'.[83] The widow is a woman metaphorically lacking a head, a husband; by way of recompense, she must literally cover her head to signify her continued subjection to an invisible patriarch, to Christ who is her spiritual husband commanding her obedience and thus maintaining her feminine subject position even in the absence of a male governing power. *The Whole Duty of a Woman,* a conduct book printed first in 1695 that claims to be written by a lady, transforms the meaning of the widow's head covering from a symbol of her subjection to a visible sign of the disciplined female mind, a transformation more in line with the autonomous material conditions of widowhood. The book instructs widows to 'put on a more retired Temper of Mind, a Stricter and Soberer Behaviour, not to be cast off with your Vail, but to be the constant Adornment of your Widowhood', a state that 'requires a great Sobriety and Degrees of Piety'.[84] Here the widow's covered head signifies a mind that is sober, strict and temperate, as well as chaste – a mind, in short, much like that marked by the portraits of the men in black. It is true that the older woman's rejection of beauty practices is a form of conformity to her culture's rejection of the sexuality of older women, but by looking like a widow before she was one and continuing when widowhood became a reality, Anne Clifford develops a framework within her culture that allows her to picture herself as men could, as independent and self-disciplined.

The more masculine meanings of black clothes to which Anne Clifford aspires with her appearance become evident in the Countess of Pembroke's account book for 1665 and 1667–1668. Her austerity in clothes and her hairstyle – her beauty practices, or perhaps more properly, her unbeauty practices – provided access to authority. Even beyond being a visual signifying system, clothing and hairstyle are the outcome of social and economic relationships, and in this account book Anne Pembroke, as she signs herself, has power. Partly in her own hand, the account book is a much more far-reaching domestic document than the account book from her youth. Where the early account book told the story of her obligations to her parents and kin, the hundreds of pages in the later account book detail her obligations to her households and her history. In it she appears as a landowner, estate manager, building contractor, farmer, family matriarch and charitable donor. It details her reception of rents and outlay on the repair of castles, including the repair of walls, roofs, windows and chimneys, and the mending of field walls, mills and barns. Improving the interior of her castles, including Pendragon, Appleby and Brough, she pays for textiles for bed sheets and curtains, for tablecloths and napkins, and for window draperies, as well as for other movables like fireplace grates, bed cords in bedsteads, plate and glasses. With regard to outdoor activity, she pays for the purchase of livestock and seeds, as well as the planting and weeding of a garden, for horses, their care, and for saddles and other riding equipment, including cartwheels for her own use. Embedded in an extended community, she enlists the services of servants, ministers and lawyers and maintains or provides gifts of money and other things, including books, to family members and other acquaintances. In addition to the many articles of clothing she acquires for other people, she also pays for clothes and haircuts for herself.

Anne Clifford's hairdressing choices at this period of her life are an extension of the sartorial and tonsorial plainness visible in portraits from the 1630s onwards. She purchases caps, and she regularly cuts off her hair. This does not appear to be a mere trim. Anne Clifford records on 13 February 1665 that she gave to George Goodgion for 'cutting off the hayer of my Head: this morninge here in my chamber in Brougham Castle six shillinges this being ye second time I had my head shaven since I came last to lye in Brougham Castle'.[85] She pays the same sum again on 25 August 1665, in an entry in her own hand, 'for cutting of all hare of my hade now here in my chamber in this Appleby Castel'. She does the same in November of the same year at Brougham Castle, and again in August 1668, probably at Appleby. An entry made on 17 November 1668 suggests that having George Goodgion cut her hair is habitual: 'for cutting and shaving off the haires of my head as usuall six shillinges'. Her 'Day-by-Day Book', a manuscript narrative account of the events of the last months of her life, from January 1676 to 21 March of the same year records a more fulsome narrative of a haircut. On 22 February, she writes:

> Before I was out of my bed did I pare off the tops of the nails of my fingers and toes, and when I was up I burnt them in the chimney of my chamber, and a little after this in the same chamber of mine did George Goodgion clip off all the hair of my head, which I likewise burnt in the fire, and after supper I washed and bathed my feet and legs in warm water, wherein beef had been boiled and brann. And I had done none of this to myself since the 13th of December that George Goodwin cut my hair for me in this chamber of mine. God grant that good may betide me and mine after it.[86]

George Williamson identifies George Goodgion as a barber, and he might have been, in that he did regularly cut her hair. Anne Clifford had a barber in her household many years before – according to a 'Catalogue of the Household And Family of the Right Honourable Richard Earl of Dorset', which covered the period between 1613 and 1624, an Adam Bradford.[87] The Earl of Dorset sent his barber to trim his daughter, Lady Margaret's hair during a period of conflict between the Earl and his wife.[88] But Goodgion is also tasked with carrying rents to Craven and buying on Anne Clifford's behalf oxen, linens designed to be made into sheets, and books of devotion for her servants, amongst other things. He appears to be a servant, as much as anything, and haircare is part of his duties. No longer a young lady with thick hair decorated in pearls, hair so long it hangs to her waist, the Baroness is bald. As an older woman, she has a male servant shave her head in a practice that seems absolutely to defy the ornamental functions of hair.

Anne Pembroke's shorn head may have a medical impetus – as suggested by its place in the narrative alongside nail clipping and a foot bath – but the physiological balance that such medical haircuts might produce is more appropriate to men than women, for whom hair is a more strictly moralized, political covering. From Helkiah Crooke's perspective, hair has four purposes: cover, defence, ornament, and to 'consume and waste away the thicke and fuliginous or sooty excrements'.[89] Because hair consumes excrements, one should not keep one's head always covered and it may be necessary, depending on the time of the year, the country and the constitution, to cut the hair or allow it to grow longer in order to achieve the desired physiological balance. Crooke is against shaving the hair off altogether, believing baldness may 'prove the cause of defluxions'.[90] William Bullein argued in favour of the medical benefits of haircuts: 'The cutting of the haire, and the paring of the nailes, cleane keepeing of the eares, and teeth, be not only thinges comely and honest, but also holsome rules of Phisicke for to be superfluous things of the excrements'.[91] Levinus Lemnius agreed and posited that haircuts might improve the memory. When the weather is mild and the country temperate,

> I myslike not (as touchinge healthynesse of bodye) shavinge of the crowne of the head. For thereby grosse vapours which hurt the Memory, have more scope and liberty to evaporate and fume oute. And therefore some in my opynion, take a holesome way for healthynesse (so they do it without anye maner of superstition otherwise) which go pollshorne and have theyr heads shaven to the hard scalpe. For by this meanes all they that are encombred wyth Rhewmes, Catarrhes, and headach, fynde much ease, and so do all they that have theyr eyesighte (through abundance of humours) dymme, and theyr hearing thicke, and theyr smelling stopped.[92]

Hair is the result of the body's physiological balance and a haircut a potential medical treatment that rebalances the body's humours. That a haircut could improve the strength and the memory might explain Anne Clifford's shaved head, given that memory is central to her writing life. The *Great Books of Record* document precisely how remembering history is a method of resisting the subordinate position in which her society wanted to place her as a woman.[93] Megan Matchinske, for instance, describes Anne Clifford as a woman whose 'sense of identity is imbricated in notions of deep history – in an ancestral connection to family origin'.[94] Anne Clifford was certainly active and physically strong in her seventies, if her prodigious record of building, her purchase of a dozen pairs of spectacles with six cases and her acquisition of safegards (clothing for riding or travelling) for herself is anything to go by.

Even if a shorn head is medically logical, it entirely rejects the feminine script of womanhood in which hair plays a feature role, its length, as we have seen in the previous chapter, starring as the sign of difference between male and female. As a widow, Anne Clifford should not, according to moralizing constructions of widowhood, treat her hair as an ornamental, visceral medium for fashion. But she is not even managing her hair as a marker of her femininity. It is simply erased as a signifier. Her hair is not just short. It is shorn. In the seventeenth century this is transgressive: a rejection not just of sexualized femininity but also of feminine propriety itself. A shaved head could be regarded as a sign of popery. John Bulwer writes that 'for a Woman to be shorne, is cleerly against the intention of Nature' and reminds readers of how the Germans and Gauls shaved the heads of the adulterous woman in order to disgrace her, 'deprived of the peculiar Ornament of her sex';[95] both chastity and hair are the ornaments of women, and the loss of one necessitates the loss of the other. For him, it is lawful to cut the hair only 'to a just moderation: and as we prune luxurious Vines, so wee may take away and freely coerce that improsicuous matter of Haire'.[96] William Prynne recalls that nuns poll their heads on entrance into holy orders, another blight on the practice which he says has pagan origins in Roman culture; there is no religious reason, in his view, for women to cut their hair so short, the establishment of gender difference being the paramount moral principle. It is 'unfit for any but lewd Adulteresses and notorious Whores, (as many polled Nonnes and shorne-frizled English Maddames are)'.[97] Thomas Wall is explicit in his claim that a woman's long hair is essential, divinely given as a 'sign of her subjection to Man [...] for her hair is given her for a covering, namely to cover her Eyes, to teach her she is under the power of Man her Husband'. Although Wall, too, acknowledges that there have been Biblical prescriptions for polled heads, that men might with the cutting of their hair be 'cleansed from the filthiness of the Flesh', this is a rule that applies to men, and not to women, for whom a shorn head is merely akin to being uncovered, both physically and socially.[98] A shaved head is a rejection of a woman's ornamental and deferential social position, for the shorn woman indicates her place outside social authority – that she has no head. For a woman to cut off her own hair, as Anne Clifford does, is to call the gendered, subordinating meanings of the female body into question.

It is important to add that there is little evidence to suggest that Anne Clifford's acquaintances understood her shorn head as a mark of sexual or religious depravity. She adopts other head coverings. Yet coupled to the material conditions of her social power and her position within a firmly Protestant household, her head seems to speak most of all to her gendered autonomy. If she cuts her hair for medical reasons, the bald pate might show the balance of her humours. She cuts her hair without concern for feminine deference. With her black clothes, she further adapts a masculine script for dressing to her feminine needs. Bald, she will not be anyone's wife and she is demonstrably not an object of desire. She is, however, fit and healthy. By cutting her hair, going even beyond the signs of widowhood, she removes herself altogether from the social conditions governing women. She is powerful, not because of the spectacle she creates and the desire she arouses. No one's mistress, she is 'Mistris of her Self'.

This phrase comes from the funeral sermon preached by Edward Rainbow, Bishop of Carlisle, who provides a clear indication of how at least one of her contemporaries reads her looks. His funeral sermon repeatedly touches on her appearance, suggesting that it was eccentric but a component of her power. In his telling, Clifford's sartorial virtues point to her prudence, charity and self-discipline. Corroborating her power in the way that men's clothes do, her clothes, however modest, do not testify to her subordination. Like Henry Peacham's great prince, she clothed herself in 'humble and mean attire' but dressed her servants well, not growing rich on their bare backs, even at times being 'clad more coursly and cheaply than most of the Servants in her House'.[99] This is an assessment of Clifford's style that is also made in more derogatory terms by George Sedgwick, who decried her 'very plain and mean apparel, far too mean for her quality' and her constant wearing of a petticoat and waistcoat of black serge.[100] The funeral sermon is, as such sermons are, somewhat hagiographic, and the account book does cast doubt on the veracity of Rainbow's claims about the meanness and Englishness of her attire (as I will show shortly), yet perhaps Rainbow's point remains. The account book does confirm that her clothing demonstrated self-discipline· 'her dress was not disliked by any, yet imitated by none [...] She was absolute Mistris of her Self, her Resolutions, Actions and Time.'[101] Rainbow is careful to say that she is plain by choice and not necessity. If she is to be considered good, Nature must have blessed her with beauty, but because of her choice to abstain from fashion, those who entered her chamber might think it a 'Temple, a Court, a Tribunal, an Almonary'. More than a dressing room, her chamber becomes a site of ecclesiastical and legal power.[102] Rainbow reinforces her power through his account of her body and of her consumption of goods. On both accounts again he emphasizes her self-discipline. 'Her Blood flowed from the Veins of three anciently eno-bled families', and if she is a woman, Nature has blessed her in her body, which is 'Durable and Healthful' and 'well ordered, as well as built'; she has what is necessary to heroic action, a 'healthful well-constituted Body fitted to serve the Commands of a great Mind'. This body has disciplined habits of consumption, too, for she is a woman who takes few pains about her body but dresses only her soul.[103] More practically, and even contradicting this assessment, Rainbow adds that Clifford knows the value of 'home-bread fare, home-growing, and home-spun manufacture', and is among those who do 'not run to France or Persia, to fetch form or matter for their Pride' – despite her ability to do so. Cognizant of sumptuary politics, Rainbow adds that she was not cen-sorious towards others who did dress grandly, of those who took the lawful liberty 'to apparel themselves according to their Rank and Place' because she knew, he says, it was possible to do so without pride.[104] Just as she might have been beautiful, she might have been fashionable, for she was not ignorant of fashionable ways. Rainbow reports that John Donne is 'to have said of this lady in her younger years, to this effect; That she knew well how to discourse of all things, from Predestination to Slea-silk'.[105] In Rainbow's telling of Anne Clifford's life, her appear-ance as Baroness is the outcome of her attitudes towards history and community. She is not a social radical, for what she expresses with her looks questions neither the utility of dress in making visible social hierarchies nor a feminine knowledge of fashion. Rather, because she is emphatically English in her loyalties and because of her self-discipline, she proves with her dress that she can govern.

The account book's records of the clothes that she buys late in life confirm Rainbow's picture of a somewhat austere dresser. Yet they also reveal how her governance is not exactly like that of the good house-wife of Proverbs (Rainbow's exemplar) but somewhat more masculine. Just as she covers and then shaves her head, she uses clothes as a way of tending to social obligations attached to her position as her father's heir, not her role as a wife and widow. She is certainly not an extrava-gant consumer of luxury goods. She has clothes mended, paying 'for mendinge my Petticoates wastcoates and Garters and silke for them one shillinge & six pence'. When she buys bodices, the making of which Beverly Lemire describes as a 'specialized trade and eminently profitable',[106] she displays little sign of indulgence. One of her bodice makers charged 3s and 6s/bodice, another costs 2s 8d and another, with a roll, ¼ yard of fustian and 2¼ yards of shag costs 9s 2d. Gregory King, a seventeenth-century mathematician and economist whom Clifford met in his youth, lists the average cost at 8s.[107] Her bodices are not an expensive version of their kind, and neither are her shoes, which cost 7s for two pairs. King estimated that people in England, on average, bought two pairs of stockings and two pairs of shoes per year – figures confirmed by N. B. Harte.[108] The older Clifford does not go over this number, whereas the younger Lady Anne Clifford did. Yet, the 'furrd gloves for my owne wearinge' do cost more than the average. Bought at York for 5s 6p, these gloves are more expensive than those she buys, for instance, from Thomas Langhorn for 3s 4d to give away to strangers.

Not quite as austere as Rainbow suggests, Anne Clifford continues to buy silk, in a world where silk itself, says Harte, was an 'expensive luxury'.[109] She repeatedly buys for herself black ducape, a particularly sturdy kind of silk. With few purchases of jewellery or metallic textiles, her clothes are not as ornamented as they were in her youth. But neither are they entirely plain and cheap, like those Brilliana Harley asks for. She continues to purchase ribbon, including red and black ribbon. The colour of the silk distinguishes it from the fashionable silks of the second half of the seventeenth century, which were lighter, printed and Asian – fabrics much more suitable to the purposes of a particularly conspicuous form of consumption.[110] Still, Clifford did buy one fashionable fabric, purchased in Penrith by Thomas Strickland: '18: yeards of Italiano for 2 Gownes for my owne weare at 3s 4d ye yeard & for silke and whale Bone & Callico & Gallowne & for trimming in all three poundes eighteene shillinges & three pence'. She buys a further 2 yards of calico to line a mantle on the same day (2s 10p). The Italiano is not a usual fabric name, but it is fair to assume that it is from Italy, a producer of silk. Besides being the epitome of the foreign textile, inspiring numerous attacks by English opponents, calico was a fashionable textile, and obviously so; it was, by the end of the seventeenth century, what Woodruff D. Smith, calls a substitute status commodity: an item that is adopted by people to demonstrate their high status, but which could be afforded even by those who could not afford commodities that the wealthiest people could afford, such as Asian silk.[111] Anne Clifford only has a trimming of calico and her gowns seem mostly to be constructed of black silk, a colour and a textile, as we have already seen, that asserts her status, discipline, governance – and wealth.

The account book confirms the picture of the Countess of Pembroke made visible in 'The Great Picture': the woman who dresses in sober but expensive black and white linen like a gentleman or a widow. No longer buying linen striped with silver, she still buys vast quantities of linen and cotton, including housewife's linen, dimity and holland, probably a local product by this time.[112] The account book also reveals something of what is invisible in the portrait, the clothes beneath her clothes. Here again we can see Anne Clifford fashioning herself in masculine terms. She buys linen to make drawers for her own use: she records a payment of £2 for 20 yards of housewife's linen and 10 yards of fustian, the linen for waistcoats and lining her drawers, and the fustian for drawers and for 'clothes to lye over my knees'. In wearing drawers, Anne Clifford is dressing like a man, for *The History of Underclothes* contends that in the seventeenth century, there is little evidence that women of any rank wore them.[113] Anne Clifford clearly does. Just as she rejects feminine hair, she also adopts the masculine practice of wearing drawers. The drawers might be linked to health and to warmth, which seem a persistent factor in her sartorial choices. Frances Bacon recommends the keeping out of air as a means to prolong life because air can cause dryness and whither the spirits; clothes can help in this, particularly linen next to the skin in summer and baize and woollen linings.[114] Perhaps to this end, Anne Clifford also buys fustian and grey and black shag for three mantles, and baize for a petticoat. In her youth, her petticoats were of silk, but baize, fustian and shag are all possibly wool, although shag might also be made of silk. In her old age, Anne Clifford has not foresworn luxury items, but they are less conspicuous than in her youth because they are black. Yet even warmth can become a treasure in a world without central heating; warm clothes that protect the body from what Francis Bacon calls 'the devouring power of the Ayre' are the garb of longevity.[115]

Finally, the clothing purchases of the older Anne Clifford demonstrate her role as governor in the way that they establish her relationships to other people. Just as in her youth, the mode of consumption was one component of the meaning of her clothes and hair, so too when she is older. Instead of being the recipient of gifts, she is now the dispenser of them. The 'Day-by-Day Book' records the frequent use of gloves as gifts and the account book records repeatedly the purchase of textiles to give away, as she confers on her servants liveries and used clothes (evident, ironically, in the 10s she pays to her laundry maids 'to have back againe the old Gowne I lately gave them I haveing promised it before to another'). Such gifts of clothing are, as Jones and Stallybrass identify, made from material 'which is richly absorbent of symbolic meaning and in which memories and social relations are literally embodied'.[116]

Clothing others embodies her power over the recipients, not her gendered subordination. Clifford also purchases vast quantities of goods from towns near her castles, especially Kendall, Penrith, Appleby and York, surely making her a significant contributor to the local economies. Only once does Clifford pay to have several boxes and trunks 'with severall commodities' sent from London to Kendall, at a cost of £7 8d for the shipping. Otherwise, as in her youth, she employs servants to make purchases, most commonly Robert Pickering, groom of her chamber, and Thomas Strickland, her secretary and receiver of rents (in 1676, she calls him 'one of my Chiefe Officers') to go to nearby towns and purchase goods.[117]

She has social relationships with some of the people from whom she vicariously purchases goods. With Thomas Langhorn, 'the Shop-keeper' of Penrith who dines at Brougham and is invited into her chamber in 1676, she appears to have a long-standing relationship, buying from him and Frances Langhorn a number of silk and linen textiles.[118] She frequently buys silk, holland, ribbons and lace from Francis Lowther, who is identified in one entry as her cousin. She also purchases textiles from women of her almshouse at Appleby, established in 1651 and endowed by 1652.[119] They make lace, sew and apparently manufacture linen and stockings. For instance, Clifford repeatedly buys bone lace from a woman named Dorothy Wyber (or Wibergh or Wiber), identified as 'the deaffe wench of my Almeshouse here at Appleby', much of it to give away and purchased in quantities of a dozen or two dozen yards at a time. Although for a total of more than 144 yards of bone lace, Dorothy Wyber receives the small sum of £3 4s, about 5d/yard, the relationship is not purely a commercial one. Clifford also records a visit by Dorothy Wyber to Brougham, who dined there on Shrove Monday in 1676: 'And today there dined without with my folks Dorothy Wiber, the Deafe woman of my Almeshouse at Appleby, and after dinner I had her into my chamber and kist her. And I saw her payd for 5 dozen yards of Bonlace, but I was very angry with her for bringing so much and told her I would have no more of her.'[120] Because Clifford died little over a month later, it is impossible to tell if the conflict was resolved. What is clear is that Clifford buys from Dorothy Wyber less because she needs bonelace than because she has a social obligation to buy from her, who by her poverty compels the baroness's charity; the relationship is severed when Wyber expects Clifford to buy more than she perceives is Wyber's due. Lace might be a luxury good, although it is produced by women working for low wages, but Anne Clifford does not buy 60 yards of it because she wants 60 yards of lace. She engages in economic transactions that are contingent on other social factors, such as kinship, community and obligation. The economies of gift exchange and the market are not entirely extricable and Anne Clifford uses clothing herself and her household as the occasion to link them. Anne Clifford's attitude towards her hair as an older woman is part of this culture of consumption where it is more important to be in control than it is to be regarded as attractive.

Conclusion

A part of the body heavily laden with symbolic significance, hair can convey individual and cultural attitudes about class, gender, religion, age, politics and aesthetics. It is a natural material excreted from the body, a consequence of the body's humoural balance, and it is a site for artificial intervention – colouring, curling, cutting, covering and sculptural rearrangement. It can exhibit beauty and just as surely articulate the wearer's questions about beauty's role in defining women's place in society. Johannes Endres wrote in a special issue of *Eighteenth-Century Studies* devoted to eighteenth-century hair that 'From a cultural–historical perspective, the interpretation of hair has only just begun. As a threadlike, many-celled type of skin, hair seems to demand consideration in terms of categories emerging from everyday life and its practical organization in relation to custom and fashion, beauty, and cosmetics.'[121] This chapter suggests that hair manifests attitudes towards consumption. Anne Clifford may have presented herself as conventionally beautiful in her youth, but when she looks back at her life, she does not construe these looks as being important to her as coin within the patriarchal economy of marriage. Rather, she sees her hair as an inheritance, the visible evidence of the blood she has received from her parents, the blood that makes her worthy of the place she occupies as a Clifford. In her youth, hair is also a medium for the revelation of her access to luxury goods, to social status and to her mother's social place. Even when she is a child, she wears the fashionable hairstyles of adult women, and her clothes and hairstyles both visually and materially connect her to kin and the friends of her family and establish her power over those who occupy a lower social position. She does not reject ornament but approaches it as a consequence of her place. Later in life, however, Anne Clifford reshapes the meaning of her hair as she covers and then cuts it off in a move that, while appropriate to the older woman in a culture anxious about the sexuality of older women, also challenges the notion that women lacked self-discipline. As the Baroness of Westmorland, Anne

Clifford controls her own head, literally. She becomes her own mistress in part by shaving her head. For Thorstein Veblen, women were an emblem of conspicuous consumption because women's clothes, even more than men's, demonstrated their leisure, their inability to work in shoes, skirts and corsets that hampered their movements, and their status as the economic dependents of men.[122] This history of consumption is too simple. The records of Anne Clifford's consumption – her account books, her portraits and her *Great Books of Record* – remind us of the fundamental importance of age in constituting gendered consumption and, most of all, that women might ascribe other meanings to the purchase and wear of luxury goods than their dependence.

Notes

Introduction

1. Petrarch, 'Sonnet 90', in *Selections from the Canzoniere and Other Works,* trans. Mark Musa (Oxford and New York: Oxford University Press, 1985), 38.
2. Philip Sidney, 'Sonnet 9', in *Sir Philip Sidney: The Major Works*, ed. Katherine Duncan-Jones (Oxford: Oxford University Press, 1989), 156.
3. Edmund Spenser, 'Sonnet XV', in *Amoretti and Epithalamion: A Critical Edition*, ed. Kenneth J. Larsen (Tempe, AZ: Medieval and Renaissance Texts and Studies, 1997), 74.
4. John Donne, 'Elegy 14', in *John Donne's Poetry,* ed. Donald R. Dickson (New York and London: W.W. Norton, 2007), 41–4.
5. John Milton, *Paradise Lost*, in *John Milton: The Complete Poems*, ed. John Leonard (London: Penguin, 1998), line 4.298.
6. William Shakespeare, 'Sonnet 20', in *Complete Sonnets and Poems*, ed. Colin Burrow (Oxford: Oxford University Press, 2002), 421, lines 5, 8.
7. ibid., *Venus and Adonis*, 175–236, line 10.
8. Christopher Marlowe, *Hero and Leander*, in *The Collected Poems of Christopher Marlowe*, ed. Patrick Cheney and Brian J. Striar (New York and Oxford: Oxford University Press, 2006), 196, lines 51, 55; John Milton, *Paradise Lost,* lines 4.300–1.
9. Nancy Vickers, '"The Blazon of Sweet Beauty's Best": Shakespeare's *Lucrece',* in *Shakespeare and the Question of Theory*, ed. Patricia Parker and Geoffrey Hartman (New York: Methuen, 1985), 96.
10. Naomi J. Miller, 'Lady Mary Wroth and Women's Love Poetry', in *Early Modern English Poetry: A Critical Companion*, ed. Patrick Cheney, Andrew Hadfield, and Garrett A. Sullivan, Jr. (New York: Oxford University Press, 2007), 195–205; Nona Fienberg, 'Wroth and the Invention of Female Poetic Subjectivity', in *Reading Mary Wroth: Representing Alternatives in Early Modern England,* ed. Naomi J. Miller and Gary Waller (Knoxville, TN: University of Tennessee Press, 1991), 175–90.
11. Katherine Duncan-Jones, 'Bess Carey's Petrarch: Newly Discovered Elizabethan Sonnets', *The Review of English Studies* n.s. 50.199 (1999): 304–19.
12. Kim F. Hall, '"I Rather Would Wish to be a Black-Moor": Beauty, Race, and Rank in Lady Mary Wroth's *Urania'*, in *Women, 'Race', and Writing in the Early Modern Period*, ed. Margo Hendricks and Patricia Parker (New York: Routledge, 1994), 178–94; Kim F. Hall, 'Beauty and the Beast of Whiteness: Teaching Race and Gender', *Shakespeare Quarterly* 47 (1996): 461–75; Kim F. Hall, *Things of Darkness: Economies of Race and Gender in Early Modern England* (Ithaca, NY and London: Cornell University Press, 1995); Dympna Callaghan, 'Re-Reading Elizabeth Cary's *The Tragedie of Mariam, Faire Queene of Jewry'*, in *Women, 'Race', and Writing in the Early Modern Period*, 163–77; Kimberly Woolsey Poitevin, '"Counterfeit Colour": Making Up Race in Elizabeth Cary's *The Tragedy of Mariam'*, *Tulsa Studies in Women's Literature*

24.1 (2005): 13–34; Catherine Gallagher, 'Oroonoko's Blackness', in *Aphra Behn Studies*, ed. Janet Todd (Cambridge: Cambridge University Press, 1996), 235–58; Barbara Bowen, 'Aemilia Lanyer and the Invention of White Womanhood', in *Maids and Mistresses, Cousins and Queens: Women's Alliances in Early Modern England*, ed. Susan Frye and Karen Robertson (New York: Oxford University Press), 274–303.

13. Elizabeth Cropper, 'On Beautiful Women, Parmigianino, Petrarchismo, and the Vernacular Style', *The Art Bulletin* 58.3 (1976): 374–94; Elizabeth Cropper, 'The Beauty of Woman: Problems in the Rhetoric of Renaissance Portraiture', in *Rewriting the Renaissance: The Discourses of Sexual Difference in Early Modern Europe*, ed. Margaret W. Ferguson, Maureen Quilligan and Nancy J. Vickers (Chicago, IL and London: The University of Chicago Press, 1986), 175–90; Mary Vaccaro, 'Parmigianino and Andrea Baiardi: Figuring Petrarchan Beauty in Renaissance Parma', *Word and Image* 17.3 (2001): 243–358; Véronique Nahoum-Grappe, 'The Beautiful Woman', in *A History of Women in the West. Vol. 3. Renaissance and Enlightenment Paradoxes*, ed. Natalie Zemon Davis and Arlette Farge (Cambridge, MA: Harvard University Press, 1993), 87–100; Ben Lowe, 'Body Images and the Politics of Beauty: Formation of the Feminine Ideal in Medieval and Early Modern Europe', in *Ideals of Feminine Beauty: Philosophical, Social, and Cultural Dimensions*, ed. Karen A. Callaghan (Westport, CT: Greenwood Press, 1994), 21–36; Mary Rogers, 'Sonnets on Female Portraits from Renaissance North Italy', *Word and Image* 2.4 (1986): 291–305.

14. Sara F. Matthews Grieco, 'The Body, Appearance, and Sexuality', in *History of Women in the West*, 58.

15. Agnolo Firenzuola, *On the Beauty of Women*, trans. Konrad Eisenbichler and Jacqueline Muray (Philadelphia, PA: University of Pennsylvania Press, 1992), 14.

16. Heather Dubrow, *Echoes of Desire: English Petrarchism and its Counterdiscourses* (Ithaca, NY and London: Cornell University Press, 1995), 163–201; Naomi Baker, '"To Make Love to a Deformity": Praising Ugliness in Early Modern England', *Renaissance Studies* 22.1 (2007): 86–109. On Italian versions of the form, see Patrizia Bettella, 'Discourse of Resistance: The Parody of Feminine Beauty in Berni, Doni and Firenzuola', *Modern Language Notes* 113.1 (1998): 192–203.

17. John Donne, 'Elegy 10: The Anagram', in *John Donne's Poetry*, 37–8.

18. William Shakespeare, 'Sonnet 130', in *Complete Sonnets and Poems*, 641.

19. Thomas Buoni, *The Problemes of Beautie*, trans. S.L. (London: G. Eld for Edward Blount and William Aspley, 1606), 26.

20. Margreta de Grazia, 'The Scandal of Shakespeare's Sonnets', in *Shakespeare's Sonnets: Critical Essays*, ed. James Schiffer (New York and London: Garland, 2000), 106. See also Marvin Hunt, 'Be Dark But Not Too Dark: Shakespeare's Dark Lady as a Sign of Color', in *Shakespeare's Sonnets*, 385.

21. Hall, *Things of Darkness*, 121.

22. William Shakespeare, 'Sonnet 130', in *Complete Sonnets and Poems*, 641, line 14.

23. Donne, 'Elegy 10: The Anagram', line 56.

24. John Collop, 'To Aureola', in *Poesis Rediviva* (London: Humphrey Moseley, 1656), 69–70.

25. Dubrow, 200–1.
26. Lowe, 29–34.
27. Baldesar Castiglione, *The Book of the Courtier,* trans. George Bull (London: Penguin, 1967), 334–45. See Plato, *The Symposium*, trans. Christopher Gill (London: Penguin, 1999), 43–50.
28. Petrarch, 'Sonnet 13', in *Petrarch's Lyric Poems: The Rime Sparse and Other Lyrics*, trans. Robert M. Durling, ed. Robert M. Durling (Cambridge, MA: Harvard University Press, 1976), 48–9; Philip Sidney, 'Sonnet 71', in *Sir Philip Sidney: The Major Works*, 182, line 4.
29. Spenser, 'Sonnet LVI', in *Amoretti and Epithalamion*, 91; Lisa M. Klein, '"Let us love, dear love, lyke as we ought": Protestant Marriage and the Revision of Petrarchan Loving in Spenser's *Amoretti*', *Spenser Studies* 10 (1992): 109–37.
30. Ovid, *The Art of Love*, in *The Erotic Poems*, trans. Peter Green (London: Penguin, 1982), 3.101.
31. Elise Goodman-Soellner, 'Poetic Interpretation of the "Lady at her Toilette" Theme in Sixteenth-Century Painting', *The Sixteenth-Century Journal* 14.4 (1983): 426–44.
32. Frances E. Dolan, 'Taking the Pencil out of God's Hand: Art, Nature, and the Face-Painting Debate in Early Modern England', *PMLA* 108.2 (1993): 236.
33. Patricia Parker, *Literary Fat Ladies: Rhetoric, Property, Gender* (London: Methuen, 1987), 154.
34. Milton, *A Masque Presented at Ludlow Castle*, in *John Milton: The Complete Poems*, 57, 67, lines 393–4, 739–41.
35. William Shakespeare, *The Rape of Lucrece,* in *Complete Sonnets and Poems*, 243–4, lines 10, 16, 27–8.
36. Samuel Daniel, 'Sonnet XXXI', in *Poems and A Defence of Ryme*, ed. Arthur Colby Sprague (Chicago, IL and London: University of Chicago Press, 1965), 26, lines 13–14.
37. Robert Herrick, 'To the Virgins, to make Much of Time', in *The Poems of Robert Herrick*, ed. L. C. Martine (London: Oxford University Press, 1965), 85, line 1; Andrew Marvell, 'To His Coy Mistress', in *Andrew Marvell: The Complete Poems*, ed. Elizabeth Story Donno (Harmondsworth: Penguin, 1981), 50–1, lines 25–8.
38. Nancy J. Vickers, 'Diana Described: Scattered Women and Scattered Rhyme', in *Writing and Sexual Difference*, ed. Elizabeth Abel (Chicago, IL: University of Chicago Press, 1982) 107.
39. William J. Kennedy, 'Sidney's *Astrophil and Stella* and Petrarchism', in *Early Modern English Poetry: A Critical Companion*, 75; Arthur Marotti, '"Love is Not Love": Elizabethan Sonnet Sequences and the Social Order', *English Literary History* 49.2 (1982): 396–428; Michael Schoenfeldt, 'The Matter of Inwardness: Shakespeare's Sonnets', in *Shakespeare's Sonnets: Critical Essays*, 305–24; Anne Ferry, *The 'Inward' Language: Sonnets of Wyatt, Sidney, Shakespeare, Donne* (Chicago, IL: University of Chicago Press, 1983); Joel Fineman, *Shakespeare's Perjured Eye: The Invention of Poetic Subjectivity in the Sonnets* (Berkeley, CA and Los Angeles, CA: University of California Press, 1986); Nancy J. Vickers, 'Diana Described', 103.
40. Michel de Certeau, *The Practice of Everyday Life*, trans. Steven Rendall (Berkeley, CA: University of California Press, 1984), 37, xix.

41. Hilda L. Smith, 'Women Intellectuals and Intellectual History: Their Paradigmatic Separation', *Women's History Review* 16.3 (2007), 365.
42. Andrea Dworkin, *Woman Hating* (New York: E. P. Dutton, 1974), esp. 112–17; Susan Brownmiller, *Femininity* (New York: Linden Press/Simon & Schuster, 1984); Robin Tolmach Lakoff and Raquel Scherr, *Face Value: The Politics of Beauty* (London: Routledge & Kegan Paul, 1984); Wendy Chapkis, *Beauty Secrets: Women and the Politics of Appearance* (Boston, MA: South End Press, 1986); Susan Bordo, *Unbearable Weight: Feminism, Western Culture and the Body* (Berkeley, CA: University of California Press, 1993); Sara Halprin, *'Look at my Ugly Face': Myths and Musings on Beauty and other Perilous Obsessions with Women's Appearance* (Toronto, ON: Penguin, 1995); Lynn S. Chancer, *Reconcilable Differences: Confronting Beauty, Pornography, and the Future of Feminism* (Berkeley, CA: University of California Press, 1998); Debra L. Gimlin, *Body Work: Beauty and Self-image in American Culture* (Berkeley, CA: University of California Press, 2002); Patricia Hill Collins, *Black Feminist Thought: Knowledge, Consciousness, and the Politics of Empowerment*, 2nd edn (New York and London: Routledge, 2000), esp. 88–92.
43. Sheila Jeffreys, *Beauty and Misogyny: Harmful Cultural Practices in the West* (New York: Routledge, 2005).
44. ibid., 111; Linda M. Scott, *Fresh Lipstick: Redressing Feminism and Fashion* (New York: Palgrave Macmillan, 1994), 118–19, 135–41.
45. Valerie Felita Kinloch, 'The Rhetoric of Black Bodies: Race, Beauty, and Representation', in *'There She is Miss America': The Politics of Sex, Beauty, and Race in America's Most Famous Pageant*, ed. Elwood Watson and Darcy Martin (New York: Palgrave Macmillan, 2004), 100.
46. Jeanine C. Cogan and Joanie M. Erickson, eds, *Lesbians, Levis and Lipstick: The Meaning of Beauty in Our Lives* (New York: Harrington Park Press, 1999).
47. Liz Frost, '"Doing Looks": Women, Appearance and Mental Health', in *Women's Bodies: Discipline and Transgression*, ed. Jane Arthurs and Jean Grimshaw (London and New York: Cassell, 1999), 122–3, 133.
48. Pamela Church Gibson, 'Redressing the Balance: Patriarchy, Postmodernism, and Feminism', in *Fashion Cultures: Theories, Explorations and Analysis*, ed. Stella Bruzzi and Pamela Church Gibson (London and New York: Routledge, 2000), 351.
49. Amanda Bailey, *Flaunting: Style and the Subversive Male Body in Renaissance England* (Toronto, ON: University of Toronto Press, 2007); Sue Vincent, *Dressing the Elite: Clothes in Early Modern England* (Oxford: Berg, 2003).
50. Daniel 13:2 in *The Holy Bible* (Rouen: John Coursturier, 1635).
51. ibid., 13:17.
52. ibid., 13:48.
53. See 'Susanna and the Elders', Victoria and Albert Museum, Museum Number T.50–1954. <http://collections.vam.ac.uk/item/O85016/embroidered-picture-susannah-and-the-elders>
54. Daniel 13:31 in *The Holy Bible*.
55. Images and information on all paintings are from ARTStor Digital Library.
56. Rozsika Parker, *The Subversive Stitch: Embroidery and the Making of the Feminine* (New York: Routledge, 1989), 96–8.

57. Susan Frye, 'Sewing Connections: Elizabeth Tudor, Mary Stuart, Elizabeth Talbot, and Anonymous Seventeenth-Century Needleworkers', in *Maids and Mistresses, Cousins and Queens*, 165.
58. Lisa M. Klein, 'Your Humble Handmaid: Elizabethan Gifts of Needlework', *Renaissance Quarterly* 50.2 (1997): 462.
59. Jennifer Munroe, '"In This Strang Labourinth, How Shall I Turne?"': Needlework, Gardens, and Writing in Mary Wroth's *Pamphilia to Amphilanthus'*, *Tulsa Studies in Women's Literature* 24.1 (2005): 35–55; Elizabeth Mazzola, *Women's Wealth and Women's Writing in Early Modern England: 'Little Legacies' and the Materials of Motherhood* (Farnham: Ashgate, 2009). See also Susan Frye, 'Maternal Textualities', in *Maternal Measures: Figuring Caregiving in the Early Modern Period*, ed. Naomi J. Miller and Naomi Yavneh (Aldershot: Ashgate, 2000), 224–36.
60. Margaret Cavendish, 'Of Painting', in *Worlds Olio* (London: J. Martin and J. Allestrye, 1655), 84–7.
61. Samuel Pepys, *The Diary of Samuel Pepys*, ed. Robert Latham and William Matthews, vol. 8 (Los Angeles, CA: University of California Press, 1974), 163, 186–7, 196, 209.
62. Pepys, vol. 8, 163, 186–7.
63. ibid., 243.
64. ibid., vol. 9, 123.
65. Margaret Cavendish, 'A True Relation of My Birth, Breeding, and Life', in *Paper Bodies: A Margaret Cavendish Reader*, ed. Sylvia Bowerbank and Sara Mendelson (Peterborough, ON: Broadview, 2000), 60.
66. This autobiography does not appear in the second edition, published in 1671.
67. Cavendish, 'A True Relation', 60–2.
68. ibid., 48.

1   'The Beautifying Part of Physic': Women's Cosmetic Practices in Early Modern England

1. See Maggie Angeloglou, *A History of Make-Up* (London: Studio Vista, 1970); Carroll Camden, *The Elizabethan Woman* (London: Elsevier Press, 1952); Richard Corson, *Fashions in Makeup: From Ancient to Modern Times* (London: Peter Owen, 1972); Annette Drew-Bear, 'Cosmetics and Attitudes Towards Women in the Seventeenth Century', *Journal of Popular Culture* 9 (1975): 31–7; Annette Drew-Bear, 'Face Painting Scenes in Ben Jonson's Plays', *Studies in Philology* 77 (1980): 388–401; Annette Drew-Bear, 'Face Painting in Renaissance Tragedy', *Renaissance Drama* 12 (1981): 71–93; Laurie Finke, 'Painting Women: Images of Femininity in Jacobean Tragedy', *Theatre Journal* 36 (1984): 357–70; Shirley Nelson Garner, '"Let Her Paint an Inch Thick": Painted Ladies in Renaissance Drama and Society', *Renaissance Drama* 20 (1989): 123–39; Dosja Reichard, '"Their Faces are not their Own": Powders, Patches and Paint in Seventeenth-Century Poetry', *Dalhousie Review* 84 (2004): 195–214; Sujata Iyengar, *Shades of Difference: Mythologies of Skin Color in Early Modern England* (Philadelphia, PA: University of Pennsylvania Press, 2005), esp. 123–39.

2. Kim Hall, *Things of Darkness: Economies of Race and Gender in Early Modern England* (Ithaca, NY: Cornell University Press, 1995), esp. 62–122.
3. Frances E. Dolan, 'Taking the Pencil Out of God's Hand: Art, Nature, and the Face-Painting Debate in Early Modern England', *PMLA* 108 (1993): 224–40; Patricia Phillippy, *Painting Women: Cosmetics, Canvases and Early Modern Culture* (Baltimore, MD: Johns Hopkins University Press, 2006).
4. For a modern point of view on the deleterious effects of mercury and lead, see John Emsley, *The Elements of Murder: A History of Poison*, (Oxford: Oxford University Press, 2005).
5. Camden, 202–4.
6. Iyengar, 135.
7. Montserrat Cabré, 'From a Master to a Laywoman: A Feminine Manual of Self Help', *Dynamis* 20 (2000): 371–93.
8. George Hartman, *The Family Physitian* (London, 1696), 511.
9. Johann Jacob Wecker, *Cosmeticks, or, the Beautifying Part of Physick* (London: Thomas Johnson, 1660); *Arts Master-piece: Or the Beautifying Part of Physick* (London: Nathaniel Brook, 1660). Except for the title page, these two works are identical. Both of them state that they are never before published, but 'long since promised' by Nicholas Culpeper. Nathaniel Brook, who printed *Arts Master-piece*, printed other of Culpeper's works after his death.
10. J. B. *Anthropometamorphosis: Man Transform'd: Or The Artificial Changling* (London: William Hunt, 1653), B2v.
11. Andrew Wear, *Knowledge & Practice in English Medicine, 1550–1680* (Cambridge: Cambridge University Press, 2000), 210–11. For more on the distinction between surgeon and physician, see Lucinda McCray Beier, *Sufferers and Healers: The Experience of Illness in Seventeenth-Century England* (London: Routledge & Kegan Paul, 1987), 10, 14; Rosemary O'Day, *The Professions in Early Modern England, 1450–1800: Servants of the Commonweal* (Harlow: Longman, 2000), 183–251. For more on surgeons and dermatological cures, see P. M. W. Copeman and W. S. C. Copeman, 'Dermatology in Tudor and Early Stuart England', *British Journal of Dermatology* 82.1 (1970): 78–88 and 82.3 (1970): 303–10.
12. Doreen A. Evenden, 'Gender Differences in the Licensing and Practice of Female and Male Surgeons in Early Modern England', *Medical History* 42 (1998): 194–216; Wear, 211; Margaret Pelling, *The Common Lot: Sickness, Medical Occupations and the Urban Poor in Early Modern England* (London: Longman, 1998), 203–29.
13. Wear, 113; Beier, 31; Doreen Evenden Nagy, *Popular Medicine in Seventeenth-Century England* (Bowling Green, OH: Bowling Green State University Popular Press, 1988), 70.
14. Thomas Tuke, *A Discourse Against Painting and Tincturing of Women* (London: Edward Marchant, 1616), B3–B4v.
15. Mary Evelyn, *Mundus Muliebris, or The Ladies Dressing-Room Unlock'd, and her Toilette Spread In Burlesque* (London: R. Bentley, 1690), 9; Margaret Cavendish, Duchess of Newcastle, *The Bridals*, in *Plays, Never Before Printed* (London: A. Maxwell, 1668), 26–7.
16. Hugh Plat, *Delights for Ladies, to Adorne their Persons, Tables, Closets, and Distillatories* (London: Peter Short, 1602), G11–G11v. After 1600, *Delights for Ladies* was printed in 1602, 1603, 1605, 1608, 1609, 1611, 1615, 1617, 1624, 1628, 1630, 1632, 1635, 1636, 1640, 1644, 1647, 1651, 1654 and 1656.

17. Hannah Wolley [or Woolley], *The Accomplish'd Lady's Delight* (London: B. Harris, 1677), 117, 171. After its first printing under this title in 1675, *The Accomplish'd Lady's Delight* was reprinted in 1677, 1683, 1684, 1685, 1686, 1696 and 1720. The section of the book containing the cosmetic recipes, 'Ladies Physical Closet', is also printed in *The Ladies Delight* (London: Thomas Milbourn, 1672).

18. Margaret Cavendish, Duchess of Newcastle, 'Of Painting', in *The Worlds Olio* (London: J. Martin and J. Allestrye, 1655), 84–7.

19. Plat, H–H*v*, H3, H3*v*.

20. *Natura Exenterata: Or Nature Unembowelled* (London: H. Twiford, 1655), 18.

21. Thomas Vicary, *The English Man's Treasure* (London: Thomas Creede, 1613), 74, 76 (misnumbered as 77), 168, 192. This work, first printed in 1586, also appeared in 1587, 1596, 1599, 1613, 1626, 1633 and 1641.

22. John Partridge, *The Treasurie of Commodious Conceits, and Hidden Secretes* (London: Richard Jones, 1591), D5. This title was published in 1573, 1584, 1586, and 1591.

23. John Partridge, *The Treasurie of Hidden Secrets* (London: Richard Oulton, 1637), F2*v*, F4, G. This title was also printed in 1596, 1600, 1608, 1627, 1633, 1637 and 1653.

24. Nicholas Culpeper, *The English Physician* (London: William Bentley, 1652). This work was first published in 1652, and thereafter in seventeenth-century editions in 1653, 1655, 1656, 1661, 1662, 1665, 1666, 1669, 1671, 1674, 1676, 1679, 1681, 1683, 1684, 1695 and 1698. It was also printed at least once, and sometimes more, in every decade of the eighteenth century.

25. ibid., 99, 121. For other recipes using 'cleanse' to refer to remedies for freckles, pimples, morphew and scurf, see pages 76, 93, 108, 132, 153, 165, 195, 202, 217.

26. 'Tartar', *LEME: Lexicons of Early Modern English*, http://leme.library.utoronto.ca.proxy.hil.unb.ca, s.v.; 'Tartar', *Oxford English Dictionary*, 2nd edn (1989). Online. Nicholas Culpeper, *A Physicall Directory, or A Translation of the London Dispensatory* (London: Peter Cole, 1649), 326. This was a very popular publication. While *Pharmacopoeia Londinensis* was printed only in 1618, 1627 and 1651, the translation, also entitled *Pharmacopoeia Londinensis: or the London Dispensatory,* was printed in 1649, 1650, 1651, 1653, 1654, 1655, 1656, 1659, 1661, 1667, 1669, 1672, 1675, 1679, 1683, 1695, 1702, 1718 and 1720.

27. Hartman, 516.

28. Culpeper, *A Physicall Directory,* 279.

29. Culpeper, *The English Physician,* 9.

30. John Tanner, *The Hidden Treasures of the Art of Physick* (London: George Sawbridge, 1659), 536.

31. See Rembert Dodoens, *A New Herbal, or Historie of Plants,* trans. Henry Lyte ([Antwerp: Henry Loë], 1578) (also printed in 1586, 1595 and 1619); John Gerard, *The Herball or General Historie of Plantes* (London: Adam Islip, Joice Norton, and Richard Whitakers, 1633) (also printed in 1597 and 1636); *Greate Herball* (London: John King, 1561) (also printed in 1539); John Parkinson, *Paradisi in Sole Paradisus Terrestris* (London: Humfrey Lownes and Robert Young, 1629) (also printed in 1635 and 1656).

32. Tuke, B3*v*.

33. Lady Frances Catchmay, *Book of Medicens,* c.1625, MS 184a, fol. 1*v*, Wellcome Library, London, hereafter Wellcome.

34. Catchmay, fols. 22, 24, 24*v*, 25*v*.
35. Jane Jackson, *A very shorte and compendious Methode of Phisicke and Chirurgery Containeinge the Cures inwardly*, 1642, MS 373, fols.1v, 4, Wellcome.
36. ibid., fols. 5–7.
37. ibid., fol. 5.
38. ibid., fols. 18*v*, 123, 57, 57*v*, 132*v*.
39. Elizabeth Digby, *Elizabeth Digby's Housebook*, c.1650, Egerton MS 2197, fol. 26, British Library, London, hereafter BL; Margaret Baker, *Medical and Culinary Recipes*, Sloane MS 2485, fols. 31*v*–32, 33*v*–34, 71, 46, BL.
40. Lady Ranelagh (Compiler), *Cookery Receipts of Lady Ranelagh*, Sloane MS 1367, fols. 4, 32, 54*v*, 36, 50, 55, BL.
41. Mary Doggett, *Book of Receipts*, 1682, Additional MS 27466, fols. 6*v*, 7*v*, 14, 24*v*, 38, BL.
42. Mary Glover, *Mary Glover, her Booke of Receipts*, 1688, Additional MS 57944, fols.1, 15*v*, 91*v*, BL.
43. Copeman and Copeman, 82.3 (1970): 304.
44. Levinus Lemnius, *The Touchstone of Complexions*, trans. Thomas Newton (London: Thomas Marsh, 1576), 90.
45. *Artificiall Embellishments. Or Arts Best Directions How to Preserve Beauty or Procure it* (Oxford: William Hall, 1665), 16–29. Although the Wing catalogue attributes the work to Thomas Jeamson, Christoph Heyl questions this. See 'Deformity's Filthy Fingers: Cosmetics and the Plague in *Artificiall Embellishments, or Arts Best Directions how to preserve Beauty or Procure it* (Oxford, 1655)', in *Didactic Literature in England 1500–1800: Expertise Constructed*, ed. Natasha Glaisyer and Sara Pennell (Aldershot: Ashgate, 2003), 137–51. For more on the 'non-naturals,' see Antoinette Emch-Dériaz, 'The Non-Naturals Made Easy', in *The Popularization of Medicine 1650–1850*, ed. Roy Porter (London: Routledge, 1992), 134–59.
46. *Artificiall Embellishments*, 39; see also Copeman and Copeman, 82.3 (1970): 304.
47. Wolley, 179–80.
48. Cavendish, 'Of Painting', 84–7.
49. Mary Trye, *Medicatrix or the Woman Physician* (London: T.R. and N.T., 1675).
50. Wear, 270.
51. Walter Pagel, *Paracelsus: An Introduction to Philosophical Medicine in the Era of the Renaissance*, 2nd rev. edn (Basel: Karger, 1982), 82–8, 100–5, 144–6, 201.
52. Paracelsus, *Of the Chymical Transmutation, Genealogy and Generation of Metals and Minerals*, trans. Robert Turner (London: Richard Moon, 1657), 37.
53. Wear, 170.
54. 'An Epilogue Collected and Gathered by John Banester', in *A Briefe and Necessarie Treatise, Touching the Cure of the Disease called Morbus Gallicus, or Lues Venerea*, by William Clowes (London: Thomas East, 1585), Oiii, Oivv.
55. John Woodall, *The Surgions Mate* (London: Edward Griffin, 1617), 301–7.
56. Vicary, 166–7, 177, 210, 211. On the use of virgin's milk, see Culpeper, *A Physicall Directory*, 102.
57. On mercury, see Culpeper, *A Physicall Directory*, 94, 275, 311, 323, 330 and 331; on lead, see 74, 331, 270, 278, 295–6, 304, 307 (misnumbered as 337) and 309 in the same.
58. *The Greate Herball*, Lviv.

59. Ranelagh, fol. 55.
60. Catchmay, fols. 41*v*, 45*v*.
61. Baker, fols. 31*v*–32, 71.
62. Doggett, fols. 24*v*, 7*v*.
63. Catchmay, fol. 41*v*.
64. ibid., fols. 11*v*, 13.
65. Ranelagh, fol. 32.
66. Montserrat Cabré, 'Women or Healers? Household Practices and the Categories of Health Care in Late Medieval Iberia', *Bulletin of the History of Medicine* 82 (2008): 18–51, esp. 49, 50.
67. Sara Pennell, 'Perfecting Practice? Women, Manuscript Recipes and Knowledge in Early Modern England', in *Early Modern Women's Manuscript Writing*, ed. Victoria E. Burke and Jonathan Gibson (Aldershot: Ashgate, 2004), 253.
68. Margaret Pelling, 'Thoroughly Resented? Older Women and the Medical Role in Early Modern London', in *Women, Science and Medicine 1500–1700: Mothers and Sisters of the Royal Society*, ed. Lynette Hunter and Sarah Hutton (Phoenix Mill: Sutton Publishing, 1997), 71. See also Margaret Pelling, *Medical Conflicts in Early Modern London: Patronage, Physicians, and Irregular Practitioners, 1550–1640* (Oxford: Clarendon Press, 2003), 194–5.
69. Elizabeth Lane Furdell, *Publishing and Medicine in Early Modern England* (Rochester: University of Rochester Press, 2002), 148–9.
70. *Medical Advertisements*, catalogue number 551.a.32, fol. 95, BL.
71. ibid., fols. 123–123*v*.
72. ibid., fol. 199.
73. Emsley, 7–19.
74. Vicary, 74, 160, 163, 206, 210; *A book of such medicines as have been approved by the special practice of Mrs. Carlyon* c.1660, MS V.a.388, 33–4, Folger Library, Washington DC; *A Booke of diuers Medecines, Broothes, Salues, Waters, Syroppes and Oyntementes of which many or the most part haue been experienced and tryed by the speciall practize of Mrs Corlyn*, 1606, MS 213, fol. 27, Wellcome Library.
75. G. Baker, 'The Nature and Property of Quicksilver', in *A Briefe and Necessarie Treatise*, Miv.
76. Woodall, 301.
77. 'An Epilogue Collected and Gathered by John Banester', Oiiiv, Oivv.
78. Wear, 271.
79. John Webster, *Metallographia, or, A History of Metals* (London: Andrew Clark, 1671), A2v; Alvaro Alonso Barba, *The Second Book of the Art of Mettals, Wherein is Taught the Common Way of Refining Silver by Quicksilver* (London: S. Mearne, 1670), esp. 1, 48.
80. Paracelsus, 45.
81. William Fulke, *A Most Pleasant Prospect into the Garden of Naturall Contemplation* (London: Edward Griffin, 1640), fol. 68; Joseph Du Chesne, *A Breefe Aunswere of Josephus Quercetanus Armeniacus, Doctor of Phisick, to the Exposition of Jacobus Aubertus Vindonis* (London: R. Robinson, 1591), fol. 12*v*.
82. Paracelsus, 26.
83. Johann Wecker, *Eighteen Books of the Secrets of Art & Nature: Being the Summe and Substance of Naturall Philosophy* (London: Simon Miller, 1660), frontispiece, a1, 82–91.

84. Sir Kenelm Digby, *A Choice Collection of Rare Chymical Secrets and Experiments in Philosophy* (London: [n.p.], 1682), A, A3*v*–A4.
85. Kenelm Digby, 132–6, 236–8.
86. *Artificiall Embellishments*, 49, 76. This work also explains the virtues of the lead plaster (184–5).
87. Richard Haydocke, 'A Discourse of the Artificiall Beauty of Women', in *Tracte Containing the Artes of Curious Paintinge*, by Giovanni Lomazzo, trans. Richard Haydocke (Oxford: Joseph Barnes, 1598), 130.
88. Hartman, 522.
89. Lynette Hunter, 'Sisters of the Royal Society: The Circle of Katherine Jones, Lady Ranelagh', in *Women, Science and Medicine 1500–1700*, 183–4.
90. Allison Kavey, 'Worlds of Secrets: Books of Secrets and Popular Natural Philosophy in England, 1550–1600', (PhD dissertation, Johns Hopkins University, 2004), 176–88.
91. Pelling, *Medical Conflicts*, 212–13.
92. ibid., 192; Pelling, 'Compromised by Gender: The Role of the Male Medical Practitioner in Early Modern England', in *The Task of Healing: Medicine, Religion and Gender in England and the Netherlands,* ed. Hilary Marland and Margaret Pelling (Rotterdam: Erasmus Publishing, 1996), 101–33.
93. Deborah E. Harkness, 'Managing an Experimental Household: The Dees of Mortlake and the Practice of Natural Philosophy', *Isis* 88.2 (1997): 249.
94. *Artificiall Embellishments*, 46–7.
95. Pelling, *The Common Lot*, 204.
96. *Medical Advertisements*, fol. 171.
97. Susan Brownmiller, *Femininity* (New York: Linden Press/Simon & Schuster, 1984), 130.
98. Sara Halprin, *'Look at my Ugly Face': Myths and Musings on Beauty and other Perilous Obsessions with Women's Appearance* (Toronto, ON: Penguin, 1995), 6.

2 'Soveraigne Receipts', Fair Beauty and Race in Stuart England

1. Karen Britland, *Drama at the Courts of Queen Henrietta Maria* (Cambridge: Cambridge University Press, 2006); Melina J. Gough, 'Courtly *Comédiantes*: Henrietta Maria and Amateur Women's Stage Plays in France and England', in *Women Players in England 1500–1600: Beyond the All Male Stage.* ed. Pamela Allen Brown and Peter Parolin (Aldershot: Ashgate, 2005), 193–215; Sarah Poynting, '"In the Name of all the Sisters": Henrietta Maria's Notorious Whores', in *Women and Culture at the Courts of Stuart Queens*, ed. Clare McManus (New York: Palgrave Macmillan, 2003), 163–85; Julie Sanders, 'Caroline Salon Culture and Female Agency: The Countess of Carlisle, Henrietta Maria, and Public Theatre', *Theatre Journal* 52 (2000): 449–64; Sophie Tomlinson, '"She that Plays the King": Henrietta Maria and the Threat of the Actress in Caroline Culture', in *The Politics of Tragicomedy: Shakespeare and After*, ed. Gordon McMullan and Jonathan Hope (London: Routledge, 1992), 189–207; Erica Veevers, *Images of Love and Religion: Queen Henrietta Maria and Court Entertainments* (Cambridge: Cambridge University Press, 1989).

2. Susan M. Pearce, *On Collecting: An Investigation into Collecting in the European Tradition* (London and New York: Routledge, 1995), 116.
3. *The Queens Closet Opened* (London: Nathaniel Brook, 1655), A4v. All subsequent references are to this edition.
4. Margreta de Grazia, 'The Scandal of Shakespeare's Sonnets', in *Shakespeare's Sonnets: Critical Essays*, ed. James Schiffer (New York and London: Garland, 2000), 101–2.
5. Valerie Babb, *Whiteness Visible: The Meaning of Whiteness in American Literature and Culture* (New York and London: New York University Press, 1998), 9–10.
6. Joyce Green MacDonald, *Women and Race in Early Modern Texts* (Cambridge: Cambridge University Press, 2002), 44.
7. Gary Taylor, *Buying Whiteness: Race, Culture, and Identity from Columbus to Hip Hop* (Basingstoke: Palgrave Macmillan, 2005), 14; Nell Irvin Painter, *The History of White People* (New York and London: W. W. Norton, 2010), xi, 104–6. See also Babb, 16–45; Laura Doyle, *Freedom's Empire: Race and the Rise of the Novel in Atlantic Modernity, 1640–1940* (Durham, NC and London: Duke University Press, 2008), 27–78; Steve Garner, *Whiteness: An Introduction* (London and New York: Routledge, 2007), 64–8.
8. Taylor, 34–5
9. Ania Loomba, *Shakespeare, Race, and Colonialism* (Oxford: Oxford University Press, 2002), 22–46.
10. Sujata Iyengar, *Shades of Difference: Mythologies of Skin Color in Early Modern England* (Philadelphia, PA: University of Pennsylvania Press, 2005), 4.
11. MacDonald, 9, 10; Loomba, 36; Kim F. Hall, *Things of Darkness: Economies of Race and Gender in Early Modern England* (Ithaca, NY and London: Cornell University Press, 1995), 6–7.
12. Loomba, 33.
13. Margo Hendricks and Patricia Parker, eds, *Women, 'Race,' and Writing in the Early Modern Period*, (London: Routledge, 1994); Kimberly Woolsey Poitevin, '"Counterfeit Colour": Making Up Race in Elizabeth Cary's *The Tragedy of Mariam*', *Tulsa Studies in Women's Literature* 24.1 (2005): 13–34; Barbara Bowen, 'Aemilia Lanyer and the Invention of White Womanhood', in *Maids and Mistresses, Cousins and Queens: Women's Alliances in Early Modern England*, ed. Susan Frye and Karen Robertson (New York: Oxford University Press, 1999), 274–303; Cristina Malcolmson, '"The Explication of Whiteness and Blackness": Skin Color and the Physics of Color in the Works of Robert Boyle and Margaret Cavendish', in *Fault Lines and Controversies in the Study of Seventeenth-Century English Literature*, ed. Claude J. Summers and Ted-Larry Pebworth (Columbia, MO: University of Missouri Press, 2002), 187–203.
14. Richard Dyer, *White* (London and New York: Routledge, 1997), 14.
15. Jesse G. Swan, '"Imbodies, and imbrutes": Constructing Whiteness in Milton's *A Maske Presented at Ludlow Castle*', *Clio* 33.4 (2004): 370, 372.
16. Peter Erickson, 'Representations of Blacks and Blackness in the Renaissance', *Criticism* 35.4 (1993): 517.
17. Kim F. Hall, 'Beauty and the Beast of Whiteness: Teaching Race and Gender', *Shakespeare Quarterly* 47.5 (1996): 466.
18. Veevers, 179.
19. Aurelian Townsend, 'Tempe Restored', in *Inigo Jones: The Theatre of the Stuart Court*, ed. Stephen Orgel and Roy Strong, vol. 2 (Berkeley, CA and

Los Angeles, CA: University of California Press; London: Sotheby Parke Bernet, 1973), 479–503; lines 361–4.

20. William Davenant and Inigo Jones, 'The Temple of Love', in *Inigo Jones: The Theatre of the Stuart Court,* vol. 2, 599–629; lines 421–2.

21. William Davenant, 'Luminalia: The Queen's Festival of Light', in *Inigo Jones: The Theatre of the Stuart Court,* vol. 2, 705–23; line 37.

22. Francis Lenton, *Great Britaines Beauties, or, The Female Glory* (London: Marmaduke Parsons, 1638).

23. William Davenant, 'Salmacida Spolia', in *Inigo Jones: The Theatre of the Stuart Court,* vol. 2, 729–85; lines 107–10, 88–92. All subsequent references are to this edition.

24. See Orgel and Strong, *Inigo Jones: The Theatre of the Stuart Court,* vol. 2, 735 for an image.

25. Taylor, 32–3; *Nicholas Hilliard's Art of Limning: A New Edition of A Treatise Concerning the Arte of Limning,* transcription by Arthur F. Kinney, commentary and apparatus by Linda Bradley Salamon (Boston, MA: Northeastern University Press, 1983), 31; Henry Peacham, *The Compleat Gentleman* (London: Francis Constable, 1634), 131.

26. Davenant and Jones, 'The Temple of Love', line 295.

27. Townsend, 'Tempe Restored', line 122; Orgel and Strong, *Inigo Jones: The Theatre of the Stuart Court,* vol. 2, 767, 434.

28. Martin Butler, 'Politics and the Masque: *Salmacida Spolia*', in *Literature and the English Civil War,* ed. Thomas Healy and Jonathan Sawday (Cambridge: Cambridge University Press, 1990), 59–74.

29. Graham Parry, *The Golden Age Restor'd: The Culture of the Stuart Court, 1603–1642* (Manchester: Manchester University Press, 1981), 201–2.

30. Veevers, 118.

31. Karen Britland, 'An Under-Stated Mother-in-Law: Marie de Médici and the Last Caroline Court Masque', in *Women and Culture at the Courts of the Stuart Queens,* ed. Clare McManus (Basingstoke: Palgrave Macmillan, 2003), 213.

32. Orgel and Strong, *Inigo Jones: The Theatre of the Stuart Court,* vol. 2, 735.

33. Kathryn Schwarz, *Tough Love: Amazon Encounters in the English Renaissance* (Durham, NC: Duke University Press, 2000), 22, 56–7.

34. Sir Walter Raleigh, *Discoverie of the Large, Rich, and Bewtiful Empire of Guiana* (London: Robert Robinson, 1596), 23.

35. Robert Harcourt, *A Relation of a Voyage to Guiana* (London: J. Beale, 1613), 4; John Smith, *The True Travels, Adventures, and Observations of Captaine John Smith, in Europe, Asia, Affrica, and America, from anno Domini 1593 to 1629* (London: John Haviland, 1630), 51.

36. *A Publication of Guiana's Plantation* (London: William Jones, 1632), 7.

37. Smith, 49.

38. Raleigh, 45, 95.

39. ibid , 94.

40. *A Publication of Guiana's Plantation,* 14.

41. Harcourt, 33–5.

42. R. Malcolm Smuts, 'Art and the Material Culture of Majesty in Early Stuart England', in *The Stuart Court and Europe: Essays in Politics and Political Culture,* ed. R. Malcolm Smuts (Cambridge: Cambridge University Press, 1996), 107.

43. Madeline Bassnett, 'Restoring the Royal Household: Royalist Politics and the Commonwealth Recipe Book', *Early English Studies* 2 (2009): 3

<http://www.uta.edu/english/ees/fulltext/bassnett2.html>. See also Laura Lunger Knoppers, 'Opening the Queen's Closet: Henrietta Maria, Elizabeth Cromwell, and the Politics of Cookery', *Renaissance Quarterly* 60.2 (2007): 464–99. For examples of receipt books with a clearly polemical and royalist stance, see Theodore Turquet de Mayerne, *Archimagirus Anglo-Gallicus: or Excellent & Approved Receipts and Experiments in Cookery* [...] *According to the French Mode, and English Manner* (1658) and *The Court & Kitchin of Elizabeth, Commonly called Joan Cromwel, the Wife of the late Usurper Cromwell* (1664).

44. Jayne Archer, 'The Queen's Arcanum: Authority and Authorship in *The Queens Closet Opened* (1655)', *Renaissance Journal* 1.6 (2002): 14–26.

45. Leah Marcus, *The Politics of Mirth: Jonson, Herrick, Milton, Marvell, and the Defense of Old Holiday Pastimes* (Chicago, IL: University of Chicago Press, 1978), 213, 214.

46. Richard Dyer, 'White', *Screen* 29.4 (1988): 44–6.

47. Sara Ahmed, 'Declarations of Whiteness: The Non-Performativity of Anti-Racism', *Borderlands* 3.2 (2004), para. 1. <http://www.borderlands.net.au/vol3no2_2004/ahmed_declarations.htm>

48. Hugh Trevor-Roper, 'Mayerne, Sir Theodore Turquet de (1573–1655)', in *Oxford Dictionary of National Biography* (Oxford: Oxford University Press, 2004). Online.

49. For more on this see P. W. M. Copeman and W. S. C. Copeman, 'Dermatology in Tudor and Early Stuart England', *History of Dermatology* 81 (1969): 303–10; Gail Kern Paster, *The Body Embarrassed: Drama and the Disciplines of Shame in Early Modern England* (Ithaca, NY: Cornell University Press, 1993), 12.

50. Thomas Vicary's *The English Man's Treasure* (London: Thomas Creede, 1613), 74; Peter Levens, *Right Profitable Booke for all Diseases, called, The Path-way to Health* (London: John Beale, 1631), 23; John Partridge's *Treasurie of Hidden Secrets* (London: [E. B.], 1627), F4, F2v.

51. *The Queens Closet Opened*, 146, 137, 138, 144.

52. Nicholas Culpeper, *The English Physician* (London: William Bentley, 1652), 35.

53. [Thomas Jeamson], *Artificiall Embellishments: Or Arts Best Directions How to Preserve Beauty or Procure It* (Oxford: William Hall, 1665), 47.

54. Ludmilla Jordanova, 'The Social Construction of Medical Knowledge', *The Social History of Medicine* 8 (1995): 362–3.

55. Margaret Pelling, *Medical Conflicts in Early Modern London: Patronage, Physicians, and Irregular Practitioners, 1550–1640* (Oxford: Clarendon Press, 2003), 234–45, 315–31.

56. Knoppers, 483–4.

57. Edith Snook, '"Soveraigne Receipts" and the Politics of Beauty in *The Queens Closet Opened*', *Early Modern Literary Studies*, Special Issue 15 (August, 2007) 7.12–19. <http://extra.shu.ac.uk/emls/si-15/snooksov.htm>

58. Townsend, 'Tempe Restored', 469.

59. Diane Purkiss, *Literature, Gender and Politics During the English Civil War* (Cambridge: Cambridge University Press, 2005), 77.

60. Kevin Sharpe, *Criticism and Compliment: The Politics of Literature in the England of Charles I* (Cambridge: Cambridge University Press, 1987), 3–22.

61. *The Wandring Beauty: A Novel* was printed by Sam. Briscoe, first in 1698 and then in 1700 in *Histories, Novels and Translations*. The 1700 edition

of *The Wandring Beauty* does not have the dedication to Edward, Earl of Derwentwater.

62. On *The Widow Ranter,* see Margo Hendricks, 'Civility, Barbarism, and Aphra Behn's *The Widow Ranter',* in *Women, 'Race,' and Writing in the Early Modern Period,* 225–39; Heidi Hutner, *Colonial Women: Race and Culture in Stuart Drama* (Oxford: Oxford University Press, 2001), 89–106. On *Oronooko,* see Laura Doyle, *Freedom's Empire,* 97–115; Laura Brown, *Ends of Empire: Women and Ideology in Early Eighteenth-Century English Literature* (Ithaca, NY and London: Cornell University Press, 1993), 23–63; Gary Gautier, 'Slavery and the Fashioning of Race in *Oroonoko, Robinson Crusoe,* and *Equiano's Life', Eighteenth Century: Theory and Interpretation* 42: 2 (2001): 161–79; Margaret W. Ferguson, 'Juggling the Categories of Race, Class, and Gender: Aphra Behn's *Oroonoko',* in *Women, 'Race,' and Writing,* 209–24.

63. The title recalls several other popular works conduct books: Phillip Stubbes' *A Crystall Glasse for Christian Women* (1590 through to 1693), Barnabe Rich's *My Ladies Looking Glass* (1616), Thomas Tolls' *The Female Duel, or, the Ladies Looking Glass* (1661), Samuel Clarke's *A Looking-Glass for Good Women to Dress Themselves By* (1677) and Edward Bury's *A Looking-Glass for the Unmarried* (1697).

64. Aphra Behn, *The Lady's Looking-Glass, To Dress Herself By: Or, the Whole Art of Charming* (London: W. Onley, 1697), 6.

65. Behn, *The Lady's Looking Glass,* 7–9, 11–12.

66. Behn, *The Lady's Looking Glass,* 8, 23.

67. Aphra Behn, *The Wandring Beauty,* in *The Works of Aphra Behn,* ed. Janet Todd, vol. 3 (Columbus, OH: Ohio State University Press, 1995), 402. All subsequent references are to this edition.

68. Judith M. Spicksley, 'To Be or Not to Be Married: Single Women, Money-lending, and the Question of Choice in Late Tudor and Stuart England', in *The Single Woman in Medieval and Early Modern England: Her Life and Representation,* ed. Laurel Amtower and Dorothea Kehler (Tempe, AZ: Arizona Center for Medieval and Renaissance Studies, 2003), 78. See also Bridget Hill, *Servants: English Domestics in the Eighteenth Century* (Oxford: Clarendon Press, 1996), 42.

69. Pamela Sharpe, 'Dealing with Love: The Ambiguous Independence of the Single Woman in Early Modern England', *Gender and History* 11.2 (1999): 209–32; Christine Peters, 'Single Women in Early Modern England: Attitudes and Expectations', *Continuity and Changes* 12 (1997): 325–45; Spicksley, 65–96.

70. Hill, 44–63.

71. Naomi Tadmor, 'The Concept of the Household-Family in Eighteenth-Century England', *Past and Present* 151 (1996): 123–5.

72. Johann Wecker, *Arts Master-piece: Or, the Beautifying Part of Physick* (London: Nathaniel Brook, 1660), 35.

73. Johann Wecker, *Eighteen Books of the Secrets of Art & Nature* (London: Simon Miller, 1660), 87.

74. Leo Gooch, 'Radcliffe, James, styled third earl of Derwentwater (1689–1716)', in *Oxford Dictionary of National Biography* (Oxford: Oxford University Press, 2004). Online.

75. Brown, 55–8.

76. *An Exact Narrative and Relation of his Most Sacred Majesties Escape from Worcester on the third of September, 1651* (London: [n.p.], 1660), 6, 8.
77. *An Exact Narrative*, 16. This description also appears in *Englands Triumph: A More Exact History of His Majesties Escape After the Battle of Worcester* (London: John Grismond, 1660).
78. Thomas Blount, *Boscobel: or the Compleat History of His Sacred Majesties Most Miraculous Preservation* (London: M. Clark, 1680), 48.
79. ibid., 61.
80. *Englands Triumph*, 19.
81. Susan Staves, 'Behn, Women, and Society', in *The Cambridge Companion to Aphra Behn*, ed. Derek Hughes and Janet Todd (Cambridge: Cambridge University Press, 2004), 19–20.
82. Frederick M. Link, *Aphra Behn* (New York: Twayne, 1968), 148.
83. Thomas Buoni, *Problemes of Beautie and all Humane Affections*, trans. S.L. (London: G. Eld, 1606), 54–5.
84 Homi Bhabha, 'The White Stuff', *Artforum* (1998): 21.
85. Anne McClintock, *Imperial Leather: Race, Gender and Sexuality in the Colonial Context* (London and New York: Routledge, 1995), 5.

3   The Greatness in Good Clothes: Fashioning Subjectivity in Mary Wroth's *Urania* and Margaret Spencer's Account Book (BL Additional MS 62092)

1. For a concise assessment of these derogatory associations, see Amanda Vickery, 'Women and the World of Goods: A Lancashire Consumer and her Possessions, 1751–81', in *Consumption and the World of Goods,* ed. John Brewer and Roy Porter (London and New York: Routledge, 1993), 274–301.
2. See for example, John Brewer and Roy Porter, eds, *Consumption and the World of Goods*; Elizabeth Kowaleski-Wallace, *Consuming Subjects: Women, Shopping, and Business in the Eighteenth Century* (New York: Columbia University Press, 1997); Beverly Lemire, *Dress, Culture and Commerce: The English Clothing Trade Before the Factory, 1660–1800* (Basingstoke: Macmillan – now Palgrave Macmillan; New York: St. Martin's, 1997); Amanda Vickery, *The Gentleman's Daughter: Women's Lives in Georgian England* (New Haven, CT and London: Yale University Press, 1998); Lorna Weatherhill, *Consumer Behaviour and Material Culture in Britain 1660–1760*, 2nd edn (London and New York: Routledge, 1996). For an important examination of women and consumption in earlier periods, see Karen Newman, 'City Talk: Women and Commodification in Jonson's *Epicoene*', *English Literary History* 3 (1989), 503–18.
3. Ann Rosalind Jones and Peter Stallybrass, *Renaissance Clothing and the Materials of Memory* (Cambridge: Cambridge University Press, 2000); Lena Cowen Orlin, ed., *Material London, ca. 1600* (Philadelphia, PA: University of Pennsylvania Press, 2000); Susan Vincent, *Dressing the Elite: Clothes in Early Modern England* (Oxford and New York: Berg, 2003); Roze Hentschell, *The Culture of Cloth in Early Modern England: Textual Constructions of a National Identity* (Aldershot: Ashgate, 2008).
4. Daniel Roche outlines five kinds of sources for the history of clothing: clothing, paintings and engravings, historical books on costume, literature

and the 'archives' – business and family account books. See *The Culture of Clothing: Dress and Fashion in the Ancien Regime,* trans. Jean Birrell (Cambridge and New York: Cambridge University Press, 1994), 7–21.

5. The only study of clothing in a pre-eighteenth-century woman's account book that I've been able to locate is Santina M. Levey, 'References to Dress in the Earliest Account Book of Bess of Hardwick', *Costume* 34 (2000): 13–28.

6. Margaret Spencer, *Spencer Accounts: Account Book for Personal Expenses of Margaret Spencer (d.1613), daughter of Robert, 1st Baron Spencer of Wormleighton,* 1610–1613, Additional MS 62092, British Library, London, UK. All subsequent references to this manuscript are noted in parenthetical citations.

7. See, for example, Nona Fienberg, 'Mary Wroth and the Invention of Female Poetic Subjectivity', in *Reading Mary Wroth: Representing Alternatives in Early Modern England,* ed. Naomi J. Miller and Gary Waller (Knoxville, TN: University of Tennessee Press, 1991), 175–90; Nona Fienberg, 'Mary Wroth's Poetics of the Self', *Studies in English Literature 1500–1800* 42.1 (2002): 121–36; Helen Hackett, '"A Book, and solitariness": Melancholia, Gender and Literary Subjectivity in Mary Wroth's *Urania*', in *Renaissance Configurations: Voices/Bodies/Spaces 1580–1690,* ed. Gordon McMullan (New York: St. Martins; Basingstoke: Macmillan – now Palgrave Macmillan, 1998), 64–85; Jacqueline T. Miller, 'The Passion Signified: Imitation and the Construction of Emotions in Sidney and Wroth', *Criticism,* 43.4 (2002): 407–21; Kathryn Pratt, '"Wounds Still Curelesse": Estates of Loss in Mary Wroth's *Urania*', in *Privacy, Domesticity, and Women in Early Modern England,* ed. Corinne S. Abate (Aldershot: Ashgate, 2003), 45–62; Amelia Zurcher Sandy, 'Pastoral, Temperance, and the Unitary Self in Wroth's *Urania*', *Studies in English Literature 1500–1800* 42.1 (2002): 103–19; Carolyn Swift, 'Feminine Identity in Lady Mary Wroth's Romance *Urania*', *English Literary Renaissance* 14 (1984): 328–48; Heather L. Weidemann, 'Theatricality and Female Identity in Mary Wroth's *Urania*', in *Reading Mary Wroth,* 191–209.

8. Linda Levy Peck mentions Margaret Spencer in *Consuming Splendor: Society and Culture in Seventeenth-Century England* (Cambridge: Cambridge University Press, 2005), 69, 70. A family monument in the parish church in Brington, Northamptonshire indicates that Margaret and Robert Spencer had four sons and three daughters: '1. John Spencer, Esq; who died at Blois in France without issue; 2. William Lord Spencer, who married Lady Penelope Eldest daughter of Henry Earl of Southampton; 3. Richard Spencer, Esq; 4. Sir Edward Spencer of Boston in the Co. of Midd. Knight, who married Dame Mary Widow of Sir William Reade of Austerby in the same co. Knight – 1. Mary married to Sir Richard Anderson of Penly in the co. of Hartforde Knight; 2. Elizabeth married to Sir George Fane of Buston in the Co. of Kent Knight, who died without issue; 3. Margaret, who died unmarried; which Robert Lord Spencer departed this life the 25 of October Anno Domini 1627 and Margaret his Wife the 17th August 1597. Robert Lord Spencer built this monument in his life Anno 1599.' See Peter Whalley, *The History and Antiquities of Northamptonshire. Compiled from the Manuscript collections of the Late Learned Antiquary John Bridges, Esq.,* vol. 1 (Oxford: Payne, 1791), 475.

9. The first entry seems to be for the previous year because it begins with the indication that she received the money 'last somer', and notes that she cannot remember how she spent 2s 4d, since it has been such a long time

(fol.1*v*). I arrive at the estimation of her age knowing that her parents were married in 1587; her brother William was born in 1591, and Mary, a sister was born in 1588. Her date of death is recorded on Margaret Spencer's grave marker, near the family monument, along with the Latin inscription '*Sola Virtus Invicta / Subjecta Nulli, Mentis / Atque animi bonum, / Florem decoris singuli car- / punt dies*' or 'Unconquered virtue alone,/Subjected to none/ Goodness in mind and spirit;/Day by day they pluck the flowers of honour.' Thanks to Adrian Tronson for the translation. See William Dugdale, *The Antiquities of Warwickshire*, vol. 1, revised William Thomas (Didsbury: E. J. Morten, n.d.); Richard Cust, 'Spencer, Robert, first Baron Spencer (1570–1627)', *Oxford Dictionary of National Biography* (Oxford: Oxford University Press, 2004). Online; Peter Whalley, *The History and Antiquities of Northamptonshire*; [http://www.althorp.com/spencer-family/familytree. pdf]; G. E. Cokayne with Vicary Gibbs, H. A. Doubleday, Geoffrey H. White, Duncan Warrand and Lord Howard de Walden, eds, *The Complete Peerage of England, Scotland, Ireland, Great Britain and the United Kingdom, Extant, Extinct or Dormant* (1910–59) (London: St. Catherine Press, 1953), I, pt. 1, 159–60.

10. The story is told that the Earl of Arundel insulted him in Parliament in 1621 by saying that 'My ancestors have suffered, and it may be for doing the King and the country good service, and in such time as when, perhaps the lord's ancestors that spake last kept sheep.' Robert Spencer is supposed to have replied that that was when the Earl of Arundel's ancestors were plotting treason. See Cust, as well as Cokayne, vol. 12, pt. 1, 159–60.

11. *The Muses Thankfulnesse, or A Funeral Elegie, Consecrated to the perpetuall memory of the late All Honourable, and All-Noble Lord, Robert, Baron Spencer, of Wormleighton* ([London: I. Jaggard, 1627]).

12. 'Spencer, Robert, first Baron Spencer of Wormleighton', in *Dictionary of National Biography* (London: Oxford University Press, 1921–1922), vol. 18, 776.

13. Edmund Spenser, *Colin Clouts Come Home Again*, in *The Yale Edition of the Shorter Poems of Edmund Spenser,* ed William A. Oram et al. (New Haven, CT and London: Yale University Press, 1989), 570; lines 537–8.

14. Ben Jonson, 'A Particular Entertainment', in *The Workes of Benjamin Jonson* (London: Will Stansby, 1616), 869–78.

15. Margaret Spencer is also, incidentally, the ancestor of Diana, Princess of Wales; Althorp is her burial place.

16. Elizabeth Hanson, *Discovering the Subject in Renaissance England* (Cambridge: Cambridge University Press, 1998), 10.

17. Pierre Bourdieu, *Outline of a Theory of Practice,* trans. Richard Nice (Cambridge: Cambridge University Press, 1977), 94.

18. Roche, *The Culture of Clothing*, 6. Susan E. Whyman also proposes that the ideals of behaviour found in the seventeenth-century conduct books had classical origins: from Cicero came the belief that outward decorum was a manifestation of inner disposition. Decorum comprises more than dress, and includes gestures, complexion and walking. *Sociability and Power in Late-Stuart England: The Cultural Worlds of the Verneys 1660–1720* (Oxford: Oxford University Press, 1999), 88.

19. Jones and Stallybrass, 2.

20. Juan Luis Vives, *A Very Fruteful and Pleasant boke callyd the Instruction of a Christian Woman,* trans. Richard Hyrde (London: Thomae Berth., 1541), 28*v*.

21. Richard Brathwait, *The English Gentlewoman* (London: B. Alsop and T. Fawcet, 1631), 7–8.
22. Giovanni Michelle Bruto, *The Necessarie, Fit, and Convenient Education of a Yong Gentlewoman*, trans. W. P. (London: Adam Islip, 1598), B4.
23. Vincent, 125–6.
24. Bruto, K2*v*, K4.
25. ibid., F8.
26. Vives, 25, 26*v*.
27. Brathwait, 9–10.
28. John Dod and Robert Cleaver, *A Godly Forme of Houshold Government* (London: R. Field, 1621), P8.
29. Mary Wroth, *The First Part of the Countess of Montgomery's Urania*, ed. Josephine A. Roberts (Binghamton, NY: Medieval and Renaissance Texts and Studies, 1995), 76. All subsequent references are to this edition.
30. For example, Emilina, a lady who loves and is abandoned by an imposter Amphilanthus, wears tawny; Amphilanthus dons a tawny livery, said to reveal his misery; another lady has her hair wound in strings of tawny, 'to shew her chance' (300, 378, 396, 416).
31. David Cressy, *Birth, Marriage, and Death: Ritual, Religion, and the Life-cycle in Tudor and Stuart England* (Oxford and New York: Oxford University Press, 2002), 440. See also, Lou Taylor, *Mourning Dress: A Costume and Social History* (London: George Allen & Unwin, 1983), 104.
32. Jones and Stallybrass, 17.
33. ibid., 276.
34. Kim F. Hall, '"I Rather Would Wish to be a Black-Moor": Beauty, Race, and Rank in Lady Mary Wroth's *Urania*', in *Women, 'Race,' and Writing in Early Modern England*, ed. Margo Hendricks and Patricia Parker (London and New York: Routledge, 1994), 187, 180.
35. Akiko Kusunoki, 'Female Selfhood and Male Violence in English Renaissance Drama: A View from Mary Wroth's *Urania*', in *Women, Violence, and English Renaissance Literature: Essays Honoring Paul Jorgensen*, ed. Linda Woodbridge and Sharon Beehler (Tempe, AZ: Arizona Center for Medieval and Renaissance Studies, 2003), 140.
36. See Miller, 'The Passion Signified', 407–21; Fienberg, 'Mary Wroth's Poetics of Self', 121–36; Sandy, 'Pastoral, Temperance, and the Unitary Self', 103–19.
37. Weidemann, 'Theatricality and Female Identity', 192.
38. Elaine Beilin, 'Winning "the harts of the people": The Role of the Political Subject in the *Urania*', in *Pilgrimage for Love: Essays in Early Modern Literature in Honor of Josephine A. Roberts*, ed. Sigrid King (Tempe, AZ: Arizona Center for Medieval and Renaissance Studies, 1999), 14.
39. On women and property law, see Sara Mendelson and Patricia Crawford, *Women in Early Modern England 1550–1720* (Oxford: Clarendon Press, 1998), 218–25. They make the point that 'wives had no legal right to dispose of the commodities they produced, nor to spend the cash they had inherited or earned'; but clothing, like other household goods women produced, inherited or used daily, could be treated as their own under a form of 'moral' proprietorship (219–20).
40. Vives, 26*v*.
41. Jones and Stallybrass, 3.

42. Robert Spencer's secretary hand is also found in *Letters and Papers Relating to the Family of Spencer, or Spenser, of Althorp*, 1522–1656, Additional MS 25079, British Library, London, UK, and *Household Accompts of the Family of Spencer*, 1599–1605, Additional MS 25080, British Library, London, UK.
43. Amy Louise Erikson, *Women and Property in Early Modern England* (London and New York: Routledge, 1993), 54.
44. Amanda Vickery, *The Gentleman's Daughter*, 134.
45. In Additional MS 25080, using a notation such as 'payd Mary Spencer' (fol. 17*v*), Mary Spencer audits the accounts (fols. 148v, 89, 100*v*–147); she also appears to have a role in directing expenditures, as suggested by an entry like 'for a cloth of valure for your ladyshyppe 26s' (fol. 38). These accounts are in the hand of a Mr Campion, a servant. Robert Spencer signs off on other account periods. Campion's name appears in a list of disbursements of servants' wages for half a year; earning £5, he occupies the head of the list (fol. 95*v*). Mary Spencer's autograph also appears in Additional MS 25079 in a letter by Mary Spencer to Robert Spencer (fol. 68).
46. Dod and Cleaver, F3*v*–4. They also instruct the husband to choose a frugal wife: 'Briefly, she must know which way to save a penny, and lay about her to save it, for many a little maketh a great deale. She must know what is meete for servants, what for workemen, and what not: what is meet for ordinarie, and what is meete for strangers. Above all, shee must know how to keepe within her compasse, and yet to avoid the reproch of a pincher' (F5).
47. *Advice to the Women and Maidens of London* (London: Benjamin Billinsley, 1678). Hannah Wolley also imagines the female accountant to be a useful servant, for the maid can disperse and receive money for her lady. *The Compleat Servant-Maid* (London: T. Passinger, 1677), 21–9.
48. Basil S. Yamey draws attention to the religious impetus of accounting evident, until the eighteenth century, in beginning account books with pious inscriptions, such as 'Laus Deo', 'The Name of GOD be our helpe', 'In the name of God' or 'Pleaseth God to geve me profytt and prosperitye'. Even after this practice declined, eighteenth-century textbooks on accounting continued to exhort accountants 'to keep their books, like their consciences, clean and tidy and in a constant state of preparedness'. *Essays on the History of Accounting* (New York: Arno, 1978), 143–7. Margaret Spencer's account book does not have these religious references.
49. Bathsua Makin, *An Essay to Revive the Antient Education of Women* (London: John Darby, 1673), 15.
50. *Advice to the Women and Maidens of London*, A.
51. ibid., A3.
52. Margaret Spufford, *The Great Reclothing of Rural England: Petty Chapmen and their Wares in the Seventeenth Century* (London: Hambledon Press, 1984), 107–30.
53. Gervase Markham, for example, imagines the housewife defending her household, outwardly from the cold with wool and inwardly with linen. The housewife is responsible for most of the labour in that process, with the exception of stages dependent on the guild structure. Gervase Markham, *The English Housewife* (London: Nicholas Okes, 1631), 167–90. Alice C. Clark also accords much value to women's productive labour within the early modern household. She observes that women were excluded from weaving worsteds

because they were thought too weak to work the heavy looms; women were more often engaged in the lower paid work of spinning. *The Working Life of Women in the Seventeenth Century* (1919; reprinted London: Kegan & Paul, 1982), 103.

54. Clark, *The Working Life of Women*, 93–149, esp. 145–6.

55. Beverly Lemire, *Dress, Culture and Commerce*, 4. Lemire also examines the important role that women played in the used clothing business as unsanctioned traders, where the household skill of needleworking could translate into a paying occupation when they recycled clothing by mending and refashioning garments and then selling them. Although Lemire's focus is on the long eighteenth-century, she does trace this sort of activity back to the sixteenth century (95–120).

56. Althorp and Wormleighton belong to her father; Buston is the home of her sister Elizabeth; Penley, of her sister Mary; and Mereworth of her 'Aunt Spencer' (fol. 2), probably Mary Neville, Baroness Le Despencer. Her sister Elizabeth married Sir George Fane, of Buston '(co. Kent)', while her other sister Mary wed Sir Richard Anderson of 'Pen(d)l(e)y (co. Hertfordshire)'. See Whalley, *The History and Antiquities of Northamptonshire*, 475. Margaret Spencer also gave 2s 'to a womman for showeinge of me Sr Thomas Whartons howes' (fol. 21*v*); she expended 5s 3d, 'Leftt behinde to paye for 21 paire of sheetes that were leftt fowle att St Johnses' (fol. 24*v*); and her father gave her money at 'chartar hous' (fol. 2). A series of connected records from after Christmas 1611/12 suggests she attended the christening of a child: she paid 20s to the midwife, 'att my cosen dallysons when I crisned her child', with a further 20s going to the child's nurse; she gave 5s to 'my cosen dallisons coche man yt daye', and 2s 6d to his footman 'att that time', and finally 6d to a woman 'for openinge the gates then' (fol. 12).

57. Spufford, 85–105, 124.

58. D. M. Palliser claims that in Elizabethan England, food items, as well as 'tables and benches, knives and nails, pots and pans, and caps and shoes' were sold within a few miles of their manufacture, although Joan Thirsk documents the fierce Dutch–English competition over the trade in pins and needles. T. S. Willan also agrees that markets sold goods that were produced locally; shops, on the other hand, sold a more diverse array of goods. See D. M. Palliser, *The Age of Elizabeth: England Under the Later Tudors 1547–1603* (London and New York: Longman, 1983), 266–7; Joan Thirsk, *Economic Policy and Projects: The Development of a Consumer Society in Early Modern England* (Oxford: Clarendon Press, 1978), 78–83; and T. S. Willan, *The Inland Trade: Studies in English Internal Trade in the Sixteenth and Seventeenth Centuries* (Manchester: Manchester University Press, 1976), 53–71.

59. Spencer pays one carrier for transporting her 'thinges' from Buston, and another to bring her 'trunke and box'; a 'maythue whitt' also transports her 'hampar with my gownes from penley' (fol. 14*v*). Willan discusses the presence of carriers in England in the early seventeenth century. While by 1637, there was, he suggests, an 'extensive carrying service between provincial towns and London' with a regular schedule, he is not certain how widespread the regular service was before then. He does show the use of carriers in early periods, however. Willan, *The Inland Trade*, 12–13.

60. Thirsk, 119.

61. According to Tim Meldrum, these sorts of payments were vails, a form of remuneration that could constitute a large, even expected, portion of a servant's wages in a period in which both the money wage and the 'moral economy of service' structured servants' lives. *Domestic Service and Gender 1660–1750: Life and Work in the London Household* (Harlow: Pearson, 2000), 199–205.

62. Whyman, 100–1. For more on coaches and display, see Meldrum, 177.

63. Palliser, 237–52.

64. Herman Van Der Wee, in collaboration with John Munro, 'The Western European Woollen Industries, 1500–1750', in *Cambridge History of Western Textiles*, ed. David Jenkins (Cambridge: Cambridge University Press, 2003), 454. Baize, one of the new draperies, and fustian were produced in England from the sixteenth century. D. M. Palliser says that the largest English export was wool and woollen cloth and that cottons and silks were mostly imported in 1600. Linen was made around Manchester, but it was not until later in the seventeenth century that there was a substantial linen industry in England because English linen had been coarse. Palliser, *The Age of Elizabeth*, 260–79. See also Alfred P. Wadsworth and Julia de lacy Mann, *The Cotton Trade and Industrial Lancashire 1600–1780* (New York: Augustus M. Kelley, 1968), 1–28.

65. Natalie Rothstein, 'Silk in the Early Modern Period, c.1500–1700', in *The Cambridge History of Western Textiles*, 528. Erik Kerridge argues that there was an English silk manufacturing industry after 1615 and that by 1639 the manufacture of broad silk in London was facilitated by the immigration of Huguenot silk workers. Erik Kerridge, *Textile Manufactures in Early Modern England* (Manchester: Manchester University Press, 1985), 128. Palliser provides something of the history of trade with Turkey: in 1581, Queen Elizabeth incorporated the Turkey Company, which became the Levant Company in 1599. The English traded cloth for raw silk and Turkish carpets. Palliser, *The Age of Elizabeth*, 290.

66. Leslie Clarkson, 'The Linen Industry in Early Modern Europe', in *The Cambridge History of Western Textiles*, 473–92. Margaret Spufford, who looks at England, argues that linen was the most important English import and that it was not until the 1690s that a commercial domestic linen industry could compete with imported French, Dutch and Flemish linens. Spufford, *The Great Reclothing of Rural England*, 90. According to Kerridge, in this period, 'The English wove some flax, hemp and waste silk [used in the manufacture of narrow-wares, such as ribbons, garters, galloons, inkles, trimmings, hatbands etc.], but had no broad silk or cotton-wool textiles manufactures, and in return for their immense exports of woollens, imported from the Continent vast quantities of linen, hempen and silken yarns and cloths and of fustians and other fabrics incorporating cotton wool.' Kerridge, *Textile Manufactures*, 24.

67. This price is less than the average prices for calico documented by Carole Shammas. She says that the average price of calico in the late sixteenth century was 28s/yard; in the early seventeenth century, calico was 13s/yard; by the late seventeenth century, the cost was 12s/yard< and it rose again in the early eighteenth century to 24s/yard because of English prohibitions on foreign calico. Carole Shammas, 'Changes in English and Anglo-American

Consumption from 1550 to 1800', in *Consumption and the World of Goods,* 192–3.

68. Calico would be one of the 'new colonial consumer products which redefined material expectations and standards of comfort'. Beverley Lemire, 'Fashioning Cottons: Asian Trade, Domestic Industry and Consumer Demand, 1660–1780', in *The Cambridge History of Western Textiles,* 495. Lemire also looks at Southampton probate inventories for evidence of calico ownership in the sixteenth century in 'Domesticating the Exotic: Floral Culture and the East India Calico Trade with England, c. 1600–1800', *Textile: The Journal of Cloth and Culture,* 1: 1 (2003), 65–85.

69. Philip Lawson, *The East India Company: A History* (London and New York: Longman, 1993), 25; Lemire, 'Domesticating the Exotic', 67.

70. Thomas Mun, *A Discourse of Trade, from England unto the East Indies* (1621), 5, 7–14. In contrast, John Cary's later work, *A Discourse Concerning the East India Trade* (1699) proposes a law banning its importation on the grounds that it hinders the English textile industry by reducing the demand for English woollens (3, 4).

71. He is probably the son of Mary Neville, Baroness Le Despencer, whose name is recorded in the manuscript on several occasions. She had a castle at Mereworth, Kent, and Margaret records visits to Mereworth, as well. Francis Fane became the first Earl of Westmoreland in 1624. Margaret's sister Elizabeth married a Sir George Fane, of Buston, Kent, but I have not been able to determine the exact relationship between these Fanes. The connection with the family appears to have been an important one, for, in addition to the gifts of clothes to the Baroness, she records a gift to one of her maids on her wedding (fol. 1) and payments to Sir Francis Fane's coachman and servant (fols. 7, 8). She also pays 12d for breaking a glass at the 'sauaye of Sr Francis fanes' (fol. 6) (for that matter, she pays her nurse 6d for breaking a cup, as well) (fol. 18v).

72. Mun, *A Discourse of Trade,* 7.

73. Murray G. Lawson, *Fur: A Study in English Mercantilism 1700–1775* (Toronto, ON: University of Toronto Press, 1943), 2. Lawson also notes that the hat was attuned to politics: 'every major political upheaval brought in its train a corresponding change in hat styles'; the kind of hat popular under James I and Charles I was a 'high-crowned broad-brimmed, rather squarish "Spanish beaver"' (4–5). See also Harold A. Innis, *The Fur Trade in Canada: An Introduction to Canadian Economic History,* rev. edn (1930; Toronto, ON: University of Toronto Press, 1962), 12; Julia Emberley, *The Cultural Politics of Fur* (Ithaca, NY and London: Cornell University Press, 1997), 67.

74. Paul Chrisler Phillips indicates that during the reign of Elizabeth, the English had little interest in the fur business and obtained what they wanted from Russia. This changed in 1606 and 160? when the Earl of Southampton, Sir Ferdinand Gorges, and first, Lord Arundel of Wardour, and then, Sir John Popham sent ships to America and obtained a number of furs. In 1611, the Earl of Southampton sent another expedition to the New England coast. Paul Chrisler Phillips, *The Fur Trade,* vol. 1 (Norman, OK: University of Oklahoma Press, 1961), 25–6. See also Peter C. Newman, *Empire of the Bay* (Toronto, ON: Penguin, 1998), 39–53; Emberley, *The Cultural Politics of Fur,* 66.

75. Innis, *The Fur Trade in Canada*, 1–42; Hugh Grant, 'Revenge of the Paris Hat: The European Craze for Wearing Headgear had a Profound Effect on Canadian History', *The Beaver* 68.6 (1988/89): 37–44.
76. For more on white beavers, see Charles Garrad, 'Michabous and the Colonel's White Beaver', *The Beaver* 67.1 (1987): 50–5.
77. Roze Hentschell, 'Treasonous Textiles: Foreign Cloth and the Construction of Englishness', *Journal of Medieval and Early Modern Studies* 32 (2002): 548.
78. Brathwait, *The English Gentlewoman*, 24–5.
79. Thirsk, *Economic Policy and Projects*, 89–91.
80. Gail Kern Paster, *The Body Embarrassed: Drama and Disciplines of Shame in Early Modern England* (Ithaca, NY: Cornell University Press, 1993); Jonathan Sawday, *The Body Emblazoned: Dissection and the Human Body in Renaissance Culture* (London: Routledge, 1995); Michael C. Schoenfeldt, *Bodies and Selves in Early Modern England: Physiology and Inwardness in Spenser, Shakespeare, Herbert, and Milton* (Cambridge: Cambridge University Press, 1999).
81. On religion, see Jones and Stallybrass, 4–5.
82. Anne Hollander, *Seeing Through Clothes* (New York: Viking Press, 1978), 311.
83. See Janet Ashelford, *Dress in the Age of Elizabeth* (New York: Holmes and Meier, 1988), 108–21.
84. Richard Brathwait's *The English Gentlewoman* offers this directive: 'there is nothing which confers more true glory on us, then in displaying our owne Countries garbe by that we weare upon us' (23). Unlike Jones and Stallybrass, who associate clothes with the dissolution of the body politic, Roze Hentschell contends that fashion can work to 'consolidate a sense of nation': 'The threat of the other, and specifically the threat of other's *clothes*, works to engender the importance of the English cloth industry for its subjects.' Hentschell, 'Treasonous Textiles', 544. See also Margaret W. Ferguson, 'Feathers and Flies: Aphra Behn and the Seventeenth-century Trade in Exotica', in *Subject and Object in Renaissance Culture*, ed. Margreta de Grazia, Maureen Quilligan, and Peter Stallybrass (Cambridge: Cambridge University Press, 1996), 235–59.
85. For more on women and textiles, see Susan Frye, 'Staging Women's Relations to Textiles in Shakespeare's *Othello* and *Cymbeline*', in *Early Modern Visual Culture: Representation, Race, and Empire in Renaissance England*, ed. Peter Erickson and Clark Hulse (Philadelphia, PA: University of Pennsylvania Press, 2000), 215–50.

4   What Not to Wear: Children's Clothes and the Maternal Advice of Elizabeth Jocelin and Brilliana, Lady Harley

1. Philippe Aries, *Centuries of Childhood: A Social History of Family Life*, trans. Robert Baldick (New York: Alfred A. Knopf, 1962), 50–61; Lawrence Stone, *The Family, Sex and Marriage in England 1500–1800* (New York: Harper and Row, 1977), 162.
2. Linda Pollock, *Forgotten Children: Parent–Child Relations from 1500 to 1900* (Cambridge: Cambridge University Press, 1983), esp. 49, 97; Patricia Crawford, *Blood, Bodies and Families in Early Modern England* (Harlow: Pearson Longman, 2004), 143–5; Kenneth Charlton, *Women, Religion and Education in Early Modern England* (London: Routledge, 1999), 188–240.

3. Betty Travitsky, 'The New Mother of the English Renaissance', in *The Lost Tradition: Mothers and Daughters in Literature*, ed. Cathy N. Davidson and E. M. Broner (New York: Ungar, 1980), 33–43; Wendy Wall, *The Imprint of Gender* (Ithaca, NY: Cornell University Press, 1993); Theresa Feroli, '"Infelix Simulacrum": The Rewriting of Loss in Elizabeth Jocelin's *The Mothers Legacie'*, *ELH* 61.1 (1994): 89–102; Kristen Poole, '"The Fittest Closet for All Goodness": Authorial Strategies of Jacobean Mothers' Manuals', *SEL* 35 (1995): 69–88; Valerie Wayne, 'Advice for Women from Mothers and Patriarchs', in *Women and Literature in Britain 1500–1700*, ed. Helen Wilcox (Cambridge: Cambridge University Press, 1996), 56–79; Catherine Gray, 'Feeding on the Seed of the Woman: Dorothy Leigh and the Figure of Maternal Dissent', *ELH* 68 (2001): 563–92; Edith Snook, 'Dorothy Leigh, the "Labourous Bee," and the Work of Literacy in Seventeenth-Century England' and 'A "Wit's Camelion": Elizabeth Grymeston and the Catholic Reader', in *Women, Reading, and the Cultural Politics of Early Modern England* (Aldershot: Ashgate, 2005), 57–114; Edith Snook, 'Dorothy Leigh's *The Mother's Blessing* and the Political Maternal Voice in Seventeenth-Century England', in *The Literary Mother*, ed. Susan Staub (Jefferson, NC: McFarland, 2007), 161–84; Megan Matchinske, 'Gendering Catholic Conformity: Equivocal History and Cultural Contexts in Elizabeth Grymeston's *Miscelanea'*, in *Women Writing History in Early Modern England* (Cambridge: Cambridge University Press, 2009), 45–73; Edith Snook, 'Maternal Advice', in *The History of British Women's Writing, 1500–1610*, ed. Caroline Bicks and Jennifer Summit, *The Palgrave History of British Women's Writing*, vol. 2 (Basingstoke: Palgrave Macmillan, 2010), 108–29.
4. Kenneth Charlton, 'Mothers as Educative Agents in Pre-Industrial England', *History of Education* 23 (1994): 129–56.
5. Margaret Spufford, 'The Cost of Apparel in Seventeenth-Century England, and the Accuracy of Gregory King', *The Economic History Review* n.s. 53.4 (2000): 677–705. This view on the relative expense of clothing is also established separately by Lorna Weatherill in *Consumer Behaviour and Material Culture in Britain 1660–1760* (London and New York: Routledge, 1988), 119.
6. Gervase Markham, *The English Housewife*, ed. Michael R. Best (Montreal and Kingston: McGill-Queen's University Press, 1986), 146.
7. Appendix 1: *The Accompte of Mr Philippe Sidney*, in *The Life of Sir Philip Sidney*, by Malcolm William Wallace (Cambridge: Cambridge University Press, 1915), 406–23; Wallace, 67.
8. *Household accounts of Anne Archer, daughter and co-heiress of Simon Crouch Alderman of London, and wife of Henry Archer*, 1600–1629, Additional MS 30494, British Library, London, UK, hereafter BL.
9. There are several children identified in the manuscript. Of these, John graduated with an MA from Cambridge in 1622 and became a judge in 1648 and Giles got an MA from Cambridge in 1634; Anne married Roger Rowley of Gray's Inn in 1638 and Magdalen married William Barkley, a merchant, in 1618. See 'Archer, Giles' and 'Archer, John (Senior)', in *Alumni Cantabrigienses. Part 1: From the Earliest Times to 1751*, compiled by John Venn and J. A. Venn (Cambridge: Cambridge University Press, 1922); 'Archer, John', *A Biographical Dictionary of the Judges of England 1066–1870*, by Edward Foss (London: John Murray, 1870), 14–15; *Allegations for Marriage Licenses Issued by the Bishop of London 1611–1828*, ed. George J. Armytage, vol. 2 (London: 1887), 62, 234.

10. Linda Levy Peck, *Consuming Splendor: Society and Culture in Seventeenth-Century England* (Cambridge: Cambridge University Press, 2005), 21–2.
11. Sue Vincent, 'To Fashion a Self: Dressing in Seventeenth-Century England', *Fashion Theory* 3.2 (1999): 197–205.
12. Elizabeth Ewing, *History of Children's Costume* (New York: Scribner, 1977), 31; Phillis Cunnington and Anne Buck, *Children's Costume in England: From the Fourteenth to the End of the Nineteenth Century* (London: Adam and Charles Black, 1965), 71; Peck, 42–5.
13. Vincent, 'To Fashion a Self', 205.
14. Anne Buck, *Clothes and the Child: A Handbook of Children's Dress in England 1500–1900* (New York: Holmes and Meier, 1996), 81.
15. Melanie Schuessler, '"She Hath Over Grown All that Ever She Hath": Children's Clothing in the Lisle Letters, 1533–40', *Medieval Clothing and Textiles* 3 (2007): 183–7; Buck, 100–1.
16. Schuessler, 181–200.
17. Kenneth Charlton, '"Not publike onely but also private and domesticall": Mothers and Familial Education in Pre-Industrial England', *History of Education* 17.1 (1988): 1; Daniel Roche, *The Culture of Clothing: Dress and Fashion in the 'Ancien Règime'* (Cambridge: Cambridge University Press, 1989), 153.
18. Alan Hunt, 'The Governance of Consumption: Sumptuary Laws and Shifting Forms of Regulation', *Economy and Society* 25.3 (1996): 411–12.
19. Wilfrid Hooper, 'The Tudor Sumptuary Laws', *The English Historical Review* 30.119 (1915): 433–49. See also Sue Vincent, *Dressing the Elite: Clothes in Early Modern England* (Oxford: Berg, 2003), 117–52.
20. Alan Hunt, 'Moralizing Luxury: The Discourses of the Governance of Consumption', *Journal of Historical Sociology* 8.4 (1985): 366.
21. Vincent, *Dressing the Elite*, 132–3.
22. Amanda Bailey, *Flaunting: Style and the Subversive Male Body in Renaissance England* (Toronto, ON: University of Toronto Press, 2007), 33.
23. See Aileen Ribeiro, *Dress and Morality* (London: B. T. Batsford, 1986), esp. 59–94 on the many moralistic treatments of dress, in conduct books, polemical treatises and literature.
24. James I, King of England, *Basilikon Doron. Or His Maiesties Instructions to his Dearest Sonne, Henry the Prince* (London: Felix Kyngston, 1603), 109–12.
25. James Cleland, *Hero-paideia, or The Institution of a Young Noble Man* (Oxford: Joseph Barnes, 1607), 215.
26. Sir Walter Raleigh, *Sir Walter Raleighs Instructions to his Sonne and to Posterity* (London: Benjamin Fisher, 1632), 75.
27. Francis Osborne, *Advice to a Son, or, Directions for your Better Conduct, Through the Various and Most Important Encounters of this Life* (Oxford: H. Hall, 1656), 17.
28. Thomas Elyot, *The Boke named the Governour* (London: Tho. Bertheleti, 1531), Oiii–Oiiiv.
29. Elyot, Nviii.
30. Thomas Carew, 'A Caveat for Craftsmen and Clothiers', *Certaine Godly and Necessarie Sermons* (London: [R. Read], 1603), S8–Y4. For a more typical approach to dress, see in the same volume, Thomas Carew, 'A Jewell for Gentlewomen', R6–S(v). See also Patrick Collinson, 'Christian Socialism in Elizabethan Suffolk: Thomas Carew and his *Caveat for Clothiers*', in *Counties*

and Communities: Essays on East Anglian History Presented to Hassell Smith, ed. Carole Rawcliffe, Roger Virgoe and Richard Wilson (Norwich: Centre of East Anglian Studies, 1996), 161–78.

31. 'An Homyly Against Excesse of Apparell', in *The Second Tome of Homelyes of such Matters as were Promised* [Certain sermons or homilies appointed to be read in churches] (London: Richard Jugge and John Cawood, 1563), fol. 112v–21.

32. John Williams, *A Sermon of Apparell* (London: Robert Barker and John Bill, 1620), 28–9.

33. Hunt, 'The Governance of Consumption', 420.

34. Michel Foucault, *The History of Sexuality, Vol. 1: An Introduction*, trans. Robert Hurley (New York: Pantheon Books, 1978), 24.

35. Susan Bordo, *The Male Body*, (New York: Farrar, Straus and Giroux, 1999), 195.

36. Thomas Goad, 'The Approbation', in *The Mothers Legacy to her Unborne Childe*, by Elizabeth Joscelin, ed. Jean LeDrew Metcalfe (Toronto, ON: University of Toronto Press, 2000), 43.

37. John Clarke, Stuart Hall, Tony Jefferson and Brian Roberts, 'Subcultures, Cultures and Class', in *Resistance through Rituals: Youth Subcultures in Post-War Britain*, 2nd edn, ed. Stuart Hall and Tony Jefferson (London and New York: Routledge, 2006), 6.

38. Clarke et al., 32.

39. Lucinda M. Becker, *Death and the Early Modern English Woman* (Aldershot: Ashgate, 2003), 195.

40. Elizabeth Joscelin, *The Mothers Legacy to her Unborn Childe*, ed. Jean LeDrew Metcalfe (Toronto, ON: University of Toronto, 2000), 76, 60. This is a parallel text edition containing both Jocelin's holograph manuscript and the printed edition of 1624. All subsequent references are to this edition. I have used 'Jocelin' rather than 'Joscelin' because the former is more common.

41. See for example, Lewis Bayly, *The Practice of Piety* (London: [R.B.], 1636), 234–6; Thomas Bentley, *The Monument of Matrones Conteining Seuen Seuerall Lamps of Virginitie, or Distinct Treatises* (London: H. Denham, 1582), 369–75, 988–9; Anon, *A Jewel for Gentlewomen Containing Diuers Godly Prayers, Fit to Comfort the Wounded Consciences of all Penitent Sinners* (London: John Beale, 1624), B3v–B4v, C16v–C2.

42. Jean LeDrew Metcalfe, 'Introduction', in *The Mothers Legacy to her Unborne Childe*, 17–25.

43. Metcalfe, 24–5; Sylvia Brown, 'The Approbation of Elizabeth Jocelin', *English Manuscript Studies* 9 (2000): 129–64.

44. Goad, 41.

45. Metcalfe, 3, 4.

46. Goad, 43.

47. Vincent, *Dressing the Elite*, 29–41, 129.

48. Bailey, 27.

49. Phillip Stubbes, *Anatomie of Abuses* (London: Richard Johns, 1595), 11, 26, 29, 40, 44, 45.

50. Joshua Scodel, *Excess and the Mean in Early Modern English Literature* (Princeton, NJ: Princeton University Press, 2002), 1–18.

51. Baldesar Castiglione, *The Book of the Courtier*, trans. George Bull (London: Penguin, 2004), 325–6.

52. Plato, *Timaeus*, in *Gorgias and Timaeus*, ed. Tom Crawford, trans. Benjamin Jowett (Mineola, NY: Dover, 2003), 197.
53. Giovanni Paolo Lomazzo, *A Tracte Containing the Artes of Curious Painting, Carving, and Buildinge*, trans. Richard Haydocke (Oxford: Joseph Barnes, 1598), 25, 26.
54. Castiglione, 134. Thomas Hoby's translation uses the word 'extreme', where George Bull says 'exaggerated'.
55. Jane Bridgeman, '"*Condecenti et netti* ...": Beauty, Dress, and Gender in Italian Renaissance Art', in *Concepts of Beauty in Renaissance Art*, ed. Frances Ames-Lewis and Mary Rogers (Aldershot: Ashgate, 1998), 44–51.
56. Margaret Cavendish, 'A True Relation of My Birth, Breeding, and Life', in *Paper Bodies: A Margaret Cavendish Reader,* ed. Sylvia Bowerbank and Sara Mendelson (Peterborough, ON: Broadview, 2000), 60.
57. Margaret Cavendish, 'New World, Called the Blazing World', in *Paper Bodies: A Margaret Cavendish Reader,* ed. Sylvia Bowerbank and Sara Mendelson (Peterborough, ON: Broadview, 2000), 245.
58. Cavendish, 'New World, Called the Blazing World', 245.
59. John Evelyn, *Diary and Correspondence of John Evelyn,* ed. William Bray, vol. 2 (London: George Bell, 1889), 25, 26.
60. 'Fantastic', *Oxford English Dictionary,* 2nd edn (1989). Online.
61. Jacqueline Eales, 'Harley, Brilliana, Lady Harley (bap. 1598, d.1643)', in *Oxford Dictionary of National Biography* (Oxford: Oxford University Press, 2004). Online; Thomas Taylor Lewis, 'Introduction', *Letters of the Lady Brilliana Harley* (Camden Society, 1854), v–xxix.
62. Raymond A. Anselment, 'Katherine Paston and Lady Brilliana Harley: Maternal Letters and the Genre of Mother's Advice', *Studies in Philology* 101.4 (2004): 431–53.
63. Patricia Crawford, 'The Construction and Experience of Maternity', in *Women as Mothers in Pre-Industrial Education*, ed. Valerie Fildes (London: Routledge, 1990), 12; Jacqueline Eales, *Puritans and Roundheads: The Harleys of Brampton Bryan and the Outbreak of the English Civil War* (Cambridge: Cambridge University Press, 1990), 25–8.
64. 'Brilliana Lady Harley to her son [Sir] Edward Harley', undated, Portland Papers, Correspondence of Sir Edward Harley, vol. CXCIII, Additional MS 70118, BL.
65. ibid., f.2.
66. ibid., f.1.
67. ibid., f.3.
68. ibid., f.4*v*.
69. ibid., f.5.
70. ibid., f.11.
71. ibid., f.7–f.7*v*.
72. ibid., f.9*v*, 10.
73. For more on the political dimensions of the letters, see Jacqueline Eales, 'Patriarchy, Puritanism and Politics: the Letters of Lady Brilliana Harley (1598–1643)', in *Early Modern Women's Letter Writing, 1450–1700*, ed. James Daybell (Basingstoke: Palgrave Macmillan, 2001), 143–58.
74. Brilliana Harley to Edward Harley, December 1640, *Letters of the Lady Brilliana Harley* (London: Camden Society, 1854), 104; Brilliana Harley to Edward Harley, 23 April 1642, *Letters of the Lady Brilliana Harley*, 154; Brilliana Harley

to Edward Harley, 23 April 1641, *Letters of the Lady Brilliana Harley*, 155; Brilliana Harley to Edward Harley, 15 July 1642, *Letters of the Lady Brilliana Harley*, 178; Brilliana Harley to Edward Harley, undated, *Letters of the Lady Brilliana Harley*, 181–2.

75. Johanna Harris, '"But I thinke and beleeve": Lady Brilliana Harley's Puritanism in Epistolary Community', in *The Intellectual Culture of Puritan Women 1558–1680*, ed. Johanna Harris and Elizabeth Scott-Baumann (Basingstoke: Palgrave Macmillan, 2010, 108–21. Thank you to Johanna Harris for sharing this essay with me before its publication.

76. *The Commonplace Book of Brilliana Conway*, 1622, MS PL F1/4/1, University of Nottingham, Nottingham, UK, f.1–132.

77. Brilliana Harley to Edward Harley, 10 May 1639, *Letters of the Lady Brilliana Harley*, 52.

78. Brilliana Harley to Edward Harley, 6 December 1639, *Letters of the Lady Brilliana Harley*, 78; Brilliana Harley to Edward Harley, 14 March 1639, *Letters of the Lady Brilliana Harley*, 86.

79. Brilliana Harley to Edward Harley, 18 October 1639, *Letters of the Lady Brilliana Harley*, 66.

80. Hugh Trevor-Roper, *Archbishop Laud: 1573–1645*, 2nd edn (1962; London: Phoenix Press, 2000), 118.

81. Brilliana Harley to Edward Harley, 5 April 1639, *Letters of the Lady Brilliana Harley*, 40.

82. Brilliana Harley to Edward Harley, 20 May 1639, *Letters of the Lady Brilliana Harley*, 55.

83. Brilliana Harley to Edward Harley, 20 July 1639, *Letters of the Lady Brilliana Harley*, 63.

84. Brilliana Harley to Edward Harley, undated, *Letters of the Lady Brilliana Harley*, 22.

85. Edward Perkins to Edward Harley, 19 April 1641, Portland Papers, Papers of Sir Robert Harley, Sir Edward Harley, and Robert Harley, 1st Earl of Oxford, vol. 3, Additional MS 70003, BL, f.90.

86. Brilliana Harley to Edward Harley, 7 May 1639, *Letters of the Lady Brilliana Harley*, 50.

87. Brilliana Harley to Edward Harley, 25 February 1642/3, *Letters of the Lady Brilliana Harley*, 190.

88. Brilliana Harley to Edward Harley, 11 February 1641/2, *Letters of the Lady Brilliana Harley*, 148–9.

89. Brilliana Harley to Edward Harley, 9 May 1640, *Letters of the Lady Brilliana Harley*, 95; Brilliana Harley to Edward Harley, 3 July 1640, *Letters of the Lady Brilliana Harley*, 99; Brilliana Harley to Edward Harley, 25 June 1641, *Letters of the Lady Brilliana Harley*, 137.

90. Brilliana Harley to Edward Harley, 7 May 1642, *Letters of the Lady Brilliana Harley*, 158; Brilliana Harley to Edward Harley, undated, *Letters of the Lady Brilliana Harley*, 160; Brilliana Harley to Edward Harley, 7 May 1642, *Letters of the Lady Brilliana Harley*, 158; Brilliana Harley to Edward Harley, 17 May 1642, *Letters of the Lady Brilliana Harley*, 161; Brilliana Harley to Edward Harley, 4 June 1642, *Letters of the Lady Brilliana Harley*, 167; Brilliana Harley to Edward Harley, 11 June 1642, *Letters of the Lady Brilliana Harley*, 169; Brilliana Harley to Edward Harley, 20 June 1642, *Letters of the Lady Brilliana Harley*, 171.

91. Jacqueline Eales, *Puritans and Roundheads*, 149–77.
92. Brilliana Harley to Edward Harley, 4 June 1642, *Letters of the Lady Brilliana Harley*, 167.
93. Brilliana Harley to Robert Harley, 24 September 1643, Portland Papers, *Letters to Sir Robert Harley from his third wife, Brilliana, 1626–1643*, vol. CX, Additional MS 70110, BL, unbound.
94. 'A Memoir of the life and writings of the Rev. Thomas Pierson, Minister of Bramton Brian in Herefordshire, in the reign of King James I', *A Miscellaneous Volume, formerly belonging to James West, esq.*, n.d. Lansdowne MS 721, BL, f.149v.
95. Brilliana Harley to Robert Harley, 25 April 1626, Additional MS 70110; Brilliana Harley to Robert Harley, 25 May 1626, Additional MS 70110; Brilliana Harley to Robert Harley, 16 June 1626, Additional MS 70110; Brilliana Harley to Robert Harley, undated, Additional MS 70110; 'Whittle', *Oxford English Dictionary*, 2nd edn (1989). Online.
96. Brilliana Harley to Robert Harley, 4 December 1629, *Letters of the Lady Brilliana Harley*, 5; Brilliana Harley to Robert Harley, 18 May 1633, *Letters of the Lady Brilliana Harley*, 7.
97. Brilliana Harley to Robert Harley, 25 April 1626, Additional MS 70110; Brilliana Harley to Robert Harley, 16 June 1626, Additional MS 70110; Brilliana Harley to Robert Harley, 11 June 1643, Portland Papers, *Papers of Sir Robert Harley, Sir Edward Harley and Robert Harley, 1st Earl of Oxford, etc., 1642–44*, vol. IV, Additional MS 70004, BL, n.p.
98. Brilliana Harley to Robert Harley, 24 September 1643, Additional MS 70110.
99. Brilliana Harley to Edward Harley, 14 December 1638, *Letters of the Lady Brilliana Harley*, 16.
100. Eales, 'Patriarchy, Puritanism and Politics', 148.
101. 'Appendix: Sir Robert Harley's "Character" of a Puritan', in Jacqueline Eales, 'Sir Robert Harley, K.B., (1579–1656) and the "Character" of a Puritan', *British Library Journal* 15 (1989): 150.
102. Eales, ibid., 157.
103. J. T. Cliffe, *Puritans in Conflict: The Puritan Gentry During and After the Civil Wars* (London: Routledge, 1988), 54–8, 185–6; Anne Laurence, 'Women, Godliness and Personal Appearance in Seventeenth-Century England', *Women's History Review* 15.1 (2006): 71.
104. Brilliana Harley to Edward Harley, 9 January 1638, *Letters of the Lady Brilliana Harley*, 22.
105. Brilliana Harley to Edward Harley, 2 January 1641, *Letters of the Lady Brilliana Harley*, 107.
106. Brilliana, Lady Harley to Sir William Vavasour, 31 July 1643, *Historical Manuscripts Commission: Calendar of the Manuscripts of the Marquis of Bath Preserved at Longleat, Wiltshire*, vol. 1. (London: Mackie, 1904), 13.
107. King Charles I to Brilliana, Lady Harley, 21 August 1643, *Historical Manuscripts Commission: Calendar of the Manuscripts of the Marquis of Bath Preserved at Longleat, Wiltshire*, vol. 1., 14; Brilliana, Lady Harley to the King, August 1643, *Historical Manuscripts Commission: Calendar of the Manuscripts of the Marquis of Bath Preserved at Longleat, Wiltshire*, vol. 1., 17.

5 The Culture of the Head: Hair in Mary Wroth's *Urania* and Margaret Cavendish's 'Assaulted and Pursued Chastity'

1. On race in early modern women's writing, see Margo Hendricks and Patricia Parker, eds, *Women, 'Race,' and Writing in the Early Modern Period* (London and New York: Routledge, 1994); Kim F. Hall, *Things of Darkness: Economies of Race and Gender in Early Modern England* (Ithaca, NY and London: Cornell University Press, 1995); Cristina Malcolmson, '"The Explication of Whiteness and Blackness": Skin Color and the Physics of Color in the Works of Robert Boyle and Margaret Cavendish', in *Faultlines and Controversies in the Study of Seventeenth-Century English Literature,* ed. Claude J. Summers and Ted-Larry Pebworth (Columbia, SC and London: University of Missouri Press, 2002), 187–203; Sujata Iyengar, *Shades of Difference: Mythologies of Skin Color in Early Modern England* (Philadelphia, PA: University of Pennsylvania Press, 2005). On feminism, race and hair, see Tracy Owens Patton, 'Hey Girl, Am I More than My Hair?: African American Women and their Struggles With Beauty, Body Image, and Hair', *NWSA Journal* 18.2 (2006): 24–51; Ayana B. Byrd and Lori L. Tharps, *Hair Story: Untangling the Roots of Black Hair in America* (New York: St. Martin's Press, 2001); *tenderheaded: A Comb-Bending Collection of Hair Stories,* ed. Juliette Harris and Pamela Johnson (New York: Pocket Books, 2001); Geraldine Biddle-Perry and Sarah Cheang, eds, *Hair: Styling, Culture and Fashion* (Oxford: Berg, 2008).
2. Georgine de Courtais, *Women's Headdress and Hairstyles in England from AD 600 to the Present Day* (London: B. T. Batsford, 1973); Robin Bryer, *The History of Hair: Fashion and Fantasy Down the Ages* (London: Philip Wilson, 2000); Richard Corson, *Fashions in Hair: The First Five Thousand Years* (1965; London: Peter Owen, 2005).
3. Geraldine Biddle-Perry, 'Hair, Gender and Looking', in *Hair: Styling, Culture and Fashion,* 97.
4. Patricia Hill Collins, *Black Sexual Politics: African Americans, Gender, and the New Racism* (London and New York: Routledge, 2004), 195. See also Orlando Patterson, *Slavery and Social Death: A Comparative Study* (Cambridge, MA: Harvard University Press, 1985), 61.
5. Patricia Hill Collins, *Black Feminist Thought: Knowledge, Consciousness, and the Politics of Empowerment,* 2nd edn (New York and London: Routledge, 2000), 89.
6. Noliwe M. Rooks, *Hair Raising: Beauty, Culture, and African American Women* (New Brunswick, NJ: Rutgers University Press, 1997), 8.
7. Ann Jones and Peter Stallybrass, *Renaissance Clothing and the Materials of Memory* (Cambridge: Cambridge University Press, 2000), 208–9. See also Marjorie Garber, *Vested Interests: Cross-Dressing and Cultural Anxiety* (New York and London: Routledge, 1992), esp. 21–40; Jean Howard, 'Cross-Dressing, the Theatre, and Gender Struggle in Early Modern England', in *Crossing the Stage: Controversies on Cross-Dressing,* ed. Lesley Ferris (New York and London: Routledge, 1993), 20–46; Laura Levine, *Men in Women's Clothing: Anti-theatricality and Effeminization, 1579–1642* (Cambridge and New York: Cambridge University Press, 1994); Stephen Orgel, *Impersonations: The Performance of Gender in Shakespeare's England* (Cambridge: Cambridge University Press, 1996); Dympna Callaghan, *Shakespeare Without Women* (London and New York: Routledge, 2000).
8. William Prynne, *The Unlovelinesse of Lovelockes* (London: [n.p.], 1628), A4v.

9. Johannes Endres, 'Diderot, Hogarth, and the Aesthetics of Depilation', *Eighteenth-Century Studies* 38.1 (2004): 18.
10. William Shakespeare, 'Sonnet 130', in *Complete Sonnets and Poems*, ed. Colin Burrow (Oxford: Oxford University Press, 2002), 641, line 4; Shakespeare, *The Rape of Lucrece*, in *Complete Sonnets and Poems*, 265, lines 400–1; Shakespeare, *Twelfth Night*, in *William Shakespeare: The Complete Works*, ed. Stanley Wells and Gary Taylor (Oxford: Clarendon Press, 1988), 1.3.95–100; Shakespeare, *Titus Andronicus*, in *William Shakespeare: The Complete Works*, 2.3.34, 39; Shakespeare, *Hamlet*, in *William Shakespeare: The Complete Works*, 1.2.241; Shakespeare, *Much Ado About Nothing*, in *William Shakespeare: The Complete Works*, 3.2.41–3; Shakespeare, *The Taming of the Shrew*, in *William Shakespeare: The Complete Works*, 5.2.170. For more on hair and *Twelfth Night*, Gustav Ungerer, 'Sir Andrew Aguecheek and His Head of Hair', *Shakespeare Studies* 16 (1983): 101–33.
11. John Milton, *Paradise Lost*, in *John Milton: The Complete Poems*, ed. John Leonard (London: Penguin, 1998), lines 2.711, 4.301–3, 4.304–8.
12. ibid., *Samson Agonistes*, 495, lines 1136–8.
13. For more on Milton and hair, see Stephen B. Dobranski, 'Clustering and Curling Locks: The Matter of Hair in *Paradise Lost*', *PMLA* 125.2 (2010): 337–53.
14. Lynn Festa, 'Personal Effects: Wigs and Possessive Individualism in the Long Eighteenth Century', *Eighteenth-Century Life* 29.2 (2005): 47–90.
15. Margaret Spencer, *Spencer Accounts: Account Book for Personal Expenses of Margaret Spencer (d.1613), daughter of Robert, 1st Baron Spencer of Wormleighton*, 1610–1613, Additional MS 62092, British Library, London, UK, fol. 17; 'Account of expenses for clothes [in the handwriting of Mary Evelyn, wife of John Evelyn] for herself and daughters', 1669–1671, Additional MS 15949, BL, Original Correspondence of the Evelyn family, of Wotton, co. Surrey, from 1634 to 1824, vol. 2, fols. 117–22v; 'Foretop', *Oxford English Dictionary*, 2nd edn (1989). Online.
16. Prynne, 17.
17. 'Advice to the Maidens of London, to Forsake their Fantastical Top-Knots' (London: J. Blare, [1683–1706]).
18. Thomas Vicary, *The English Man's Treasure* (London: Thomas Creede, 1613), 10–11.
19. Helkiah Crooke, *Mikrokosmographia: A Description of the Body of Man* (London: William Jaggard, 1615), 66–70.
20. Rembert Dodoens, *A Niewe Herball, or Historie of Plants*, trans. Henry Lyte (London: Gerard Dewes, 1578), 121, 684, 699 and 686, 687, 768.
21. Dodoens, 409, 599, 649, 710, 734 and 331, 354, 624, 638, 657, 687.
22. John Parkinson, *Paradisi in Sole. Paradisus Terrestris* (London: Humfrey Lownes and Robert Young, 1629), 566.
23. Galen, *Galen's Art of Physic*, trans. Nicholas Culpeper (London: Peter Cole, 1652), 46.
24. Crooke, 68.
25. ibid., 69.
26. Robert Greene, *A Quip for an Upstart Courtier* (London: John Wolfe, 1592), D3v, D4.
27. Margaret Pelling, *The Common Lot: Sickness, Medical Occupations and the Urban Poor in Early Modern England* (New York and London: Longman, 1998), 215.
28. Wendy Cooper, *Hair: Sex, Society, Symbolism* (London: Aldus Books, 1971), 161, 167.

29. *Medical Advertisements,* catalogue number 551.a.32, fol. 87, BL.
30. ibid., fol. 43.
31. Corson, 198–259.
32. Thomas Hall, *The Loathsomnesse of Long Haire* (London: J. G., 1654), 28.
33. J. B.[John Bulwer], *Anthropometamorphosis: Man Transform'd: or, the Artificial Changling* (London: William Hunt, 1653), B2*v*,
34. Bulwer, 58.
35. Thomas Hall, 24.
36. [T. H.], *A Looking-Glasse for Women* (London: R. W., 1644).
37. *Hic Mulier: Or, The Man-Woman* (London: J. T[rundle], 1620), B3.
38. ibid., A4*v*.
39. ibid., B2.
40. Edward Phillips Stratham, *A Jacobean Letter-Writer: The Life and Times of John Chamberlain* (London: Kegan Paul, 1920), 182–3.
41. Thomas Hall, 26–7, 39–40.
42. ibid., 66.
43. Prynne, esp. 17 and 51.
44. ibid., 1, 7.
45. ibid., a1*v*, A3*v*.
46. J. B. [Bulwer], 63, 59.
47. Bulwer, C.
48. Florio qtd. in Ania Loomba, *Shakespeare, Race, and Colonialism* (Oxford: Oxford University Press, 2002), 22.
49. Loomba, 7.
50. Lady Mary Wroth, *The First Part of the Countess of Montgomery's Urania,* ed. Josephine A. Roberts (Binghamton, NY: Medieval and Renaissance Texts and Studies, 1995), 19. All subsequent references are to this edition.
51. Sheila T. Cavanagh, '"What is my nation?" Lady Mary Wroth's Interrogations of Personal and National Identity', in *Early Modern Prose Fiction: The Cultural Politics of Reading,* ed. Naomi Conn Liebler (New York: Routledge, 2007), 114.
52. Kim F. Hall, 198.
53. ibid., 207.
54. Lady Mary Wroth, *The Second Part of the Countess of Montgomery's Urania,* ed. Josephine A. Roberts, completed by Suzanne Gossett and Janel Mueller (Tempe, AZ: Renaissance English Text Society with Arizona Center for Medieval and Renaissance Studies, 1999), 76.
55. ibid., 168.
56. John Thorie, *The Theatre of the Earth* (London: Adam Islip, 1599), Ddiiv; George Abbot, *A briefe description of the whole worlde* (London: T. Judson, 1599), C.
57. John Frampton, *A Discouerie of the Countries of Tartaria, Scithia, and Cataya, by the Northeast* (London: Thomas Dawson, 1580), 3.
58. Pierre d'Avity, sieur de Montmartin, *The Estates, Empires, and Principallities of the World,* trans. Edward Grimeston, (London: Adam Islip, 1615), 705.
59. Bulwer, 55.
60. Thomas Herbert, *A Relation of Some Yeares Travaile, Begunne Anno 1626* (London: William Stansby, 1634), 146, 147.
61. Baldesar Castiglione, *The Courtier,* trans. George Bull (London: Penguin, 1967), 67.
62. ibid., 86.

63. Sir Philip Sidney, *The Countess of Pembroke's Arcadia (The New Arcadia)*, ed. Victor Skretkowicz (Oxford: Clarendon Press, 1987), 84.
64. ibid., 329.
65. ibid., 69.
66. ibid., 68.
67. Prynne, A3–A3v. For more on this scene and connections between Wroth and Sidney, see Orgel, 79 and Sue Starke, 'Love's True Habit: Cross-Dressing and Pastoral Courtship in Wroth's *Urania* and Sidney's *New Arcadia*', *Sidney Journal* 24.2 (2006): 27.
68. Stephen Greenblatt, *Shakespearean Negotiations: The Circulation of Social Energy in Renaissance England* (Berkeley, CA and Los Angeles, CA: University of California Press, 1988), 76.
69. Margaret Cavendish, 'Letter 2', in *Sociable Letters*, ed. James Fitzmaurice (Peterborough, ON: Broadview, 2004), 47.
70. Margaret Cavendish, 'Assaulted and Pursued Chastity', in *Natures Picture Drawn By Fancies Pencil*, 2nd edn (London: A. Maxwell, 1671), 394. All subsequent references are to this edition.
71. Dobranski, 348.
72. Michael Shapiro, *Gender in Play on the Shakespearean Stage: Boy Heroines and Female Pages* (Ann Arbor, MI: University of Michigan Press, 1996), 15.
73. Howard, 22, 26. See also Shapiro, 16–20.
74. *A Looking-Glasse for Women*, 9.
75. Marina Leslie, 'Evading Rape and Embracing Empire in Margaret Cavendish's *Assaulted and Pursued Chastity*', in *Menacing Virgins: Representing Virginity in the Middle Ages and Renaissance*, ed. Kathleen Coyne Kelly and Marina Leslie (Cranbury, NJ: Associated University Press, 1999), 192.
76. Shapiro, 212–13.
77. Kathryn Schwarz, 'Chastity, Militant and Married: Cavendish's Romance, Milton's Masque', *PMLA* 118.2 (2003): 280.
78. Samuel Purchas, *Purchas His Pilgrimage: Or Relations of the World* (London: William Stansby, 1626), 713, 714.
79. Herbert, 6.
80. Aphra Behn, *Oroonoko* in *Oroonoko and Other Writings* ed. Paul Salzman (Oxford: Oxford University Press, 1994), 53.
81. Margaret W. Ferguson, 'Feathers and Flies: Aphra Behn and the Seventeenth-Century Trade in Exotica', in *Subject and Object in Renaissance Culture*, ed. Margreta de Grazia, Maureen Quilligan and Peter Stallybrass (Cambridge: Cambridge University Press, 1996), 253–5.
82. Alexander Butchart, *The Anatomy of Power: European Constructions of the African Body* (London and New York: Zed Books, 1998), 51.
83. Stephen Greenblatt, *Marvelous Possessions: The Wonder of the New World* (Chicago, IL: University of Chicago Press, 1991), 22, 23.
84. Valerie Traub, 'Mapping the Global Body', in *Early Modern Visual Culture: Representation, Race, and Empire in Renaissance England,* ed. Peter Erickson and Clark Hulse (Philadelphia, PA: University of Pennsylvania Press, 2000), 97.
85. Iyengar, 13.
86. Constance C. Relihan, *Cosmographical Glasses: Geographic Discourse, Gender, and Elizabethan Fiction* (Kent, OH and London: Kent State University Press, 2004), 3.

87. For early modern catalogues of human colours (tawny, black, dusky, ash, olive, white), see Purchas, 723; Margaret Cavendish, *The Description of a New World, Called the Blazing World* in *The Blazing World and Other Writings*, ed. Kate Lilley (London: Penguin, 1992), 133; Cavendish, 'Assaulted and Pursued Chastity, 421.
88. Purchas, 503, 538, 568, 587, 718, 896, 952.
89. Frampton, 4.
90. Bulwer, 49.
91. Herbert, 14.
92. Iyengar, 229.
93. Herbert, 146, 147.
94. Charles de Rochefort, 'From *The History of the Caribby-Islands* (1658)', in *Versions of Blackness: Key Texts on Slavery from the Seventeenth Century*, ed. Derek Hughes (Cambridge: Cambridge University Press, 2007), 325.
95. Richard Blome, *A Geographical Description of the Four Parts of the World, Taken from the Notes and Workes of the Famous Monsieur Sanson* (London: T. N., 1670), 49, 54.
96. Behn, 7, 12.
97. Byrd and Tharps, 14.
98. ibid., 2. See also Roy Sieber, 'History', in *Hair in African Art and Culture*, ed. Roy Sieber and Frank Herreman (New York: Museum for African Art, 2000), 18–23.
99. Blome, 49, 54, 9, 11.
100. Kim F. Hall, 25.
101. William Strachey, 'For the Colony in Virginea Britannia (1612)', in *Race in Early Modern England: A Documentary Companion*, ed. Ania Loomba and Jonathan Burton (New York and Basingstoke: Palgrave Macmillan, 2007), 188.
102. Richard Ligon, 'A True and Exact History of the Island of Barbados (1657)', in *Race in Early Modern England: A Documentary Companion*, ed. Ania Loomba and Jonathan Burton (New York and Basingstoke: Palgrave Macmillan, 2007), 256.
103. Tony Ballantyne and Antoinette Burton, 'Introduction: Bodies, Empires, and World Histories', in *Bodies in Contact: Rethinking Colonial Encounters in World History*, ed. Tony Ballantyne and Antoinette Burton (Durham, NC and London: Duke University Press, 2005), 6.
104. Anne McClintock, *Imperial Leather: Race, Gender and Sexuality in the Colonial Context* (New York and London: Routledge, 1995), 61.
105. Philip Sidney, 'Sonnet 12', in *The Poems of Sir Philip Sidney*, ed. William A. Ringler, Jr (Oxford: Clarendon Press, 1962), page 170, line 2. For more on this motif, see Ungerer, 117–18.
106. Lisa Jones, *Bulletproof Diva: Tales of Race, Sex, and Hair* (New York: Anchor Books Doubleday, 1994), 11–12.

6   An 'absolute Mistris of her Self': Anne Clifford and the Luxury of Hair

1. Mihoko Suzuki, ed., *Anne Clifford and Lucy Hutchinson* (Aldershot: Ashgate, 2009); Julie Crawford, 'The Case of Lady Anne Clifford; or, Did Women have a Mixed Monarch', *PMLA* 121.5 (2006): 1682–1689; Elizabeth V. Chew,

'Si(gh)ting the Mistress of the House: Anne Clifford and Architectural Space', in *Women as Sites of Culture: Women's Roles in Cultural Formation from the Renaissance to the Twentieth Century*, ed. Susan Shifrin (Aldershot: Ashgate, 2002), 167–82. Anne Clifford's name changed throughout her life, from Lady Anne Clifford, to the Countess of Dorset, to the Countess of Pembroke; in her late account books, she identifies herself as Anne Pembroke. She was also Baroness Westmorland after 1646. I use all of these names as different attributes of her identity, but for the sake of consistency through the analysis and in concord with most scholarly analyses of her work, I use the name Anne Clifford throughout this chapter.

2. Marina Warner, *From the Beast to the Blonde: On Fairy Tales and their Tellers* (London: Chatto & Windus, 1994), 371.

3. Christopher J. Berry, *The Idea of Luxury: A Conceptual and Historical Investigation* (Cambridge: Cambridge University Press, 1994), 11–44.

4. Grant McCracken, *Big Hair: A Journey into the Transformation of Self* (Woodstock, NY: Overlook Press, 1995), 131.

5. Louisa Cross, 'Fashionable Hair in the Eighteenth Century: Theatricality and Display', in *Hair: Styling, Culture and Fashion,* ed. Geraldine Biddle-Perry and Sarah Cheang (Oxford: Berg, 2008), 23.

6. Linda Levy Peck, *Consuming Splendor: Society and Culture in Seventeenth-Century England* (Cambridge: Cambridge University Press, 2005), 2–3, 6–10.

7. Woodruff D. Smith, *Consumption and the Making of Respectability, 1600–1800* (New York and London: Routledge, 2002), 31–43, 64. Smith outlines religious attitudes towards luxury which bifurcate along the same lines (79, 80).

8. Berry, 87–98.

9. Alan Hunt, 'Moralizing Luxury: The Discourses of the Governance of Consumption', *Journal of Historical Sociology* 8.4 (1995): 355–6.

10. Will Fisher, *Materializing Gender in Early Modern English Literature* (Cambridge: Cambridge University Press, 2006), 156.

11. Gustav Ungerer, 'Sir Andrew Aguecheek and his Head of Hair', *Shakespeare Studies* 16 (1983): 117.

12. Juan Luis Vives, *A Verie Fruitfull and Pleasant Booke Called the Instruction of a Christian Woman*, trans. Richard Hyrde (London: John Danter, 1592), G3–G3v.

13. [T.H.], *A Looking-Glasse for Women, or, A Spie for Pride* (London: [R.W.], 1644), 3–4, 8.

14. Robin Bryer, *The History of Hair: Fashion and Fantasy Down the Ages* (London: Philip Wilson, 2000), 51; Fisher, 143–7; Stephen B. Dobranski, 'Clustering and Curling Locks: The Matter of Hair in *Paradise Lost*', *PMLA* 125.2 (2010): 337–8.

15. William Prynne, *The Unloveliness of Lovelockes* (London: [n.p.], 1628), 29, 50.

16. *New Anatomie, or Character of a Christian, or Round-head* (London: Robert Leybourne, 1645), 12.

17. George C. Williamson, *Lady Anne Clifford, Countess of Dorset, Pembroke and Montgomery, 1590–1676: Her Life, Letters and Work* (Kendal: Titus and Son, 1922), 494, 506.

18. For more on the textual history of the *Great Books of Record*, see Richard T. Spence, *Lady Anne Clifford Countess of Pembroke, Dorset and Montgomery*

(1590–1676) (Phoenix Mill: Sutton, 1997), 160–75. D. J. H. Clifford printed one section of the third volume of *The Great Books of Record*, c.1649–1652 as 'The Kendal Diary'. Katherine Acheson also edited 'The Life of Me' from the *Great Books of Record* for her edition.

19. *Great Books of Record*, c.1649–52, Hothfield MS WD/Hoth/A988/10, 3 vols. Cumbria Record Office, Kendal, UK, 1.1.
20. *The Great Books of Record*, vol. 3, 157, 158.
21. Williamson, 386–92, 404–10.
22. Ann Rosalind Jones and Peter Stallybrass, *Renaissance Clothing and the Materials of Memory* (Cambridge: Cambridge University Press, 2000), 35.
23. Aileen Ribeiro, *Fashion and Fiction: Dress in Art and Literature in Stuart England* (New Haven, CT and London: Yale University Press, 2005), 7.
24. Richard T. Spence identifies the current colour as dark purple and suggests that it might easily be mistaken for brown; an analysis of the pigmentation might help to clarify the issue of the original colour (185). An inscription on the painting indicates that the portraits of her parents were based on originals done in 1589. This appears to be roughly accurate, although Roy Strong argues that it is not precisely so, for the original of her mother (National Portrait Gallery no. 41) was painted in 1585. *Tudor and Jacobean Portraits*, vol. 1 (London: Her Majesty's Stationery Office, 1969), 58–9.
25. 'Appendix D: From Anne Clifford, "A Summary of the Records and a True Memorial of the Life of me the Lady Anne Clifford" (1652)', in *The Memoir of 1603 and The Diary of Lady Anne Clifford*, ed. Katherine O. Acheson (Peterborough, ON; Broadview, 2007), 220.
26. Williamson, 490.
27. *The Great Books of Record*, vol. 3, 150.
28. ibid., vol. 3, 159.
29. ibid, vol. 3, 164.
30. Williamson, 499.
31. Baldesar Castiglione, *The Book of the Courtier*, trans. George Bull (London: Penguin 2003), 330.
32. *The Great Books of Record*, vol. 3, 165.
33. Williamson, 489–90.
34. Ribeiro, 7.
35. These portraits are discussed by Roy Strong in *Tudor and Jacobean Portraits*, 2 vols, 1: 57–9, 2: plates 100–6.
36. 'Armor of George Clifford, Third Earl of Cumberland, ca. 1580–1585', Metropolitan Museum of Art Collection Database, http://www.metmuseum. org/works_of_art/collection_database>. Accessed 7 May 2008.
37. Anne Clifford, *Account Book*, 1600–02, Osborn MS B27, Beinecke Library, Osborn MS B27, New Haven, CT.
38. Anne Clifford, 'The Diary of 1616–1619', in *The Memoir of 1603 and The Diary of 1616–1619*, 135.
39. According to the OED, cypress is the name of several textiles imported from or through Cyprus, a cloth of gold, satin or cobweb lawn. 'Cypress[3]', *Oxford English Dictionary*, 2nd edn (1989). Online.
40. Anne Buck, *Clothes and the Child: A Handbook of Children's Dress in England, 1500–1900* (New York: Holmes & Meier, 1996), 100–1.

41. Anne Clifford, 'Memoir of 1603', in *The Memoir of 1603 and The Diary of 1616–1619*, 43.
42. Thom Hecht, 'Hair Control: The Feminine "Disciplined Head"', in *Hair: Styling, Culture and Fashion*, ed. Geraldine Biddle-Perry and Sarah Cheang (Oxford: Berg, 2008), 211.
43. Phillip Stubbes, *The Anatomie of the Abuses* (London: Richard Jhones, 1595), 39–40.
44. Daniel Roche, *The Culture of Clothing: Dress and Fashion in the 'Ancien Regime'*, trans. Jean Birrell (Cambridge: Cambridge University Press, 1989), 169.
45. *Looking-Glasse for Women*, 6.
46. Ribeiro, 70, 71.
47. Hugh Latimer, 'A Sermon Preached by M. Hugh Latimer on S. Stevens day at Grimsthorp. An. 1552', in *Fruitfull Sermons Preached by the Right Reverend Father, and Constant Martyr of Jesus Christ M. Hugh Latimer* (London: John Day, 1584), f.280*v*–1.
48. Thomas Carew, 'A Jewell for Gentlewomen', in *Certaine Godly and Necessarie Sermons, Preached by M. Thomas Carew of Bilston in the Countie of Suffolke* (London: [R. Read], 1603), S7.
49. Carew, R6*v*, R7.
50. *Pleasant Quippes for the Upstart New-fangled Gentlewoman* (London: Richard Jhones, 1595), A4, B.
51. Susan Vincent, *Dressing the Elite: Clothes in Early Modern England* (Oxford and New York: Berg, 2003), 38.
52. Karen Newman, 'City Talk: Women and Commodification in Jonson's *Epicoene*', *English Literary History* 56.3 (1989): 506.
53. Anne Taylor was 'newly put away' at the time of the coronation. She is remembered in 1646 when her portrait appears, with that of Samuel Daniel, on the wall in the panel of the 'The Great Picture' depicting the 15-year-old Anne Clifford. Clifford, 'The Memoir of 1603', 55.
54. Laura Gowing, '"The Freedom of the Streets": Women and Social Space, 1560–1640', in *Londinopolis: Essays in the Cultural and Social History of Early Modern London*, ed. Paul Griffiths and Mark S. R. Jenner (Manchester and New York: Manchester University Press, 2000), 143–5.
55. Mihoko Suzuki, 'Anne Clifford and the Gendering of History', *Clio* 30.2 (2001): 219.
56. Anne Clifford, 'A Summary of the Records and a True Memorial of the Life of me the Lady Anne Clifford', 220.
57. Richard Steele, *A Discourse Concerning Old Age* (London: J. Astwood, 1688), 140.
58. Williamson, 499.
59. Henry Cuffe, *The Differences of the Ages of Mans Life* (London: T[homas] H[arper], 1640), 210–211.
60. Francis Bacon, *The History of Life and Death* (London: Humphrey Mosley, 1638), 121.
61. See also Erik Gray, 'Severed Hair from Donne to Pope', *Essays in Criticism* 47.3 (1997): 222–3.
62. Angela Rosenthal, 'Raising Hair', *Eighteenth-Century Studies* 38.1 (2004): 2.
63. Mary Chan and Nancy E. Wright, 'Marriage, Identity, and the Pursuit of Property in Seventeenth-Century England: The Cases of Anne Clifford and

Elizabeth Wiseman', in *Women, Property, and the Letters of the Law in Early Modern England*, ed Nancy E. Wright, Margaret W. Ferguson and A. R. Buck (Toronto, ON: University of Toronto Press, 2004), 165.

64. Vincent, 52.
65. Ribeiro, 7–8.
66. Elizabeth Honig, 'In Memory: Lady Dacre and Pairing by Hans Eworth', in *Renaissance Bodies: The Human Figure in English Culture c.1540–1660*, ed. Lucy Gent and Nigel Llewellyn (London: Reaktion Books, 1990), 60–9.
67. Lou Taylor, *Mourning Dress: A Costume and Social History* (London: George Allen & Unwin 1983), 66.
68. Sheila ffolliott, 'Catherine de Medici as Artemisia: Figuring the Powerful Widow', in *Rewriting the Renaissance: The Discourses of Sexual Difference in Early Modern Europe*, ed. Margaret W. Ferguson, Maureen Quilligan and Nancy J. Vickers (Chicago, IL: University of Chicago Press, 1986), 228.
69. Allison Levy, 'Framing Widows: Mourning, Gender and Portraiture in Early Modern Florence', in *Widowhood and Visual Culture in Early Modern Europe*, ed. Allison Levy (Aldershot: Ashgate, 2003), 229.
70. Williamson, 343.
71. See for example the portraits of Inigo Jones (NPG 603); John Finch, 1st Baron Finch, a Royalist judge (NPG 2125); John Pym, a parliamentarian (NPG 6650); John Evelyn, the diarist (NPG L148); Sir Henry Vane the Elder, a diplomat and administrator (NPG 1118); Sir William Waller, parliamentary army officer (NPG 5819); William Harvey, the physician (NPG 60) and even Charles I (NPG 1924). <http://www.npg.org.uk/collections.php>
72. M.A. Tierney, *The History and Antiquities of the Castle and Town of Arundel*, vol. 2 (London: G. & W. Nicol, 1834), 487.
73. Edward Hyde, Earl of Clarendon, *History of the Rebellion* qtd. in Graham Parry, *The Golden Age Restor'd: The Culture of the Stuart Court, 1603–42* (Manchester: Manchester University Press, 1981), 109.
74. Parry, 121; Henry Peacham, *The Compleat Gentleman* (London: Francis Constable, 1634), 220–1
75. Peacham, 3.
76. David Howarth, 'The Patronage and Collecting of Aletheia, Countess of Arundel 1606–54', *Journal of the History of Collections* 10.2 (1998): 132.
77. Anne Clifford, 'The Diary of 1616–1619', 64, 65, 105, 149, 155.
78. Richard Brathwait, *The English Gentlewoman* (London: John Dawson 1641), Mm2v.
79. Erin J. Campbell, '"Unenduring" Beauty: Gender and Old Age in Early Modern Art and Aesthetics', in *Growing Old in Early Modern Europe: Cultural Representations*, ed. Erin Campbell (Aldershot: Ashgate, 2006), 154.
80. *Great Books of Record*, vol. 3, 47, 49.
81. Vives, Cc4v.
82. Fulvius Androtius, *The Widowes Glasse: Abridged*, in The *Treasure of Vowed Chastity in Secular Persons. Also the Widowes Glass*, by Leonard Lessius and Fulvius Androtius, trans. by I. W. P. (St. Omer: English College Press, 1621), 231, 265, 310.
83. Androtius, 273.
84. *The Whole Duty of a Woman: Or a Guide to the Female Sex From the Age of Sixteen to Sixty* (London: J. Gwillim, 1696), 93, 94 [misnumbered as 64].

85. 'Lady Anne's Account Book for 1665 and 1667–1668', in *The Papers of Lady Anne Clifford (1590–1676)*. Cumbria Record Office, Hothfield MS WD/Hoth/A988/17. All citations are to this document. No page numbers are provided.

86. Anne Clifford, 'The Last Few Months of Lady Anne's Life [Day-By-Day Book]', in *Lady Anne Clifford, Countess of Dorset, Pembroke and Montgomery, 1590–1676*, 275.

87. Williamson, 327, 478

88. ibid., 118.

89. Helkiah Crooke, *Mikrokosmographia: A Description of the Body of Man* ([London]: printed for William Jaggard, 1615), 70.

90. Crooke, 70.

91. William Bullein, *The Government of Health* (London: Valentine Sims, 1595), fol. 24.

92. Levinus Lemnius, *The Touchstone of Complexions*, trans. by Thomas Newton (London: Thomas Marsh, 1576), 123*v*–124.

93. See Suzuki, 195–229.

94. Megan Matchinske, *Women Writing History in Early Modern England* (Cambridge: Cambridge University Press, 2009), 86.

95. J.B. [John Bulwer], *Anthropometamorphosis: Man Transform'd: or, the Artificial Changling* (London: William Hunt, 1653), 58.

96. Bulwer, 59.

97. William Prynne, *Histrio-mastix: The Players Scourge, or, Actors Tragaedie, Divided into Two Parts* (London: Edward Allde, 1633), 202–4.

98. Thomas Wall, *Spiritual Armour to Defend the Head* (London: William Marshal, 1688), 4, 13.

99. Edward Rainbow, *A Sermon Preached at the Funeral of the Right Honorable Anne Countess of Pembroke, Dorset, and Montgomery* (London: R. Royston, 1677), 30–1.

100. qtd. in Spence, 213.

101. Rainbow, 53.

102. Rainbow, 42.

103. Rainbow, 16, 18.

104. Rainbow, 32, 43.

105. Rainbow, 38.

106. Beverly Lemire, *Dress, Culture and Commerce: The English Clothing Trade Before the Factory, 1660–1800* (New York: St. Martin's Press, 1997), 62–3.

107. Anne Clifford met Gregory King (1648–1712) on 24 February 1665. She gave 30 shillings to King, 'Mr Dugdales Boy, who is so ingenious in takeing ye formes of Castles & townes'. King's later work, particularly his calculations of the clothing expenditures in England, has proved essential to the economic historians of today.

108. N. B. Harte, 'The Economics of Clothing in the Late Seventeenth Century', *Textile History* 22.2 (1991): 288.

109. ibid., 290.

110. Smith, 55.

111. ibid., 56.

112. Harte, 290; Joan Thirsk, *Economic Policy and Projects: The Development of a Consumer Society in Early Modern England* (Oxford: Clarendon Press, 1978), 144–5.

113. C. Willett and Phillis Cunnington, *The History of Underclothes* (New York: Dover Publications, 1992), 65.
114. Bacon, 189, 194.
115. ibid., 195.
116. Jones and Stallybrass, 20.
117. Anne Clifford, 'The Last Months', in *The Diaries of Lady Anne Clifford,* ed. D. J. H. Clifford (Phoenix Mill: Sutton Publishing, 2003), 269.
118. ibid., 256.
119. Spence, 146–7.
120. Clifford, 'The Last Months', 258.
121. Johannes Endres, 'Diderot, Hogarth, and the Aesthetics of Depilation', *Eighteenth-Century Studies* 38.1 (2004): 17–38.
122. Thorstein Veblen, *The Theory of the Leisure Class* (Oxford: Oxford University Press, 2007), 118–24.

Index

Illustrations are indicated in bold

Druck:
Customized Business Services GmbH
im Auftrag der
KNV Zeitfracht GmbH
Ein Unternehmen der Zeitfracht - Gruppe
Ferdinand-Jühlke-Str. 7
99095 Erfurt